Russia 1881–1921

From Tsarism to Communism

From Tsarism to Communism

LONGMAN

Oliver and Boyd
Longman House
Burnt Mill
Harlow
Essex CM20 2JE
An imprint of Longman Group UK Ltd

First published 1994

British Library Cataloguing in Publication Data
McColgan, Martin
    Russia, 1881–1921: From Tsarism to Communism —
    (Higher Grade History Series)
    I. Title II. Wood, Sydney III. Hardlines
    IV. Series
    947.08

ISBN 0-05-005087-7

Set in 10/12 Bembo Linotron
Produced by Longman Singapore Publishers Pte Ltd
Printed in Singapore

The publisher's policy is to use paper manufactured from sustainable forests.

Acknowledgements

We are grateful to the following for permission to reproduce photographs;
Archiv Gerstenberg, pages 71 and 101; Bildarchiv Preussicher Kulturbesitz, page
89; Jean-Loup Charmet, page 131; Mary Evans Picture Library, pages 30 and 65;
Hulton Deutsch Collection, pages 5 (and 31), 35, 57, 132, 161 above, 171 and
cover right (Keystone Press); David King Collection, pages 23 above, 34 (and
42), 49, 59 (and 60), 72, 82 (and 92), 87, 102, 103, 112, 114 above, 115, 123, 128
(and 133), 135, 159, 161 below, 162 (and cover left), 170, 181 (and 200), 190,
191, 196, 197, 198, 202, 211 and 212; Mansell Collection, page 178; Musée de
l'Homme, Paris, pages 6 and 7; Novosti Press Agency, pages 62, 67, 75, 144, 149
(and 180); Popperfoto, page 19 below; The Royal Collection © 1993 Her
Majesty the Queen, page 11; Topham Picture Source, pages 19 above, 160, 193
and 213; Victoria and Albert Museum, pages 12 and 29; Roger Viollet, Paris,
pages 106 (and 114 below) and 107; Weidenfeld and Nicholson Archive, page
137.

The cover photograph on the left shows a political meeting held by troops at the
front during the summer of 1919 (David King Collection) and Lenin making a
speech in Moscow (date unknown).
Cover design Martin Adams.
Illustrated by Hardlines.

Contents

Introduction   4

Issue 1   How did the Tsars control their
          empire?   5
Issue 2   How did Alexander III rule?   34
Issue 3   Political challenges to Tsarism   59
Issue 4   Why did Russia change?   82
Issue 5   The Duma and the Stolypin
          reforms   106
Issue 6   Why did the Revolution of
          February 1917 occur?   128
Issue 7   The Bolsheviks seize power   149
Issue 8   A new authority   181

Conclusion   212

General essays   214
Extended essays   215
Bibliography   216
Index   218

Introduction

The Later Modern sections of the revised Higher history syllabus are based upon the concepts 'Ideology, Identity, Authority'. The study of Russian history between 1881 and 1921 is ideally suited to developing an understanding of these concepts: within those four decades, the Tsarist empire collapsed and a Communist régime came into power. This, apparently, represented a dramatic change in 'Ideology, Identity and Authority' within the empire. But what do these words mean?

- *Ideology* can loosely be defined as the set of beliefs, usually political, which a group of people share.
- *Identity* is how people see themselves, perhaps in the context of national or ethnic background, or perhaps in terms of class.
- *Authority* is the source of power which people are either persuaded to accept, or forced to accept.

One can define, after a fashion, an *ideology* behind the institution of Tsarism in Russia. One can also explain the *ideology* behind Communism. The two are very different. There was a recognisable change in official *ideology* in Russia between 1881 and 1921. However, despite superficial appearances to the contrary, it is questionable if the *identities* of the peoples of the Russian empire changed much in the period. Most tellingly of all, the nature of the type of *authority* exerted in Russia in 1921 seemed very similar to that exerted in 1881. The significant difference was that different people were exerting that *authority*.

This book is divided into eight chapters (Issues 1 to 8) which cover the transformation from Tsarism to Communism. A task comes at the beginning of each chapter. Essay titles at the end of each chapter offer pupils further opportunities to develop their understanding of the material presented. A selection of broader essay titles, similar in style to those in Paper I of the revised Higher exam, is presented at the end of the book. In addition, suggestions for extended essay preparation and a relevant reading list are provided.

How did the Tsars control their empire?

Issue 1 will set the scene by asking:

1. How had the enormous Tsarist empire evolved by 1881?
2. Who were the people in the empire?
3. How was the empire run?

Answering these questions requires consideration of the key concepts: ideology, identity, and authority. Was there an *ideology* behind Tsarism? Did the peoples of the Tsar's empire share a common *identity*? What was the basis of the Tsar's *authority*? How was that *authority* exercised throughout the empire?

TASK

It is 1881. You have returned to Britain after having spent a year in Russia. You are asked to produce a magazine article describing what the Russian empire is like. The magazine editor requests that your article should be about 1000 words in length and should mention:

1. the geography of the empire.
2. the people.
3. the Tsar and his government.

As you work through Issue 1, make notes which will allow you to produce such an article. Write up your article when you have finished reading the chapter.

The Tsarist empire at the end of the nineteenth century

Fig 1.1   A school run by Buryat Mongols in eastern Siberia in 1882.

Figures 1.1 and 1.2 show some of the people of the Russian empire as it was inherited by Tsar Alexander III in 1881. Figure 1.1 shows a school run by Buryat Mongols in eastern Siberia. The photo was taken in 1882, one year after the accession of the new Tsar. Figure 1.2 shows a Kazan mullah and his wives. Kazan was the capital city of the Tatar or Tartar region in central Asia which was conquered by Russia in 1552.

These pictures give an indication of the wide national and cultural varieties of the subjects of Tsar Alexander III.

Figure 1.3 shows the Russian empire in 1900. The empire covered a territory of over twenty million square kilometres – a sixth of the land mass of the world. From east to west, it spanned a distance of eight thousand kilometres, from Europe to the Pacific coast. From north to south, at its widest point, it stretched for over three thousand kilometres. Only a quarter of the empire could be classified as European. Approximately two hundred different nationalities lived within the empire.

Fig 1.2   A Kazan mullah and his wives.

Fig 1.3   Map showing the Russian empire in 1900.

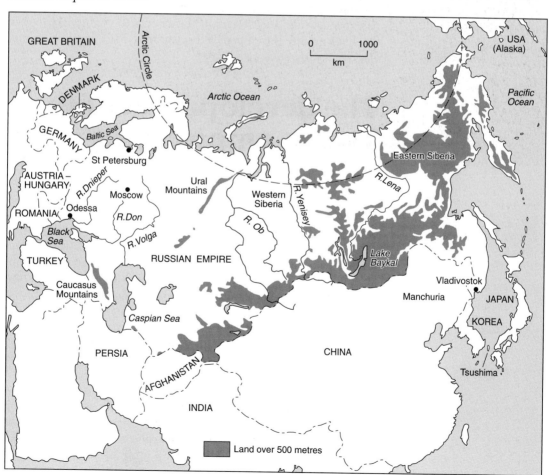

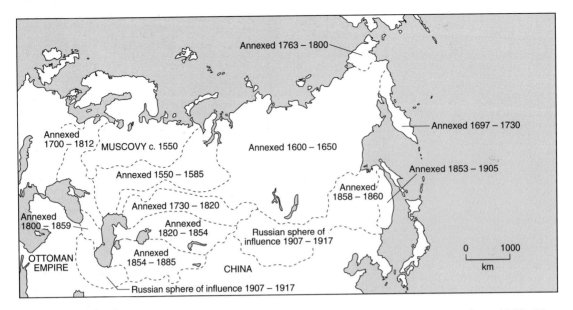

Fig 1.4   Map showing how the Russian empire had expanded between 1550 and 1917.

Figure 1.4 shows how the empire grew in size from 1550. Note how it expanded significantly every century, and was continuing to expand in the early years of the twentieth century. How had this huge empire developed? Who was this 'Tsar' whose authority extended across such a vast area?

The development of the Tsarist empire

The origins of the Russian empire can be traced back to the first Slav peoples, from whom European Russians evolved. They came from the region of the Carpathian Mountains to the area which we now know as European Russia in the sixth and seventh centuries AD. This land had been occupied by ethnic groups such as the Huns and the Khazars for hundreds of years before the Slavs arrived. A further presence in the territory was of Varangians from Scandinavia, who crossed the region to do trade in Byzantium (now Istanbul) at the mouth of the Black Sea. Relations between the various peoples in the area were uneasy in the absence of any recognised authority. In the ninth century, in an attempt to establish order, the Slavs invited the Varangians to control the region. The Varangians agreed. The centre of Varangian authority became the area around Kiev, known as Kiev Rus.

Over the next two centuries there occurred two events which ensured that Kiev Rus, and eventually Russia, would develop differently from the rest of Europe. The first of these events was religious. When the Christian church split in AD 1054, Kiev Rus retained the eastern, or 'Orthodox', form of the faith, whilst western Europe remained Roman Catholic. The second event which made Kiev Rus different was the Mongol invasion in 1223. Kiev Rus, under the control of these people of Asiatic origin, developed under the influence of eastern, rather than western, culture.

For over two centuries Kiev Rus was very much apart from the rest of Europe. An important effect of the Mongol invasion was that the influence of Kiev Rus diminished, while the influence of the territory of Muscovy, the Moscow region, grew. This was because the Prince of Muscovy was appointed as chief tax-collector of the Mongols. In any case Muscovy was increasing in importance because of factors to do with trade: it was connected to all the important river systems of northern and western Russia. For a long time its aim had been to expand in order to allow it access to the sea. With Mongol assistance, Muscovy continued to pursue this aim.

Supremacy over all Russia by the Grand Duchy of Moscow was established by two notable figures, Ivan the Great (1462–1505) and Ivan the Terrible (1547–1584). Between them, they managed to expel the Mongol presence from the Muscovite empire and to bring the whole area of Rus under Muscovite control.

The map sequence in Figures 1.5 to 1.9 shows the development of the Russian empire in Europe between 1462, when Ivan the Great took control of Russia, and 1914. Figure 1.5 shows the principality of Moscow inherited by Ivan the Great. Figure 1.6 shows how much it had grown by the time of the death of Ivan

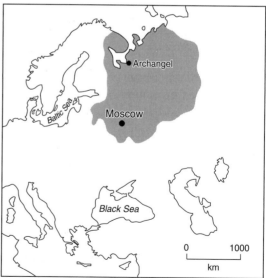

Fig 1.5   Map showing the principality of Moscow at the accession of Ivan the Great in 1462.

Fig 1.6   Map showing how the principality of Moscow had expanded by the time of Ivan the Great's death in 1505.

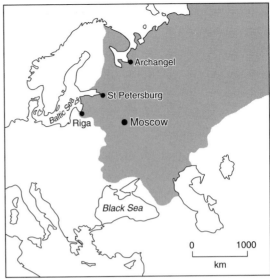

Fig 1.7 (above left)   Map showing the Russian empire in Europe at the time of Ivan the Terrible's death in 1584.

Fig 1.8 (above)   Map showing the Russian empire in Europe at the time of the accession of Catherine the Great in 1762.

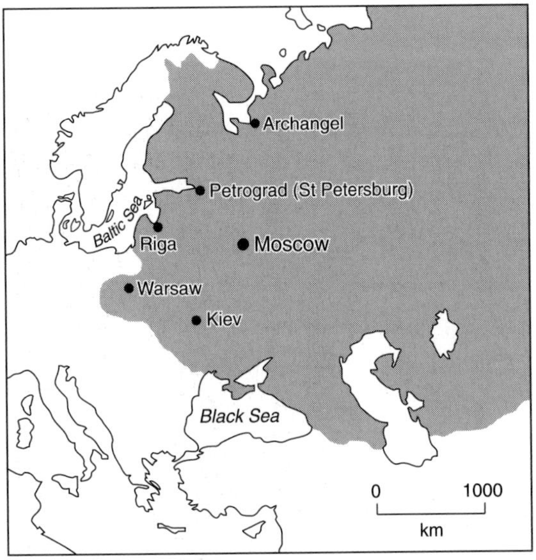

Fig 1.9   Map showing the Russian empire in Europe in 1914.

the Great. Figure 1.7 indicates the enormous tracts of land added to his empire by Ivan the Terrible. Figures 1.8 and 1.9 show how the empire continued to grow thereafter.

Ivan the Great and Ivan the Terrible used the term 'autocrat' to describe themselves. An autocrat is one who rules by his own power, an absolute sovereign, so by this, they meant that the power which they held over their subjects was unlimited. Ivan the Terrible adopted as his title the Slavonic form of the word 'Caesar', meaning 'Emperor': he called himself 'Tsar'.

The death of Ivan the Terrible in 1584 and the accession of his weak son, Theodore, led to almost thirty years of court intrigue and uncertainty before a new dynasty appeared. Michael

Romanov became Tsar of Russia in 1613. Tsar Michael, related through marriage to Ivan the Terrible, was the choice of the great families of the empire, and his aim was to re-establish Tsarist authority in difficult times. The Romanov dynasty was to remain in power until 1917.

Under the Romanovs in the seventeenth century, Russia became strong and organised, with Romanov authority being extended into every aspect of Russian life. Increasingly trade, industry and government were directed and controlled by the Tsar and his advisers.

One of the most dynamic of the Romanov Tsars was Peter the Great (1696–1725). Tsar Peter wished to modernise Russia by introducing European ways into the empire. He also wished to secure access to the Baltic Sea. This was duly won through victory in what became known as the Great Northern War. You will see in Figure 1.3 that the city founded by him and named after him, St Petersburg, gives access to the Baltic. Peter travelled extensively in Europe, learning things which he believed would be beneficial for his empire. Figure 1.10 shows a portrait of him, which was painted when he was in England in 1698.

Fig 1.10 Peter the Great painted by Sir Godfrey Kneller in 1698.

Although Tsar Peter wished to westernise Russia, Europeans believed that Russia was backward and barbaric. Here are some observations made by an English traveller to Russia at the time of Peter the Great. They concern the Moscow upper classes:

'Intellectual life and discussion were entirely lacking ... Heavy drinking was the only amusement of the nobility, and banquets ... invariably ended as orgies. Travellers were disgusted by the drunkenness and general bestiality of the Muscovites ... Their ordinary manners were those of savages ... Filthily dirty, clad in long, cumbersome garments which prevented all free movement, with their unkempt hair down to their shoulders and matted beards, they behaved hoggishly at table, dipping their black and greasy fingers indiscriminately into plates and dishes, always eating too much and drinking noisily and greedily out of unwashed vessels.'

(Quoted in C. Marsden, *Palmyra of the North: the First Days of St Petersburg*, 1942)

Figure 1.11 is a photo of a wood-carving made in 1576, showing a procession of Russian ambassadors to the court of the Austrian Emperor Maximillian II. Notice how the ambassadorial nobles at the front of the procession are followed by merchants carrying furs. This was because Russian ambassadors in Europe usually had very little money, and they relied on the sale of Russian furs to pay their way. Note too the costumes and beards of the nobles. Both the quotation just given and Figure 1.11 show how the Russians were regarded as remote, alien people by developed western Europeans.

Fig 1.11   A wood carving made in 1576, illustrating how Russian nobles were viewed by western Europeans.

The peoples of the empire

By 1881 the Russian empire could claim to have under its jurisdiction some 200 different nationalities. Some of these were primitive tribesmen, numerically small and living in remote parts of the empire. The total population of the empire in the late nineteenth century numbered in the region of 123 million people. The 1897 census calculated that the dominant national groups were as follows:

The major nationalities (in millions)	
Great Russians	44.3
Ukranians	17.8
Polish	6.3
Belorussians	4.7
Jews	4.0
Turkic	10.8
Finns	2.8
Germans	1.4
Latvians and Lithuanians	2.5
Estonians	1.0
Armenians	0.9
Georgians	1.0

This table shows the preponderance of Europeans in the empire. By far the major nationality was Great Russian. However, it is worth noting that over 55 per cent of the total number of people in the empire were *not* Russian. Another point concerns religious differences. Probably a fifth or more of the Tsar's subjects were not Christian. It is estimated that between twenty and twenty-five million of the peoples of the empire were Muslim, for example, and the four million Jews referred to in the table are defined categorically as being Jewish by faith. It is clear that amongst the people of the Russian empire there were huge diversities of ideologies and identities. For the Tsar to retain his authority over all these different peoples required considerable skill.

As the Russian empire entered the nineteenth century and as it continued to expand, nationalism became an increasingly important issue within it. Over the centuries, the Tsars were aware that their empire contained different peoples with different outlooks. That, by itself, was not a problem. Different national groups only became a problem when they began to have ambitions which seemed to challenge the Tsar's authority and the security of the empire. As Hugh Seton-Watson observes:

> 'Loyalty to the dynasty was binding on all subjects of the empire, whether Russian or not. It was perhaps to be expected that Russians would be more enthusiastically loyal than others, but from the Tsar's point of view a Baltic German, a Pole, or a Tatar who served him loyally was not less acceptable or praiseworthy a subject than a Russian.'
>
> (H. Seton-Watson, *The Russian Empire 1801–1917*, 1967)

Tension with Russia's national minorities was especially a problem in frontier territories where the Tsar's subjects were part of a national group whose identity had more in common with their neighbours outside the empire than with Russians within it. One might take the obvious example of Poland. Russia's six million Poles saw themselves as a conquered part of an alien empire who would have preferred to join up with the rest of the Polish people and establish their own nation.

The Tsar and his government

Some idea of how the Tsar viewed his authority can be derived from the set of Tsarist decrees called the Fundamental Laws of the Empire. Article One of the Fundamental Laws declared:

> 'The Emperor of all the Russias is an autocratic and unlimited monarch. God commands that this supreme power be obeyed, out of conscience as well as fear.'

Such an emphatic statement about the limitless power of one man allowed no room in the minds of any of the Tsar's subjects, noble or peasant, priest or layman, about the nature of the authority of the Tsar. A Tsar in possession of such power needed to be strong and able. Many of Russia's Tsars had been such leaders. Some of them were prepared to be brutal to emphasise their displeasure at any challenge to their authority. Ivan the Terrible and Peter the Great were capable of great cruelties against anyone who questioned or challenged them. Peter the Great, for example, personally supervised the torture and execution of 1200 plotters against him in 1698 and actively participated in the beheadings.

The concept of the absolute power of the Tsar remained an essential part of Tsarist ideology until 1917. However, over the centuries, the increasing complexities of managing the Tsarist empire meant that the Tsars required assistance to govern. Tsars had traditionally ruled with the help of the Russian nobility. The Russian nobles ensured that the taxes necessary for the upkeep of the Tsar's armies were collected and presented to the Tsar. Ivan the Terrible took the process a stage further and introduced feudalism – a system of lords and serfs – into Russia. He did this to ensure that his subjects, who were spread over an enormous area, could be kept in check, and hence could be relied upon to pay their taxes. The Russian nobles, therefore, became feudal lords, rather like the barons in mediaeval England. As such, they played a vital role as intermediaries between the Tsar and his people, ensuring that order was maintained in the countryside and that taxes were collected. The nobles, however, had no political power. The only political body which worked with the Tsar was a Senate of Nobles which operated with various officials who administered state business. This Senate and the Tsar's officials had no real authority. Their function was to assist the Tsar and to advise him. The Tsar could accept or dismiss their advice at will. His decision was final.

By the beginning of the nineteenth century, the feudal aristocrats were beginning to be replaced in importance by a different type of noble. The reason for this change was war. Russia was involved in the wars against Napoleon Bonaparte between 1802 and 1815. In 1802 Tsar Alexander I decided that Russia's resources had to be better used in the war, and he appointed eight ministers to do the job. These included Ministers of War, of Finance and of Internal Affairs. After 1802 the ministries became the essential tool of the Tsar by which his authority could be exercised over the Russian empire. However, the role of the nobles who occupied ministerial office remained similar to that of the nobles of the original Senate: they could advise the Tsar and they were expected to function efficiently, but they were not a government or a cabinet in the way that is commonly understood in Britain nowadays. The Tsar could hire and fire ministers at will. Ministers were appointed by the Tsar and were responsible to him alone. They did not act in unison: indeed, different ministries often fell out with each other and sought to win the Tsar's favour, one at the expense of the other.

As the administrative tasks of the ministries developed, they increased their manpower accordingly. By the middle of the nineteenth century, Russia had twelve civil servants per thousand people and one of their essential duties was tax-collection. What was clearly developing in Russia in the nineteenth century was a bureaucracy – an administration of Tsarist officials. The implication of this development was clear: the role of Russia's feudal aristocracy – the old landed nobles – was rapidly disappearing. Bureaucrats, rather than landed nobles, could arrange tax-collection and establish ways of keeping order in the countryside.

The question of the land
The serfs

Until 1861 the vast majority of the Tsar's subjects were not the owners of the land upon which they worked. Instead, they were serfs who worked the lands of their lords, the Russian nobles. The rights of Russia's peasants had been systematically removed by successive Tsars from the time of Ivan the Terrible. In 1767 a decree was passed by Catherine the Great forbidding serfs even to complain about their conditions:

> 'The Governing Senate . . . has deemed it necessary to make known that the landlords' serfs and peasants . . . owe their landlords proper submission and absolute obedience in all matters . . . should it so happen that . . . serfs and peasants should cease to give the proper obedience to their landlords . . . and should make bold to submit unlawful petitions complaining of their landlords, and especially to petition Her Imperial Majesty personally, then both those who make the complaints and those who write up the petitions shall be punished by the knout [flogged] and forthwith deported to Nerchinsk to penal servitude for life.'
>
> (Quoted in G. Vernadsky (ed.), *A Source Book of Russian History from Early Times to 1917*, 1972)

The landlords' ownership of serfs was absolute. For example, they could buy and sell serfs; if they so wished, they could split up families in the process.

Buying and selling serfs also occurred in Russian cities. This advertisement appeared in the *Moscow Gazette* in 1801:

> 'TO BE SOLD, three coachmen, well-trained and handsome; and two girls, the one eighteen and the other fifteen years of age, both of them good-looking and well acquainted with various kinds of handiwork. In the same house there are for sale two hairdressers: the one twenty-one years of age can read, write, play on a musical instrument, and act as huntsman; the other can dress ladies' and gentlemen's hair. In the same house are sold pianos and organs.'
>
> (D. Mackenzie Wallace, *Russia*, 1912)

Other European leaders were astounded at the control exercised over Russia's peasants. In 1787 Emperor Joseph II of Austria observed:

> 'Everything seems easy when one wastes money and human lives. We in Germany or France could not attempt to do what they dare do here without hindrance. The Lord commands; hordes of slaves obey. They are paid little or nothing; they are badly fed; they do not dare to protest, and I know that in these

years fifty thousand persons were destroyed in these new
[southern] provinces ... without their being lamented, even
without anyone mentioning it.'

(E.N. Williams, *The Ancien Régime in Europe*, 1970)

The peasants themselves did not always accept their lot in life.
They hated their existence which, as has just been seen, was just
like slavery. Protests against oppressive serfdom took many forms.
For example, peasant families might attempt to flee from their
estates, although barbaric punishments awaited those unfortunate
enough to get caught. Occasionally organised peasant risings
would develop. These were invariably and brutally repressed.

At the beginning of the nineteenth century, about half of
Russia's peasants were owned by nobles. Most of the rest were
classified as State Peasants, who were directly owned by the Tsar.
These could be given by the Tsar as gifts to landowners.

The nobles

When Tsar Alexander I introduced his bureaucracy in 1802, the
role of Russia's landed nobility in Tsarist Russia clearly decreased
in importance. And at this time there was an even greater cause for
concern amongst their ranks: there were too many of them. In
addition, the vast majority of Russia's nobles were in financial
difficulties. The main reason for this was that when a member of
the Russian nobility died, his estate was divided equally among his
sons. The inheritance process meant that estates were increasingly
becoming sub-divided into ever-diminishing units. The effect of
this over generations had become quite devastating by the late
1850s. The following table illustrates the scale of the problem:

Serf-owning landlords in European Russia, 1858–59		
	Number	Percentage
1. Grand seigneurs (Over 1000 souls)	1,032	1.1
2. Gentry (501–1000 souls)	1,754	2.0
3. Gentry (101–500 souls)	15,717	18.0
4. Impoverished gentry (21–100 souls)	30,593	35.1
5. Impoverished gentry (Fewer than 20 souls; on average 7)	38,173	43.8

(Figures taken from R.Pipes, *Russia under the Old Régime*, 1987)

The census of 1858–59 showed that there were almost 90,000 serf owners in Russia. Serfs were referred to as 'souls'. A noble required at least 100 'souls' to be allowed to vote in any of the representative assemblies of the landed gentry at that time. Those with fewer than 100 'souls' could be classified as impoverished gentry. Those with fewer than 20 'souls' could not operate a viable economic unit on the land.

These hordes of land-owning gentry clearly had no function within the Tsarist system by the mid-nineteenth century. The Tsar had his ministers and his civil servants to cater for tax-collecting and for the maintenance of law and order. Meanwhile, the peasants were protesting vehemently about serfdom, and Tsarist economic advisers were suggesting that serfdom was keeping Russia backward. In this situation, the whole concept of feudalism and its relevance to Russia came into question.

The cities of the Tsarist empire

The capital city of Tsarist Russia in 1881 was St Petersburg. Figure 1.12 shows the city's main street, the Nevsky Prospect, in the late nineteenth century, while Figure 1.13 shows part of Moscow at the same time. Notice how the buildings on the Moscow skyline feature eastern-style domes and towers while the architecture of St Petersburg is very western-European in appearance.

St Petersburg was built under the personal direction of Tsar Peter. It was to be Russia's new capital, built to help Peter to achieve his long-term ambition of 'westernising' Russia, of making it into a modern, dynamic state. Work commenced in 1709.

Russia's new capital required people to build it and people to live in it. There were few volunteers who wished to move to an area regarded as dangerous and uninviting, but Peter solved this problem in typically Tsarist fashion. In 1712, he ordered the transfer of 1000 landed gentry and 1000 merchants and tradesmen to St Petersburg. These persons were then told to pay for the construction of expensive houses out of their own pockets. The design of these houses was set down by Peter's own architect. Forced labour was then brought in under military escort to build the city. Many of these were worked to death or caught fatal diseases in the inhospitable environment. Tsar Peter, however, completed his new capital, which he referred to as Russia's 'window on the west'.

Russia's other cities developed much more normally. Primarily they were centres of trade. However, as the nature of the cities of

Fig 1.12   The Nevsky Prospect, in the late nineteenth century.

Fig 1.13   Part of Moscow in the late nineteenth century, with the Ivan the Great belfry dominating the scene as it still does today.

the rest of Europe changed in the course of the nineteenth century, largely in response to the impact of industrialisation, Russia's cities began to appear backward in comparison. According to the 1897 census, only 1.5 per cent of Russia's population could be classified as being of the business classes and only 4 per cent belonged to the urban working classes; 82 per cent of Russia's people were classified as peasants.

But to suggest that Russia had no industry of note, little trade and few professionally qualified people would be inaccurate. It is true that few of the key personnel or activities associated with industrial development existed in Russia's cities. They *did* exist on Russia's landed estates. This happened because of a succession of Tsarist decrees which placed penalties on people who tried to establish industry in towns. In 1762, for example, Tsar Peter III passed legislation which forbade merchants from using serf labour: they had to use hired labour, which was expensive. Within six months, Peter's successor, Catherine the Great, decreed that estates could establish industry anywhere except in Moscow and St Petersburg. The purpose of these measures, and others like them, was not to penalise industrialists: it was to bring about the stimulation of trade and industry throughout the empire, and not just in Russia's major cities. Of course, the effect was rather damaging because such legislation removed from Russia's cities the role soon to be taken up by the cities of Britain and, eventually, by those of the rest of western Europe. Russia's cities were not the force behind industrial expansion.

The process whereby rapid industrialisation was brought to Russia in the 1890s will be examined in Issue 4. It will be emphasised that there *was* industry within the Tsarist empire before 1890. But it remains the case that Russia in the late nineteenth century was primarily an agricultural nation and that her cities were undeveloped by the standards of the rest of Europe. The industrialisation programme of the 1890s came from a Tsarist initiative, not from the cumulative effect of the activities of a middle class of industrial businessmen based in Russia's cities.

The army

The Russian empire established by Ivan the Great was reasonably compact and allowed powerful Tsars to exert their authority over it. The empire expanded, the main impetus being the need to find fresh agricultural land to replace the exhausted fields of the centre of Russia, and it grew primarily by military means. A powerful and loyal army became a vital aspect of Tsarist authority. The extremities of the empire were always subject to attack and the army was essential for security. In the sixteenth and seventeenth centuries, there was seldom a single year in which Russia was not extensively involved in warfare along its southern and south-eastern borders as

Turks and Mongols fought to defend or win back territory which they regarded as their own.

The structure of the Russian army in the nineteenth century was based upon that established by Peter the Great. The officers came from the nobility. Sons of nobles were registered with the Imperial Guard at the age of ten, were called up for training at fifteen, and were subsequently transferred to a regiment for life. The soldiers came from conscripted villagers: each village was required to supply its quota of men to a military depot established in the chief town of each district.

By the end of his reign, Peter the Great had established a standing army of 210,000 regulars – an enormous force by contemporary European standards. The ability of the Tsars to amass huge armies remained until Tsardom disappeared in 1917.

The role of the Russian army in the nineteenth century was to defend the empire from attacks from abroad and to defend the Tsar's authority from attacks from within. During the period from 1881 to 1917, the army was often called upon for the latter reason. Fortunately for Alexander III and Nicholas II, the army remained loyal to Tsardom. But between 1914 and 1917, when Russia was embroiled in the First World War, the situation changed.

The Church

With as many as twenty-five million Muslims and four million Jews in the Russian empire at the end of the nineteenth century, not to mention numerous other minority religions, it would clearly be wrong to suggest that there was only one church in Russia. However, the majority population was European Russian; and their religion, which was the recognised religion of the Tsarist state, was Russian Orthodox Christian.

The Russian Orthodox Church was a vitally important part of the Tsarist empire. The head of the Russian Orthodox Church was the Tsar. One only has to refer back to Article One of the Fundamental Laws to see how the religious element was a vital ideological buttress to the Tsar's authority: 'God himself commands that this supreme authority be obeyed.' Russian Orthodoxy was an integral part of Tsarist ideology.

As has already been mentioned on page 8, Russia became religiously different from the rest of Europe in AD 1054. Russia kept to the Byzantine form of Christianity that had been introduced by Vladimir in AD 988. From 1054, Russia no longer accepted the authority of the Pope in Rome, while western Europe remained loyal to Rome. A further split occurred in 1453 when Constantinople, as Byzantium had been renamed, fell to the Muslim Turkish empire. This meant that Russia's Orthodox Church was no longer subject to any outside authority. In other words, Russia's Orthodox Church became a national church, controlled from within Russia itself. The implication of this turn of events was clear. In an empire controlled with absolute authority by the Tsar, it was logical that the Church, too, would come under Tsarist control. This duly occurred. Peter the Great introduced the Church Statute of 1721 by which the Russian Orthodox Church was placed under the control of the Most Holy Directing Synod, a department of the Tsar's government.

In 1881 the Orthodox Church in Russia had at its head the Tsar. It also had the captive membership of all of the Tsar's Russian subjects because it was made a criminal offence to abandon Russian Orthodoxy. Other religious groups were tolerated with different levels of compassion at different times. Tsars tended to resent other religions which might imply allegiance to an outside or alien authority. This hold over their subjects was the source of great strength to the Tsars. Some historians believe that the Russian Orthodox Church by the nineteenth century had become spiritually dead, and that it had allowed the Tsarist state to take control. As such, it was in no position to champion what might be called Christian values in a worldly sense – by, for example, speaking out against the evils of serfdom. One historian goes as far as to suggest that the absence of leadership from the Church in the quest for social justice in Russia was one reason for the appeal which revolutionaries had by the end of the nineteeenth century:

'The ultimate result of the policies of the Russian Orthodox Church was not only to discredit it in the eyes of those who cared for social and political justice, but to create a spiritual vacuum [emptiness]. This vacuum was filled with secular [worldly] ideologies which sought to realise on this earth the paradise that Christianity had promised to provide in the next.'
(R. Pipes, *Russia under the Old Régime*, 1987)

However, one should be wary of being totally critical of the Orthodox Church in Russia. Amongst its millions of clerics and adherents there were many committed and genuine believers in a long-established faith. Figure 1.14 shows an impoverished village priest and one of his parishioners, with whom he shared a similar life with similar hardships, and Figure 1.15 is of a penal settlement for priests. These pictures do not suggest a Church which had become the cause of a 'spiritual vacuum', as suggested by R. Pipes. It may have been the case that the hierarchy of the Church in Russia had become too much under state control, but Orthodoxy was an essential part of the lives of many of the people.

The Tsar was regarded by Orthodox believers as a great spiritual leader. This role of Tsardom can be traced back at least to the time of Ivan the Great. When Constantinople fell to the Turks in 1453, and since western Europe no longer followed Orthodox Christianity, Ivan the Great was the only significant ruler who remained loyal to Orthodoxy. Orthodox Christianity believed that

Fig 1.14   An impoverished village priest and a parishioner.

Fig 1.15   A community where sinning Russian priests expiated their crimes.

it needed a powerful emperor to ensure its survival without persecution. That role had, by necessity, fallen to Ivan. A learned monk declared:

> '. . . it is from the supreme and the all-powerful, the
> all-supporting right hand of God, that Tsars reign . . . thy
> sovereign power, which [extends] to the ends of the earth
> in the Orthodox Christian faith, shines everywhere under
> the heavens more brightly than the sun . . . thou alone in all the
> earth art Tsar to the Christians . . .'
>   (Quoted in T. Anderson, *Russian Political Thought*, 1967)

Those subjects of the Tsar who were committed Orthodox Christians believed that the Tsar was indeed a spiritual leader and protector. They believed that, as he was guided by God and compelled to do his Christian duty, the Tsar was a holy man. It was the duty of his God-fearing subjects to obey his decrees.

The ideology of Tsarism

As the nineteenth century progressed, academic and intellectual supporters of the Tsar began to feel a greater urgency about clarifying and promoting in the minds of the people an accepted Tsarist ideology. In part, this came about in response to the ideological challenges brought about by the French Revolution of 1789, with its rallying cry of 'Liberty, Equality, Fraternity'. The invading French revolutionary armies – of which Russia was a victim in 1811–12 – brought about the collapse of monarchies of every type. Even when revolutionary France was defeated in 1815, the ideological legacy of the Revolution remained. The demand for 'liberal' governments, operating with constitutions which established the rights of all people, was a familiar one throughout Europe for the rest of the nineteenth century.

In 1825 Tsar Nicholas I was shocked to discover a plot against his autocratic rule by a group of Russian military nobles. This revolt, which became known as the Decembrist Rising, was designed to overthrow the Tsar; to transform the institution of Tsardom into a constitutional monarchy, such as that which existed in Britain; to remove serfdom; and to bring in other reforms, such as equality before the law. It was successfully put down by the Tsar's supporters, but Nicholas I was determined that western-style liberal revolt would never again be allowed to occur in Russia. His most immediate method of removing the revolutionary threat was a policy of repression. But he and his supporters preferred the idea of persuasion: the people of the empire should be made to realise that Russian ways, distinct and removed from those of the decadent and corrupt west and also from those of the backward and barbarian east, were superior to all others.

In 1833 Nicholas appointed as his Minister of Education the learned Count Sergei Uvarov. Uvarov held this position for the next sixteen years. He, more than anyone, established the three-word formula which was accepted as constituting the essence of Tsarist ideology in the nineteenth century:

> 'In the midst of the rapid collapse in Europe of religious and civil institutions, and at a time of the general spread of destructive ideas . . . it has been necessary to establish our Fatherland on firm foundations, on which the well-being, strength, and life of the people can be based . . . Fortunately, Russia has retained a warm faith in the sacred principles without which she cannot prosper . . . Orthodoxy . . . Autocracy . . . Nationality.'
>
> (Quoted in N. Riasanovsky, *Nicholas I and Official Nationality in Russia 1825–55*, 1959)

Uvarov was not attempting to say very much that was new. What he was doing was emphatically reaffirming the cornerstones of Tsarist ideology in a format which he believed would appeal to all Russians. Instead of Liberty, Equality and Fraternity, he was insisting that Russia should be ruled by Orthodoxy, Autocracy and Nationality.

Orthodoxy

Uvarov was stating that Russian Orthodoxy was the true faith and the backbone of Russian society. Russia was a theocracy – in other words, God ruled Russia, and the instruments through which He ruled were the Tsar and the Church. To rebel against either the Tsar or the Church was to rebel against God.

Autocracy

Uvarov was insisting that the unlimited and arbitrary power of the Tsar must be accepted by all his subjects. The Tsar alone, God's servant on earth, should govern Russia. God would guide the Tsar to do only what was best for his people.

Nationality

Uvarov was pointing out that the subjects of the Tsar should see themselves as belonging to a superior culture, a unique Russian culture which embodied Orthodoxy and Autocracy. Russian culture should be protected and nourished. It should be spread throughout the empire.

As Minister of Education, Uvarov saw it as an essential task to promote Orthodoxy, Autocracy and Nationality through schools and universities. Any political opposition, he believed, should be forcibly repressed. Government, according to Uvarov, was a straightforward process. Arguments in favour of representative government, such as that which existed in Britain, were dismissed as nonsense. This point in particular was subsequently expanded upon by the other great developer of Tsarist ideology in the nineteenth century, Konstantin Pobedonostsev, of whom more will be said in Issue 2. Uvarov and Pobedonostsev shared the opinion that the Tsar's government knew what best to do in every aspect of running the empire. The Tsar's government needed to have exclusive power in directing policy. Even comment from outside the Tsar's government about the wisdom of any government decision should be banned. In this respect, Tsar Nicholas I declared:

> 'Neither praise nor blame is compatible with the dignity of the government or with the order that fortunately exists among us; one should obey and keep one's reflections to one's self.'
> (Quoted in N. Riasanovsky, *Nicholas I and Official Nationality in Russia 1825–55*, 1959)

Therefore, when Alexander II became Tsar in 1855, he inherited an ideology which had been actively developed and promoted by his predecessor. But he also inherited immense practical problems to resolve. His apparent preparedness to depart from Orthodoxy, Autocracy and Nationality was viewed with deep misgivings by some of his advisers.

Alexander II: The 'Tsar Liberator'

An empire requiring a change in direction?

When Alexander II became Tsar in 1855, Russia was involved in a war on her own territory against an invasion force which included armies from Britain and France. This war, the Crimean War (1854–56), resulted in a humiliating defeat for Russia. A clear message was thus delivered to the new Tsar and his advisers: a nation which could not win a war fought on its own territory against an invading army – which itself was poorly organised – was a weak nation.

Alexander II surveyed his empire. There were many problems evident, but the main source of them seemed clear to him: the way that Russia's society was structured. Clearly the powerful western European nations were advancing, both socially and economically, with much greater vigour than Russia. Central to the process was that they had long ago dispensed with feudalism. Russia had not.

The landed nobility who controlled the estates had long passed the stage where they offered any real service to the state; instead, they were becoming an ever-increasing mass of troublesome, bankrupt gentry. And feudalism stopped any chance of Russian industrialisation, because it prevented the peasants from going to the towns to work in factories. Economic strength which came from industrialisation was regarded as the backbone of the power of nations such as Britain. The final consideration was that serfdom in Russia was apparently on the verge of disintegration anyway. In increasing numbers serfs were fleeing from their nobles' estates: indeed, more laws existed to combat flight by serfs than to control any other aspect of life in Russia. The position seemed clear to the Tsar and he acted accordingly. On 30 March 1856, Alexander II made a declaration of intent:

> 'It is better to begin to destroy serfdom from above than to wait until it begins to destroy itself from below.'

The key word in Alexander's declaration was 'begin'. The Tsar appreciated the extent of the change which he wished to bring to Russia, and he realised that the abolition of serfdom, with all which that entailed, would be a long and difficult task. It took a further five years before the decree was passed.

The Emancipation of the Serfs of 1861 was probably the most significant piece of legislation in nineteenth-century Russia. The aim was not merely to free the Russian peasantry: it was also to revolutionise Tsarist society so that Russia would become strong enough to take her place with the great powers of the world. Serfs would certainly be affected, but in addition it was assumed that the outdated landed nobility would gradually disappear, and it was hoped that the Russian economy would dramatically improve. The Tsar and his government hoped to emerge from this transformation at the head of a modern, powerful empire, ready to face the challenges of a rapidly changing world. The problem with all this, of course, was that the great social changes which were sure to occur might threaten Tsarism itself. The more conservative of the Tsar's advisers urged caution, but Alexander was determined to continue with reform.

According to the terms of the 1861 Emancipation, serfs were to continue with their duties to their former masters for the next two years. Then they were required to buy an allocation of land from their masters. The Tsar insisted on this point to ensure that the peasants stayed on the land. He did not wish them to drift towards Russia's cities looking for work which did not yet exist and eventually to become a social problem there. The Tsar and his advisers believed that peasants who owned their own land would eventually become a conservative, stable force who would continue to support the Tsar.

Peasants were to purchase land according to the following conditions. In the short term, the land remained the property of the landowner but the peasants were allowed to use their former holdings, paying either a cash rent or providing labour for the landowner. This was referred to as a period of 'temporarily obligated' status, a period which the peasant could leave only when he had 'redeemed' his holding.

'Redemption' came about by two main methods. Either the peasant could agree to accept an amount of land which was a quarter of the size to which he was entitled, in which case he got the land free; or he could pay the landowner a quarter of the value of the land himself and have the other three-quarters paid for by the state. The catch with the second method, which in most cases was the only way that a peasant could get enough land to survive upon, was that the money provided by the state had to be repaid, with interest, over a long period of time.

The issue of redemption payments became the main source of peasant discontent for the remaining years of Tsarist rule in Russia. The value of the land which the peasants were forced to buy was invariably set at inflated prices, and to meet their debts peasants often had to take work from employers as well as to work on their land. Often the employers were former serf-owners who had become quite wealthy in the process of emancipation and who could now hire their former serfs at cheap wage rates. The peasants, who had been expecting so much from the promised emancipation, felt cheated by what had happened. Over a thousand peasant riots were recorded just in 1861.

Administration of the former peasant villages also required attention. This was done by establishing the idea of the peasant commune in each village. The commune, called the 'obshchina' or 'mir' in Russian, was designed to ensure that decisions affecting each village were discussed by village representatives. At least as important from the point of view of the Tsar and his government was that the 'obshchina' or 'mir' took collective responsibility for the payment of taxes and of course for redemption payments. Figure 1.16 is a photo of a peasant 'obshchina' taken during the reign of Alexander III. People such as these found great difficulty in meeting redemption payments. Furthermore, they were set in their ways and were hardly likely to bring much-needed improvements to Russian agriculture.

Most of the former serf-owners, too, were dismayed by serf emancipation. They were of the opinion that serfdom was an integral part of the Tsarist empire and that it was vital for maintaining social order. The few who were in favour were those who profited from the process. Reference to the table on page 17 will clearly suggest that such nobles were very much in the minority, and that, with the disappearance of serfdom, most of Russia's impoverished landed aristocracy lost any remaining illusions of importance that they might still have had. By 1900 most of the Russian landed nobility had disappeared, and their land had been taken over by the peasants.

Fig 1.16   A peasant 'obshchina'

The national minorities

The problems arising from the empire's national minorities were clearly growing as the nineteenth century progressed. One of the main reasons why Nationality was part of the ideology promoted by Uvarov was that he understood that making all the Tsar's subjects see themselves as being primarily Russian would serve to unify the empire. This process was referred to as Russification. By the time of Alexander II's accession, the concept of Russification was becoming very popular in the minds of the Tsar's advisers. Clearly, a population which was Russian Orthodox in outlook, spoke the Russian language, and was educated in Russian ways would be much more accessible to Tsarist control than a variety of ethnic groups who regarded Russia as an alien power.

In the 1830s, in response to Uvarov's desire to promote Orthodoxy, Autocracy and Nationality throughout the empire, attempts were made to influence the educational structure of the minor nationalities. For example, Russian teachers replaced Polish teachers in the districts of Belorussia and Kiev, and in 1836 teaching of the Polish language was stopped. Furthermore, strenuous efforts were made by the Orthodox Church to win converts in the Baltic provinces: between 1845 and 1847 74,000 converts were made. Jews were pressurised into accepting Orthodoxy and were ordered to do business using only Russian, Polish or German – not Hebrew. These attempts to Russify might well have appeared to the Tsar to be showing a dividend of sorts, but their negative side was that they infuriated many of the national minorities. Alexander II soon learned that the minorities were prepared to fight back.

In January 1863 there was a rebellion in Poland. Fortunately for the Tsar, the rebels had neither the organisation nor the strength to mount a serious challenge to his authority. Moreover, the foreign assistance which the rebels had hoped for failed to materialise. Instead, a guerrilla campaign against impossible odds was carried out. Figure 1.17 shows the ambush of a Russian train. Notice how the rebels are armed with makeshift weapons, such as pikes made out of scythe blades. Figure 1.18 shows the outcome of the rising – a parade of Cossacks in Warsaw, emphasising the Tsar's control of Poland. (See page 48 for more information about the Cossacks.)

The Polish rebellion made Alexander II look more closely at neighbouring imperial territories, such as the Ukraine to the south, and the Baltic provinces and Finland to the north. Alexander's approach to the national minorities became more conciliatory whilst still remaining firm. The warning signs of the inherent dangers of the national minorities were clearly in place during Alexander II's reign, but his generally liberal approach removed any cause of immediate crisis.

Fig 1.17   The ambush of a Russian train during the rebellion in Poland in January 1863.

Fig 1.18   A parade of victorious Cossacks in Warsaw, after the suppression of the 1863 rebellion.

The Tsar Liberator's attempt to establish a state based on law

Tsar Alexander's more liberal approach to running the empire took a dramatic turn when he began examining the nature of Russia's legal system. The rights of individual Russians were not subject to legal protection under autocracy. While the vast majority of the Tsar's subjects were serfs, legal rights were not a terribly important issue in Russia. With emancipation, however, this situation changed. An important question had arisen: would the former serfs be controlled, in future, by Tsarist decree backed up by force, or by a system of law? This led to the next question: if a system of law were introduced, how was Russia to be policed?

Russia did have policing of a type. It came into existence following the Decembrist Rising. So shocked was Nicholas I to discover that such a rebellion could even be considered by his own military aristocracy that he set up a political police unit of some thirty to forty men who were to infiltrate potential sources of future revolt and to report accordingly. Russia's police force was little more than a group of Tsarist spies. The group rapidly grew in number. Its function was not to uphold any law of the land: it was to destroy any political opposition to the Tsar. The law was designed to fulfil a similar function. For example, a Criminal Code passed in 1845 proposed harsh punishments for those guilty of participating in crimes classed as 'political' and made any debate about political issues which challenged the Tsar's authority illegal.

Alexander II was critical of such legislation. He believed that the world was changing and that Tsarist Russia needed to change with it. His empire, he believed, was becoming much too dependent upon police control. The future lay with a more modern outlook, more in keeping with the way that the major European states were organised.

Supporters of Orthodoxy, Autocracy and Nationality were horrified by this type of thinking. Nonetheless, Alexander II was determined to change things. His Emancipation of the Serfs had been passed in 1861. In January 1864, he attempted to placate the old landed nobility by passing a statute bringing into existence organisations known as 'zemstva' (singular 'zemstvo'). A Scot who visited Russia in the 1870s, D. Mackenzie Wallace, described the zemstvo of Novgorod in 1870 as follows:

'The zemstvo is a kind of local administration... Its principal duties are to keep the roads and bridges in proper repair, to provide means of conveyance for the rural police and other officials, to elect the justices of the peace, to look after primary education and sanitary affairs, to watch the state of the crops and take measures against approaching famine, and in short to undertake, within certain clearly defined limits, whatever seems likely to increase the material and moral wellbeing of the population. In form the institution is parliamentary... In accordance with this analogy my friend the president is sometimes jocularly termed the prime minister.'

(D. Mackenzie Wallace, *Russia*, 1912)

The creation of the zemstva caused a notable transfer of power by the Tsar, but of course their authority appeared to be very localised and limited. Critics, however, saw dangers even in this slight transfer of authority from the Tsar. What would happen, they asked, if political elements infiltrated the zemstva organisations and used them for their own purposes? This possibility might have seemed unlikely – yet the warnings were not entirely unfounded. The zemstva needed to hire professional people to carry out work in specialist areas – people such as scientists, tradesmen and teachers. These professional people found in the zemstva reasonable employment, but they brought with them political ideas which were far beyond anything ever previously considered by the old landed gentry. By 1900 approximately 47,000 professional personnel were employed by zemstva throughout Russia. The zemstva became a focus of much of the discontent with Tsarist Russia which appeared with a vengeance in the early twentieth century.

In his own lifetime, Alexander II soon began to appreciate that a loosening of the reins of autocratic Tsardom was a very risky venture, especially at a time of political unrest. Reforms such as removing some of the more barbarous punishments meted out in the army and reducing significantly the length of service in the army were humane, and did more good than harm. Relaxation of censorship was potentially more dangerous, although the vast majority of the population was illiterate so the impact may well have been minimal. His Judiciary Law, passed in 1864, was perhaps the most dangerous of all. In future all crimes in Russia, including those classified as 'political', were to be tried in courts and before juries. This experiment was a failure for Alexander for several reasons. Firstly, political opponents of Tsardom rapidly learned of the publicity value of using court trials as a public platform to speak out against Tsardom. Secondly, it rapidly became clear that juries tended to be made up of critics of Tsardom who were reluctant to find any politically accused person guilty of anything, no matter how severe the crime had been. Perhaps the most famous case occurred in 1878, when a revolutionary called Vera Zasulich, who had shot and wounded the Governor of St Petersburg, was acquitted, despite her obvious attempt at political murder.

This kind of decision played directly into the hands of critics of Alexander's liberalism. Events seemed to prove such critics correct. In March 1881, representatives of a terrorist group, the 'People's Will', assassinated Alexander II (see page 64). The Tsar's son took the throne of the empire shortly afterwards.

The new Tsar, Alexander III, was to prove anything but the Liberator his father had set out to be.

ESSAY

At the end of each chapter there are four essay titles. When you have finished working through each chapter, choose one of the essay titles and construct a plan of how you would provide an answer to it. In class, using the essay plans made up by everyone, discuss each of the essays in turn. When this has been done, choose one of the four essays and write an answer to it of approximately 1200 words.

1. What challenges to Tsarist authority developed during the reign of Alexander II and how effectively did he deal with them?

2. Why did Alexander II believe that, 'It is better to begin to destroy serfdom from above than to wait until it begins to destroy itself from below' (see page 27) and how successful was the legislation which he passed to solve the problem?

3. Why did Alexander II believe it necessary to modernise the Russian empire, and how successful was he in his attempt to do so?

4. How appropriate is it to describe Tsar Alexander II as the 'Tsar Liberator'?

2

How did Alexander III rule?

Alexander III believed that his father had been mistaken in his attempt to 'liberalise' the Russian empire. He set out to reverse many of the changes brought to Russia by the 'Tsar Liberator' and to re-establish in full Orthodoxy, Autocracy and Nationality. The following issues will be considered in this chapter:

1. In what ways did Alexander III differ from his father?
2. What was 'Russification' and how successful was Alexander III in applying it to his empire?

These issues will lead us towards a fuller understanding of the *ideology* of Tsarism and how Tsarist *authority* was applied. An examination of the problems faced by Alexander III when he attempted, through Russification, to change the *identities* of many of his subject nationalities will demonstrate how difficult it was to rule the Russian empire.

TASK

Plan and write an essay of approximately 1200 words on the following:

'Alexander III did much to restore stability to the Russian empire.' Discuss.

In preparing for this essay, you should consider:

1. From your knowledge and understanding of Issue I, why, in your opinion, was there instability in the Russian empire?
2. What did Alexander III believe to be the cause of instability within the empire?
3. What policies did Alexander III apply in order to tackle political problems?

4. How did Alexander III deal with the national minorities?
5. How successful were Alexander III's policies?

While you are preparing and writing this essay, you should be thinking about the *ideology* of Tsardom, the emphasis placed upon Tsarist *authority* by Alexander III and his advisers, and the attempt by the new Tsar to mould the *identities* of all the people of the empire into what the Tsar wanted, both for himself and, he believed, for the good of the empire.

The new Tsar

Alexander III became 'Tsarevich', or heir to the Tsarist throne, in 1865, at the age of twenty. This was because his elder brother Nicholas died in that year. In 1866, the Tsarevich married a Danish princess, who took up the Orthodox faith and the name Maria Fyodorovna. Tsar Alexander, Maria Fyodorovna and their five children are shown in Figure 2.1.

Fig 2.1 Tsar Alexander III, his wife and their five children. The future Tsar Nicholas II is standing immediately behind his father.

The new Tsar was already set in his ways when he succeeded his father in 1881. To a large extent, his ideas had been formulated under the guidance of his tutor, Konstantin Pobedonostsev, of whom more is said on page 38. The manner of his father's assassination merely reinforced what the new Tsar already believed.

First of all, he was an uncompromising supporter of unchallengeable Tsarist authority. He regarded his father's experiment with the idea of a liberal empire as a disaster. During the reign of Alexander II, political assassination had become almost commonplace in Russia. Alexander III regarded this collapse of order within the empire as an indication of the folly of departing from autocratic rule. He was determined to reassert his authority throughout Russia. This would require him to stamp out the problem of political terrorism, which to him meant stamping out all signs of political opposition. He regarded such measures as a duty of the office that he held. The new Tsar despised the political ambitions of the opponents of Tsardom. These ambitions seemed to him to be based upon those western European systems of government which were alien to Russia. Alexander genuinely believed that the Russian empire had no place for western European types of representative government and law. He was convinced that Russia's peasant masses had no possible use for such institutions, and that those who promoted the idea of such institutions in the empire were no more than a handful of troublemakers.

Secondly, and going hand in hand with his contempt for western political systems, Alexander III was a firm believer in the innate superiority of all things Russian, including of course the Russian Orthodox form of Christianity. As head of the Russian Orthodox Church, and as a firm and genuine believer in Russian Orthodoxy, he was determined to champion his faith throughout the empire. The new Tsar wanted to turn away from his father's attempt to modernise Russia along western European lines. This idea that Russia should look west for the inspiration which would determine the development of the empire had been an aim of many of Russia's Tsars, going back at least to the time of Peter the Great. The last two Tsars of Russia – Alexander III and Nicholas II – saw things differently. Alexander III was very keen that Russia should modernise, especially through industrialisation, but he firmly believed that Russia should industrialise in distinctly Russian ways. He also believed that the Russian empire as a whole should be developed along recognisably Russian lines. This would require that new energy be put into the process of Russification.

If it seems that Alexander III was a very reactionary figure, that is to say opposed to change and keen to turn back the clock, then that is perhaps being over-critical of the new Tsar. Alexander III, in areas where he believed it to be appropriate, was a modernising Tsar who wanted to make his empire strong and powerful. For example, Alexander III was the Tsar who began Russia's programme of industrialisation in the 1890s, as we shall see in more detail in Issue 4. But, as we shall also see in Issue 4, Russian industrialisation under Alexander III was carried out in very Russian ways – or, more precisely, in very Tsarist ways. It was not to be carried out by the actions of independent businessmen in a largely free-market economy, as had happened in western Europe. It was instead to be supervised 'from above' – controlled by the Tsar and his government: the Tsar's *authority* should be evident throughout the process.

Russian industrialisation provides an excellent example of Alexander III's two-sided approach: he was a truly modernising Tsar in *some* respects, but he insisted that his autocratic authority be retained in full in *every* respect.

During his own lifetime as Tsar, it seemed to Alexander III that he was achieving much of what he set out to do. Peace and stability apparently descended upon the empire. The Tsar, although not regarded as especially clever, was liked and respected by his ministers as a well-meaning man who could be relied upon. His own style of living was always modest and unassuming. Sergei Witte, the Minister of Finance who supervised Russia's programme of industrialisation in the 1890s, later wrote of the Tsar:

'Alexander III was undeniably a man of limited education. I cannot agree, however, with those who would class him as unintelligent. Though lacking perhaps in mental keenness, he was undoubtedly gifted with the broad sympathetic understanding which in a ruler is often far more important than rational brilliancy.

Neither in the Imperial family nor among the nobility was there anyone who better appreciated the value of a rouble or a kopek than Emperor Alexander III. He made an ideal treasurer for the Russian people, and his economical temperament was of incalculable assistance in the solution of Russia's financial problems...

Alexander III's prudence in government expenditures was matched by his personal thrift. Abhorring luxury and lavish spending, he led an extremely simple life. When he grew tired of his own table, he would ask for a common soldier's or a hunter's meal. This economy was sometimes carried too far. The Imperial table was always relatively poor, and the food served at the Court Marshal's board was sometimes such as to endanger health...

I would often catch glimpses of His Majesty's valet mending the Emperor's trousers. On one occasion I asked him why he didn't give his master a new pair instead of mending the old so often. "Well, I would rather have it that way," he answered, "but His Majesty won't let me. He insists on wearing his garments until they are threadbare. It is the same with his boots. Not only does he wear them as long as possible, but he refuses to put on expensive ones . . ."

The Emperor's dislike of the expensive included gorgeous rooms. For this reason he never stayed at the Winter Palace, but always occupied the unpretentious quarters of Anichkov or Gatchina. There he took small rooms and lived frugally. He tolerated the Court's luxury as an unavoidable formality, but he always longed for a different mode of existence and created it for himself in his private life.

Alexander himself led an unimpeachable life and his family was a splendid example of the old-fashioned, godfearing Russian type.'

(Quoted in W. B. Walsh (ed.), *Readings in Russian History*,
Vol II, 1963)

This, then, was Russia's new Tsar. His genuineness and honesty impressed his court and his ministers, and there is every indication that he was much liked and respected. He was a big, clumsy man, who as a child was known to his family as the 'Little Bull'. Although austere in his style of living, he was regarded as warm-hearted and generous with his emotions. His favourite pastime was carpentry, and he loved wearing simple, peasant clothes at his workbench. He was fervently religious, family-loving and totally Russian in every way, and even the scandalmongers of St Petersburg and Moscow could find nothing with which to taint his record.

As a boy, he had loved endlessly repeating a slogan planted upon his impressionable mind by Pobedonostsev: 'Russia is for the Russians'. For the next thirteen years, the new Tsar attempted with great zeal to ensure that Russia was indeed for the Russians, and that other aspects of the ideology of Tsarism held by himself and Pobedonostsev were firmly established and reinforced.

The influence of Pobedonostsev

From an early age the new Tsar had been guided by Konstantin Pobedonostsev, a committed supporter of Orthodoxy, Autocracy and Nationality. Pobedonostsev had been appointed as Procurator of the Holy Synod in 1886 – which meant that he was the Tsar's minister with particular responsibility for the running of the Orthodox Church – and he held this post until 1905. And of course, as one of the Tsar's ministers, his influence could easily extend far beyond the remit of his own department.

As the reign of Alexander II had continued, Pobedonostsev had looked on in dismay at what he regarded as the cost of attempting to 'liberalise' the Tsar's empire. His views became more and more entrenched. By 1881 he had become a vehement Russian nationalist, intolerant of any faith outside Russian Orthodoxy, and totally convinced that Tsarist autocracy was the only means of effective government for the Russian empire. Moreover, he was convinced that these views were the views of all true Russians. He believed that Alexander II had made a fatal mistake during his years as Tsar: he had listened to the opinions of unrepresentative, self-seeking people who had advised him wrongly and whose opinions were totally at odds with those of the great mass of the Russian people. It was the duty of Alexander III, he declared, to re-establish Tsarist autocracy in full and to dispense with the liberalism of his father. Such a course of action would gradually find the mass support of the Russian people.

At a time of great political turmoil in Russia and the empire, Pobedonostsev was contemptuously dismissive of the aims of liberals and revolutionaries. He believed that these political opponents were attempting to win support for ideologies which would mean the destruction of Tsarist authority throughout the empire. As a political theorist and legal expert, Pobedonostsev was not merely an uncompromising defender of Tsarist autocracy: he was also fiercely critical of the very concept of any kind of alternative political system for Russia. For example, he dismissed with derision demands for a form of parliamentary government for Russia. In his book, *Reflections of a Russian Statesman*, he called parliamentary representation 'the great falsehood of our time':

> 'Such is the complicated mechanism of the Parliamentary farce; such is the great political lie which dominates our age. By the theory of Parliamentarianism, the rational majority must rule; in practice, the party is ruled by five or six of its leaders who exercise all power... Such is the Parliamentary institution, exalted as the summit and crown of the edifice of State. It is sad to think that even in Russia there are men who aspire to the establishment of this falsehood amongst us...'
> (K. Pobedonostsev, *Reflections of a Russian Statesman*, 1898)

Pobedonostsev firmly believed that those who proposed the implementation of such 'falsehoods' into Russia had to be dealt with uncompromisingly. They had to be routed at every turn – censored, outlawed, defeated, crushed. By 1885 Pobedonostsev was urging Alexander III to abolish trial by jury and bring the whole Russian legal system more directly under Tsarist control.

In fact Pobedonostsev was instrumental in altering the nature of Tsarist Russia from the liberal empire of Alexander II to the police state of Alexander III.

Alexander, Pobedonostsev and Tolstoy: establishing control

From the beginning of Alexander III's reign, the Pobedonostsev outlook was evident. Within weeks of Alexander III's accession, Pobedonostsev had won his first, telling victory with a decision which clearly earmarked the end of the approach of the 'Tsar Liberator'. The point at issue was whether or not a Council of Ministers would be set up to carry out government policy. This was proposed by Alexander II's Minister of the Interior, Loris-Melikov, a man of whom Pobedonostsev disapproved. The implication of such a Council was that a group of ministers would meet, rather like a cabinet, and plan and put into operation Tsarist government policy. It must be remembered that up to this time the Tsar's ministers were appointed personally by the Tsar to departments which were independent one of the other. If the Tsar disapproved of any individual minister, he would simply dispense with that minister, and replace him with someone more to his liking. The Council of Ministers proposed by Loris-Melikov might not seem too radical a shift from this position, but Pobedonostsev convinced Alexander III that any lessening of Tsarist authority, no matter how slight, had to be opposed vigorously in order to ensure the maintenance of autocracy in full. He drew up for Alexander a proclamation which contained the following statement:

> 'The voice of God orders us to stand boldly by the task of governing, relying on Divine Providence, with faith in the strength and truth of autocratic power, which we have been called to confirm and protect for the good of the people, against all encroachments.'
> (Quoted in H. Seton-Watson, *The Russian Empire*, 1967)

During the meeting to discuss the proposed Council of Ministers, the Tsar's proclamation was read out. The rebuff to Loris-Melikov was clear, and he resigned. He was replaced as Minister of the Interior by Count Ignateyev, a strong nationalist and a conservative. But the Tsar's proclamation was not merely a rejection of the Council of Ministers: it was a clear statement of the direction which Alexander III would be taking. The 'truth of autocratic power' was confirmed 'against all encroachments', which is to say that any person or group wishing to see political change in Russia would face outright opposition from the Tsar.

Within a short period, Count Ignateyev himself had gone from the Ministry of the Interior, because he had suggested that the Tsar might consider working with a consultative assembly. This assembly was in no way envisaged by Ignateyev as any kind of political body: it was supposed to enable the Tsar 'to hear directly from the elected persons about the needs of their homelands, and in general for the sovereign to consult with the whole land'. Pobedonostsev immediately convinced Alexander that *any* kind of assembly representing the people was potentially dangerous and should not even be contemplated.

Ignateyev was replaced in May 1882 by Count Dmitri Tolstoy, a man whose views were much more in line with those of Pobedonostsev. From that time onwards, Pobedonostsev and Tolstoy determined the nature of the Tsar's government: it would not be of a liberal outlook.

A Tsarist régime headed by Alexander III and guided by Pobedonostsev and Tolstoy, intent as it was on restoring the powers of autocratic Tsardom in full, could only look critically at the changes made by the 'Tsar Liberator' and attempt to reverse those viewed as undesirable. It gradually became clear that any source of power which did not stem directly from the Tsar fitted this category.

One focus of attention was the Russian countryside in the wake of the 1861 emancipation. Alexander II had wanted to free Russia's serfs as a preliminary step towards modernising the state. An additional consideration had been that the Tsar would rid himself of the troublesome landed gentry; but in the short term the nobles were included in the zemstva system of local government. All this did not fit into the scheme of things in Alexander III's Russia. Tolstoy began to redress the balance: he set out to bring the Russian peasantry back under the control of Tsarist autocracy, while at the same time removing much of the remaining influence of the nobility. This required the elimination of the authority of the zemstva.

The process by which the zemstva were stripped of influence was a subtle one. In 1889 an act was passed which abolished the zemstva justices of the peace, the key officers who acted as a link between the elected zemstva and the peasants. In their place were to be appointed 'land commandants', who were members of the hereditaty nobility and who had to be acceptible to the Ministry of the Interior – in other words, to Tolstoy and the Tsar. These 'land commandants' held considerable authority over peasant villages and were introduced to ensure that no self-government, either through the zemstva or through any other organisation, existed there.

Alexander III, Pobedonostsev and Tolstoy were determined to wipe out political opposition. The law and the courts were an early focus of attention, but the Tsar and his key ministers were of the opinion that this required much keener attention than simply ensuring that those caught defying Tsarist authority would be duly punished: it required active opposition within the revolutionary underground itself.

As previously noted on page 31, Russia's political police first appeared as Tsar Nicholas I's response to the Decembrist Rising of 1825. Alexander III took policing considerably further when in 1883 he established a Department of Police as part of the Ministry of the Interior headed by Tolstoy. Over the next few years, a transformation developed in Russia's legal situation. The main thrust of this transformation was that the law courts were systematically removed from jurisdiction over what were classified as political crimes. And the only definition of a political crime was any crime which the Tsar decreed was political. Political criminals were dealt with directly by the Ministry of the Interior, which had the power to sentence offenders without in any way having to refer to the judiciary. Within a short period, the extent of the growth of Alexander III's police state was such that even minor police figures could imprison or send into exile those just suspected of political crimes. Figure 2.2 shows a dissident being put in chains by members of the Tsar's secret police force, which was called the okhrana. Very often such dissidents were exiled, without trial, by the police. They were sent to remote parts of the empire, such as Siberia, simply to remove them from Russia's cities where they might stir up trouble against the Tsar.

Fig 2.2   Inhumane treatment of a dissident.

In 1885, George Kennan, who had lived in Russia as a young man, returned to the empire to do a report on the prison system. Here he describes the journey of prisoners and political exiles to Siberia:

> 'Marching parties of convicts three or four hundred strong leave Tomsk for Irkutsk weekly throughout the whole year, and make the journey of 1040 miles [1660 kilometres] in about three months . . . Each prisoner receives five cents a day in money for his subsistence and buys food for himself from peasants along the road who make a business of furnishing it . . . No distinction is made between common convicts and political convicts, except that the latter, if they are nobles or belong to one of the privileged classes, receive seven and a half cents a day instead of five and are carried in carts instead of being forced to walk.'
>
> (G. Kennan, *Siberia and the Exile System*, 1891)

From this it is easy to see how commonplace exile was during the reign of Alexander III. Figure 2.3 shows how Tsarist Russia's treatment of its people was viewed from abroad. In Siberia, summers can be very hot and winters very severe, with temperatures often falling well below zero. Remember that most of the people sent to these places were sent without trial, and often on the orders of fairly minor police officials.

Fig 2.3 'Russian civilisation'. An English cartoon showing prisoners travelling under escort to Siberia.

It is, of course, easy to be critical of the measures passed by Alexander III, but it should not be overlooked that it seemed to the Tsar that Russia was under threat from elements which he genuinely believed were directly opposed to his people. The Tsar was not an evil monster intent on keeping Russia's people under rigid control for the sake of it. He was a genuine believer in an ideology based upon centuries of Tsarist control of Russia; upon fervent religious belief; and upon a sense of duty and purpose. He believed that he had to restore in full Tsarist authority on Russia and to pass on intact the reins of the empire to his successor, the Tsarevich Nicholas. Those whom he penalised he believed were a threat to the very essence of Russia, and he was honestly convinced that it was his God-given duty to oppose them.

Relations with European states

Alexander III realised that Russia was not strong enough to pursue an aggressive foreign policy, nor did Russia have anything in particular to gain from such a policy. For that reason, Russia adopted a conciliatory approach to the other European powers which clearly showed that her main priority was self-protection.

Soon after Alexander III became Tsar, he joined Germany and Austria-Hungary in an arrangement called the League of the Three Emperors. The main part of this arrangement was that all parties agreed not to oppose each other by allying with any enemy which went to war against a League power. Unfortunately the agreement collapsed within four years because of differences between Russia and Austria, Russia having bitterly accused Austria of plotting against Tsarist interests in Bulgaria. This developing antagonism between Russia and Austria over Balkan territories grew progressively over the next three decades, and in 1914 played a decisive part in bringing about the First World War.

Following the accession of Kaiser Wilhelm II of Germany in 1890, relations between Russia and Germany rapidly deteriorated, and the Tsar became receptive to French approaches. France, which was fearful of German development and was keen for a strong ally which would hem in Germany from the other side, had patiently awaited her opportunity to approach Russia. In 1892 a Franco-Russian Convention was signed, and by this Russia and France pledged each other support should either of them be involved in a war with Germany. This arrangement was confirmed in 1894. An essential part of it was that French capital and expertise should be made available to Russia to assist with Russian industrialisation, and more will be said about this in Issue 4.

Russification

The policy of Russification

As indicated in Issue I, aspects of Russification were clearly evident during the reigns of Nicholas I and Alexander II. Undoubtedly, however, the movement accelerated greatly during Alexander III's reign. This met with the approval of Russian nationalist intellectuals, who saw the Russian nation as representing the best of everything, including religion, culture, and even language:

> 'The Russian language was quickly raised to the touchstone of Nationality. Not only did Russian writers from Turgenev to Gogol extol the objective characteristics of their language; they implied that all other languages were markedly inferior. "One can confidently affirm," wrote Grech, the grammarian, "that our language is superior to all the modern European languages." "The Russian language," wrote Bulgarin, "which without doubt holds first place in melodiousness and in the richness and ease of word construction, is the language of poetry and literature in all the countries of the globe." '

(Quoted in N. Davies, *God's Playground: A History of Poland*, 1981)

The Tsar, Uvarov, Pobedonostsev and others like them were genuinely convinced of the correctness of Russian Orthodox Christianity and of the superiority of all things Russian. Academic support which suggested that the Russian language was 'superior to all the modern European languages' could only add to their conviction. Russification, they believed, could do nothing but good for all concerned. Once begun in earnest, the process in some ways took on the appearance of a missionary movement.

Military strategists approved of Russification as a means of making the vulnerable parts of the empire more secure. This was particularly the case in vital strategic areas, such as the Baltic coastline, where many of the Tsar's subjects were of German extraction. But throughout the border areas of the empire there was always a danger of the Tsar's subjects being tempted to rebel and join with their fellow nationals.

Alexander III and his advisers continued to promote the development of a great Russian empire as part of their policy. They did not doubt the civilising influence of Russifying underdeveloped parts of the world. They believed that Russians should take pride in the empire and in its achievements. They wanted the empire itself to adopt Orthodoxy, Autocracy and Nationality, so that it could become everything that the Tsar envisaged.

The process of Russification was applied in different ways at different speeds in different parts of the empire. The main aims of those who promoted Russification were that

1. the Russian language should be used throughout the empire.
2. the Russian Orthodox religion should be the faith of all the Tsar's subjects.
3. education throughout the empire should be provided in the Russian language and should be geared towards producing subjects loyal to the Tsar.
4. the legal system used throughout the empire should be the Russian legal system.
5. bureaucracy and administration in every part of the empire should be Russian in nature and preferably run by Russians.
6. all subjects of the Tsar should be eligible for conscription into the Tsar's Imperial Army.
7. all subjects of the Tsar should pledge their loyalty not only to the Tsar himself, but to the Russian nation.

By transforming his empire along the lines indicated by guiding principles such as these, the Tsar hoped to bring about internal security for all his people. In return, he expected total loyalty from them. Gradually, all the subjects of the empire would appreciate the superiority of Russian ways and the sacred truth of Russian Orthodoxy. That was the goal, but achieving it proved to be immensely difficult, as the following examples illustrate.

Poland

Polish territory at the time of Alexander II and Alexander III was divided amongst three empires: Russia, Prussia (soon to become Germany) and Austria-Hungary. But by far the biggest part of Poland lay under the authority of the Tsar.

At the time of Alexander III Poles in Russia numbered over six million. They regarded themselves as a distinctive people with a distinctive identity whose lands were occupied by enemy powers. Rebellions, such as that of 1863 mentioned in Issue 1, had long been a feature of the Polish situation, but the failure of that of 1863 had convinced the strongly nationalistic Polish intelligentsia that further outbreaks of active opposition to Tsarist rule were futile. A resigned acceptance had begun to set in: it was believed that the occupation of Polish lands was an unavoidable fact of life to which Poles needed to respond in a positive manner, by making the best of their situation. However, the policy of Russification adopted by Alexander III reawakened Polish nationalism with a vengeance. From being largely compliant at the time of Alexander's accession in 1881, Poles from every class of society became vehemently hostile to all things Russian by 1885. Even the Polish peasantry became 'nationalist' in outlook because of the sheer insensitivity of Alexander's process of Russification.

The architects of Russification in Poland were the Governor-General, Gurko, and the Curator of the Warsaw educational district, Apukhtin. They made Poland's educational system an immediate target. For some time, schools in Poland had been the subject of insensitive Russification. The following extract from the biography of the famous Polish scientist, Marie Curie, written by her daughter, illustrates the kind of activity which had caused great resentment amongst Poles during the reign of Alexander II:

'M. Hornberg [the Warsaw school inspector], accepting the chair offered to him . . ., seated himself heavily.
   "Please call on one of these young people."
   [Marya, the young Marie Curie, was selected.]
   "Your prayer," snapped M. Hornberg.
   Marya recited "Our Father" in a voice without colour or expression. One of the subtlest humiliations the Tsar had discovered was to make the Polish children say their Catholic prayers every day in Russian . . .
   "Name the Tsars who have reigned over our Holy Russia since Catherine II."
   "Catherine II, Paul I, Alexander I, Nicholas I, Alexander II."
   The inspector was satisfied. This child had a good memory . . .
   "Who rules over us?"
   To conceal the fire in their eyes, the directress and superintendant stared hard at the registers they held before them. As the answer did not come quickly enough, Hornberg, annoyed, asked again in louder tones:
   "Who rules over us?"
   "His Majesty Alexander II, Tsar of all the Russias," Marya articulated painfully. Her face had gone white.
   The session was over. The functionary rose from his chair, and, after a brief nod, moved to the next room.'

(E. Curie, *Madame Curie*, 1936)

Gurko and Apukhtin supervised a further intensification of measures affecting education in Poland. In 1885 a law was passed which decreed that all school subjects except Catholic religious education and the Polish language had to be taught in Russian. The idea here was to ensure that those who wanted the necessary educational qualifications to succeed were Russian speakers. Eventually, it was hoped, the Polish language would disappear. What actually happened was that the quality of Polish education, which had formerly been regarded as well in advance of anything in Russia, deteriorated. Perhaps more importantly for Alexander III, Poles everywhere reacted strongly against what the Tsar was obviously attempting to do and opposition to Russification rapidly escalated.

Polish nationalism proved to be a great rallying force which cut through political barriers in Poland. The first political movement which actively opposed Alexander III appeared in 1885. It was called 'Proletariat' and was Socialist in outlook. Another group appeared in 1887. It was called the 'National League' and its aim was to unite all the Polish peoples, taking advantage whenever possible of the rivalry among Russia, Germany and Austria-Hungary.

When Alexander III died in 1894, Russification of Poland continued under his successor, Nicholas II. Resistance also grew, and Russia's last two Tsars were never left in any shadow of doubt about Poland's determination to oppose Russian domination.

The Ukraine

The Ukranians were a people with a long history and a distinctive identity within the Russian empire. They could trace their ancestry to the Slav peoples who arrived in the sixth and seventh centuries AD. Their capital, Kiev, had been the centre of Varangian authority over Russia, or 'Kiev Rus', from the ninth century.

The development of Muscovy and the growth of the Russian empire under the Tsars overshadowed developments in the Ukraine. The region gradually became part of the Tsarist empire, often under circumstances which appeared to be to the benefit of both parties. For example, in 1651, after a decade of devastating wars against Poles and Cossacks, the Hetman (Leader) of the Ukraine appealed to the Tsar to bring his territory under the protection of Muscovy. Muscovy continued the war against Poland and, in 1667, won half the Ukraine, including Kiev. Under Peter the Great, much of the rest of the region was taken over. The Ukraine was finally absorbed into the Russian empire by Catherine the Great.

The geographical location of the Ukraine, coupled with its economic importance, meant that it had complex national problems even before nineteenth-century Russification. The Tsar's Ukranian subjects numbered over twenty-two million in the late nineteenth century, but the national mix was very varied. Poles, Russians and Jews had long-established presences in the Ukraine. As Russian's programme of industrialisation took off in the 1890s, considerable immigration occurred by people seeking work in the relatively developed Ukraine.

There were also the Cossacks of the Ukraine. These Cossacks, a group of whom are shown in Figure 2.4, were the descendants of runaway serfs, criminals and adventurers both from the Tsar's empire and from the Sultan's Turkish empire who had found refuge in the Ukraine. They had developed a very distinctive identity, almost to the extent of being a different national group, in their villages on the Dnieper River. The word 'Cossack' comes from the Turkic 'kazac', meaning a rebel or freebooter. The Cossacks were brave and skilled fighters, renowned for their horsemanship, and uncompromisingly independent people.

Catherine the Great was persuaded to appreciate the potential

Fig 2.4   A group of Cossacks.

usefulness of the Cossacks as loyal subjects of the Tsar. In 1785, Cossack army officers were awarded the same privileged status as Russian gentry nobles. From that time onwards, Cossacks, and Ukranians generally, fitted comfortably into the Russian empire. Indeed Ukranians could be found holding official posts all over the empire. Cossacks were traditionally loyal to the Tsar, and were often called upon to suppress revolts against Tsarist rule.

Ukranian nationalism can be traced back to the 1820s. In its origins, it was primarily cultural, emphasising the distinctive nature of the Ukranian people and their language. Alexander II had felt it necessary to keep developments in the Ukraine in check, but his actions (such as the banning in 1876 of the printing of any books, pamphlets or plays in the Ukranian language) were not heavy-handed and affected few people.

Alexander III's programme of Russification was designed to be a more emphatic declaration of intent to consolidate the empire's control of the Ukraine. It occurred because Ukranian nationalists became more evident during his reign, and their ambitions were apparently more dangerous to him. Some Ukranian nationalists were seeking an independent Ukraine within the Russian empire. Others were attempting to join up with ethnic Ukranians in the

Austro-Hungarian empire. By 1900 a Revolutionary Ukranian Party had been formed, joining together revolutionary and nationalist ambitions. These were the activities which the Tsars and their agents were determined to crush.

The Ukraine was far too vital to the empire for the Tsar to compromise over. Firstly it was strategically important, as it provided access to the Black Sea. In addition it was the main grain-producing area of the empire. And finally, as a supplier of raw materials such as coal, it was of increasing significance as Russia's programme of industrialisation took off in the 1890s.

Probably Alexander III's intensification of Russification in the region caused offence to relatively few Ukranians and Belorussians. Those who did take exception to the Tsar tended to join the political underground and to veer towards Socialism as a solution to the problems of the Ukraine.

The Baltic provinces: Estonia, Latvia and Lithuania

The Baltic provinces became part of the Tsar's empire in the eighteenth century, and they accounted for three and a half million subjects under Alexander III. Many of the people were of German extraction. This was especially the case in Estonia and Latvia; Lithuania was more Polish in outlook. In Estonia and Latvia, the official language was German and the education system was based upon Germany's. Their church was the Lutheran Protestant Church. Although loyal to the Tsar, the gentry of these Baltic provinces tended to see German culture as being superior to Russian culture. But not all the people in Estonia and Latvia were German. Indeed, most saw themselves as Estonians or Latvians who resented the German élite who ruled over their countries. Many of the peasants, for example, were easy converts to Orthodoxy because they disliked the Lutheran Church run by German nobles. The legacy of German occupation of the Baltic provinces was that nationalist sentiment in the region was as much anti-German as it was anti-Russian.

In such a situation, Alexander III, with a sympathetic approach, could have won over the hearts and minds of his Baltic subjects. Instead, clumsy Russian heavy-handedness resulted in vigorous Baltic nationalism which was emphatically opposed to both Germany and Russia.

The geographical location of the Baltic provinces – their proximity to St Petersburg and the access to the Baltic Sea which they provided – ensured that Russification was applied there in a particularly energetic fashion. Language, education, law and religion received special treatment, the idea being to purge anything German from the provinces and replace it with something recognisably Russian. In 1885 the schools of the Baltic states were placed under the direct control of the Tsar's Ministry of Education in St Petersburg. In 1887 a law was passed which decreed that Russian should be made the language of instruction for all subjects. In 1889 the Russian system of law was introduced and all law courts were required to conduct their business in the Russian language. Pobedonostsev secured the Tsar's co-operation in insisting that any new Protestant churches in the Baltic provinces could be built only with the specific permission of the Most Holy Directing Synod. At the same time, funds were made readily available for the building of Russian Orthodox churches should Russia's Baltic governors request them. This was the beginning of a sustained campaign in the Baltic provinces to win converts to Orthodoxy. The task was made all the more easy because, whilst converts to Orthodoxy were allowed, converts from Orthodoxy to another faith were not. In other words, once the Lutheran Church lost a soul to Orthodoxy, it was thereafter barred from welcoming him back into their fold. Russification in the Baltic provinces was then spread into local administration and policing. Russian officials were imported to replace Germans.

Lithuania fared even worse than Latvia and Estonia because, being Polish and Catholic in ethnic origin, it represented an even greater threat than German Protestantism. For example, Lithuanians had actively participated in the 1863 Polish rebellion. The response then had been to send in a Tsarist hangman to root out the troublemakers. A number of executions and deportations were arranged, the Catholic Church was persecuted, and widescale forced conversions to Orthodoxy were carried through. Pobedonostsev and his associates reasserted their preparedness to continue with this process, with renewed vigour, and the standard measures of Russification – the removal of the Polish language in education, the elimination of Catholic education, the conversions to Orthodoxy, the sacking of Poles from key positions in education and administration and their replacement by Russians, and so on – were implemented.

In all the Baltic provinces, the reaction to Russification was similar. Estonians, Latvians and Lithuanians who felt that they had done nothing to merit such unwelcome attention resented the actions of the Tsar and Pobedonostsev. Churches were appalled at the deliberate attempt to seduce their peasant members away from them. Gentry officials took great exception to being replaced by alien personnel whose only qualification, it seemed to them, was that they were native Russians.

All these elements turned with new vigour towards nationalist movements which sought to break away from the suffocating overlordship of the Tsarist empire.

Finland

Finland had a distinctive identity within the Tsarist empire. During the Napoleonic Wars, Finland and Russia came to an agreement which they believed would be to their mutual advantage. Tsar Alexander I, having pledged to uphold the liberties of the Finnish people, was accepted by them as Grand Duke of Finland. This arrangement was concluded in March 1809 by an Act of Assurance:

> '. . . Providence having placed Us in possession of the Grand Duchy of Finland, We have desired, by the present Act, to confirm and ratify the religion and fundamental laws of the Land, as well as the privileges and rights which each estate [etc.]. . . have hitherto enjoyed according to the constitution. We promise to maintain all these benefits and laws firm, unchanged, and in full force. In confirmation whereof We have signed this Act of Assurance with our own hand.
>
> Given . . . March 15 1809.
>
> Alexander.
>
> (Quoted in F. Singleton, *A Short History of Finland*, 1989)

What this assurance appeared to guarantee was that the Tsar was the Head of State of Finland, but not in the same capacity as he was within the Russian empire. Finland continued to regard itself as an independent nation, with its own laws and institutions. It retained its own Diet, or Parliament, and an entirely Finnish government. Its constitution remained in force. Its Lutheran Church and schools were left untouched. The Tsar's representative in Finland was to be a Governor-General. A Secretary of State for Finland, based in St Petersburg, would deal with Finnish affairs in Russia. This equable relationship, apparently mutually satisfactory, remained the case until Alexander III decided that his leadership of Finland needed to become much more rigid in nature. This was probably one of the Tsar's greatest mistakes in his policy of Russification. The loyal Finns had given the Tsars nothing but co-operation and help throughout the nineteenth century. Alexander succeeded in alienating them for no recognisable purpose.

Russification of Finland started in earnest in 1891. In that year, the Russian language was decreed the official language of selected government departments, and Russians were appointed to the Finnish civil service. This was just the beginning of a process which really took off under Alexander's successor, Nicholas II. In 1898, Nicholas appointed the reactionary Bobrikov as Finnish Governor-General with a clear remit to bring Finland under closer Tsarist control. The key document in the process was the Imperial Manifesto of 1899. This decreed that in effect the Tsar could bypass the Finnish Diet and impose Tsarist legislation on Finland. One further measure which really upset the Finns was the Tsarist decree that they could now be conscripted into the Tsar's armies.

The Finns were absolutely outraged by these events. Finnish nationalism became a unifying and binding force. Further insults to the Finns added to their disgust. The Governor-General, it was decreed, could dismiss Finnish judges, police officers or civil servants suspected of being disloyal to the Tsar. Russians were given the right to purchase land in Finland. Even the Finnish postal service was to be incorporated into the imperial post office of the Tsar.

At first Finnish resistance was non-violent, but that ended in 1904, when Bobrikov was assassinated by a young Finnish patriot. By that time Finnish nationalists were in contact with revolutionary groups throughout the empire. Clearly the Tsar had gone too far, and even Nicholas II realised that it had become necessary to take some of the heat out of the situation. An Imperial Manifesto of 1905 reversed most of Bobrikov's measures, including the degree requiring military service. The Finnish Diet was allowed to exist again. All this smoothed over the situation to some extent, but Russification in Finland under Alexander III and Nicholas II had done much damage to relations with a former loyal ally, and the situation was never able to be restored to what it had been.

Quite incredibly, Russia's last two Tsars had managed to turn formerly peaceable friends into outright enemies.

Armenia

Amongst the most loyal friends of Tsarist Russia were the Armenians, who lived in the south of the empire beside the Caspian Sea. The million or so Christian Armenians, who had their own Armenian Church, had long been wary of Muslim Turkey and Persia, with whom they shared common borders. Indeed, some Armenians lived in territories which were part of the Turkish empire and were subject to bouts of religious persecution. This continued to be a feature of the region during the reign of Alexander III. For example, a massacre of Armenians by Turkish Muslims occurred in the 1890s.

Armenia had become Christian in the third century AD. Antagonism and rivalry between Christians and Muslims had long been a feature of the region. When much of Armenia became part of the Tsarist empire in the early nineteenth century, the Armenians gladly accepted the protection of the Orthodox Christian Tsar. In addition, they pressed for Tsarist support for the remaining Armenian peoples still under the control of the Turkish empire. Under different circumstances, Tsar Alexander III might have been sympathetic to Armenian aims, but in the late nineteenth century events in the far east of the empire so dominated Tsarist foreign policy that the Tsar wished to placate Turkey and to have a stable working relationship with the Sultan: this was one reason why Russification of the Armenians was embarked upon. A state of effective civil war seemed to exist between Armenians and Turks in the eastern provinces of the Turkish empire: Armenians were being slaughtered by Muslim

Kurds, and Kurds were being massacred by Armenian nationalist bands. By taking strong action to keep the Armenians in check, the Tsar had a ready way to win favour with the Sultan.

The techniques of Russification applied in Armenia were of the type already used in other parts of the Empire. Forced conversions to Orthodoxy were attempted, schools were interfered with, and the legal system was altered to fit in with Russian ways. If the process of Russification in Armenia was begun under Alexander III, it took off with a vengeance under Nicholas II. In 1896 all schools operating under the control of the Armenian Church were closed and were replaced by Russian schools supervised by the Tsar's Ministry of Education. In 1903 the funds of the Armenian Church were confiscated. In his passion to Russify Armenia, Nicholas II and his Commander-in-Chief in Armenia, Golitsyn, became totally reckless, indeed vicious, and the turning point came when Armenians began to offer passive resistance to Russification. What the Armenians did was to boycott Russian schools, law courts and administrative offices, and to set up unofficial equivalents operated by themselves. With the backing of the Tsar, Golitsyn encouraged the Muslims in Armenia (mainly the Tatars of Azerbaijan) to attack Armenian property. The Tatars responded enthusiastically, and by 1905 a situation of virtual civil war between Muslims and Christians existed in Armenia.

Turkestan and the steppe region

By the time of the accession of Alexander III in 1881, the region of Central Asia referred to by the Russians as Turkestan had become securely consolidated as part of the Tsar's empire. The policies of Russification referred to so far would not work with the peoples in this area: a different approach would be required in Turkestan.

Initially Turkestan was important to Russia because it secured the frontier borders between the empire and Persia and Afghanistan, and allowed the free flow of trade within the empire between east and west. Gradually the region increased in importance for economic reasons. It was rich in mineral resources. It was the source of much of the raw cotton which supplied the growing textile industry in the 1890s: by the end of the nineteenth century, it supplied over 80 per cent of Russia's raw cotton. In addition it became a vital area for resettlement for people from the overcrowded agricultural land in the west of the empire. For all these reasons Turkestan and the steppe region mattered to Russia.

The problem for the Russians was that they were a small minority in a vast region where the peoples were fanatically Muslim and very different in culture and outlook from themselves. The Tsar was aware that any attempt at Russification in such a region would have to rely upon caution and subtlety: the uncompromisingly ruthless techniques adopted in the European parts of the empire had no place in Turkestan. Nonetheless, Russification was deemed desirable by the Tsar and the process began under Alexander III.

Russification began with administrative reorganisation. A Governor-General was appointed for Turkestan and another for the steppe region. These Governors-General were both military men, and part of their remit was to look after the military forces of the areas. In effect, the Russian military were placed in control of administration, although the military dimension was kept at a low profile. Administrative control of Turkestan and the steppe region tended to end at village level, where the native headmen were left in control. This created the impression that there was little change in how most of the native population lived their lives.

This kind of approach was continued in vital areas such as the law. The law in Turkestan and the steppe region was reorganised along Russian lines, and manned by Russian personnel at higher levels, although local Muslim courts retained control over local criminal cases. All land was nationalised, but then reassigned to the people who actually worked on it. The tax system was modified in such a way as to benefit the peasantry, although corrupt tax officials rapidly ensured that the benefits were enjoyed largely by themselves. Conscription into the Imperial Army was not forced on the native peoples. The education system was approached diplomatically: in 1884 Russian-native schools were established, and these allowed for a primary education in the native language, a Muslim religious education, and instruction in Russian language. The native schools already in existence were not closed, but they were deprived of state support. The Tsar obviously hoped that these schools would gradually die out, but he was mistaken: Muslim schools supported by private funds continued to prosper – further clear evidence that the Muslims were determined to retain their own identity.

The Tsar believed that an important part of the process of Russification in the steppe region would be an influx of Russian peasants attracted by the availability of land; this was not really an option in Turkestan itself, which was already extensively populated. By 1911 about a million and a half peasants had moved to the steppe region. Russian immigration into Turkestan itself tended to be by railway and factory workers, but by 1911 there were only just over 400,000 of these in a population of 6.5 million. So in both the steppe region and Turkestan the predominant native characteristic was far from being Russian in character.

By the early twentieth century, Turkestan and the steppe region were far from being Russified in the way that the Tsars had hoped. On the contrary, in spite of improving transport and communications in the regions, the provision of education and medicine, and the tax situation, the native peoples were progressively becoming alienated from Tsardom. This was mainly because of the Tsar's administrators, the military men whose task was to govern the regions sympathetically and to ease through the process of Russification. In reality, most of the people concerned were incompetent and corrupt. Russian settlers in the region were another source of bitter native antagonism: they were greedy for land and sought to maximise their holdings wherever possible: this inevitably brought them into conflict with the native peasants.

The last Tsarist Governor-General of Turkestan, Kuropatkin, observed in retrospect that the policies of the empire had singularly failed to make the native peoples loyal servants of the Tsar.

The Jews

There were approximately four million practising Jews in the empire when Alexander III became Tsar. Russia's Jews had never been made especially welcome. During Alexander's reign their position became significantly worse. Nicholas II continued with policies which were recognisably anti-Semitic, in other words opposed to Jews.

Anti-Semitic sentiment had long been evident in Tsarist Russia. The Russian Orthodox Church, and especially its hierarchy, despised the Jews as the murderers of Christ. The ordinary people in parts of the empire where there were Jewish settlements disliked the Jews for the business activities in which they engaged – activities which seemed to lead to the limited incomes of peasants and workers disappearing into the pockets of the Jews. Such resentment placed Russia's Jews in a very vulnerable position: they were a readily available scapegoat to use when things were going badly. The accession of Alexander III was preceded by an ominous foreboding of what was to come: the assassination of Alexander II was vaguely attributed to the Jews, and a succession of pogroms – attacks on Jews and their property, including instances of murder – occurred throughout the rest of the year. The new Tsar and his régime turned a blind eye to what was happening, particularly in the Ukraine where most Jewish settlements were.

Russian Jews were severely restricted in their movements throughout the empire. Since the eighteenth century, they had been limited to a strictly defined region referred to as the Pale of Settlement. This lay in the south-western and north-western parts of the empire. They were also barred from buying landed property or from settling outside towns. In effect they were forced into 'ghetto' areas of towns, and because of prejudice against them, they had to rely on their own means of earning a living.

Following the pogroms of 1881, the Minister of the Interior, Tolstoy, restored order, but he also carried through a succession of policies designed to ensure that Orthodox Russians should be protected from Jewish influence. Jews had to keep to their ghettos. Severe restrictions were placed on the number of Jews who could be admitted to secondary schools or universities. Barriers were placed against Jews entering professional life in areas such as medicine and the law. They were denied a vote in zemstvo elections. Massive Jewish expulsions from Kiev in 1886 and from Moscow in 1891 occurred under heartless and uncompromising circumstances.

Nicholas II was even more harsh towards Russia's Jews than his father had been. This was partly because, as Russia entered the twentieth century, the problems facing the Tsar and his government were becoming progressively more intense. The authorities in Russia found it convenient to turn opposition away from themselves on to the Jews. Pogroms became widespread, for example following the defeat of Russia in the war against Japan of 1904–05. Organised groups of thugs, with names such as the 'Union of the Russian People', consciously picked out vulnerable Jewish settlements to attack. Murders were commonplace during these raids. Figure 2.5 shows some of the victims of a pogrom in 1905.

Fig 2.5   Victims of a pogrom of 1905.

When more enlightened members of Russian society attempted to interfere in such pogroms, they were frustrated to learn that the pogroms had apparently been given official sanction:

> 'One day our head watchman Yegor suddenly disappeared, returning after a few days with a large stock of jewellery. Then we learned . . . that the most ghastly Jewish pogroms had taken place . . . in which he had taken part . . . As soon as my mother discovered [this] . . . she sent off a mounted messenger asking to have Yegor arrested. Hereupon the local authority replied to my mother that not only was Yegor's arrest impossible in consequence of the order given by a higher authority that members of the "Union of the Russian People" were not to be arrested . . . but that they were as far as possible not to interfere in Jew pogroms . . .'
>
> (V. Kovostovetz, *Seed and Harvest*, 1931)

As the Jews had no political rights, it was a logical development that Jewish intellectuals in Russia should turn ever more towards revolutionary groups. In 1897 The General Union of Jewish Workers in Russia and Poland was formed; it was known as the Bund. Issue 3 will illustrate how this group played a significant role in the development of revolutionary politics in Russia.

The Russification policy embarked upon by Alexander III and developed further by his successor, Nicholas II, could not be called a success. Those opposed to the Tsarist empire were not quelled. Perhaps more importantly, valued friends such as the Finns and the Armenians were alienated. The vast Russian empire, with its many diverse national groups, required a respected figurehead in the person of the Tsar to act as a unifying force. Instead, it was presented with three decades or more of frantic, bullying oppression, and this has to be regarded as one of the great mistakes made by Russia's last two Tsars.

ESSAY

1. What political problems did Tsar Alexander III inherit and how effectively did he deal with them?
2. Was Count Witte accurate when he wrote that Tsar Alexander III 'led an unimpeachable life' (see page 38)?
3. How successfully did Alexander III extend his authority throughout the Russian empire?
4. Did Russia's last two Tsars respond appropriately to the problem of the national minorities?

Political challenges to Tsarism

Not everybody in Russia agreed that autocratic Tsardom was the system of government which was best for the empire. Orthodoxy, Autocracy and Nationality had many political opponents. In this chapter the following issues will be examined:

1. The revolutionary ideologies of the Populists and Marxists.
2. The Liberals and the demand for a Russian constitution.
3. The influence of the Tsar's opponents.

In looking at these issues, we shall be examining the development of new *ideologies* in Russia. These *ideologies* were an obvious and direct challenge to Tsarist *authority*. The revolutionaries aimed to establish a new *authority* in Russia by which the great mass of the people of the empire would be able to develop new *identities* as liberated citizens able to control their own destinies. By contrast, Liberals sought to place limits on the Tsar's *authority* which would allow the Tsar to remain in office whilst ruling a people who had greater personal freedoms and their own representation in government.

The revolutionary parties got their message across to the Russian people by holding demonstrations, as in Figure 3.1, or by producing pamphlets which were handed around secretly, read at meetings, or scattered amongst the crowds during the demonstrations. Each party's pamphlets explained what that particular party would do if it were in power. They criticised the Tsar and his government, of course, but they also attacked the other political parties who were trying to win the favour of the Russian people.

Fig 3.1   A revolutionary party demonstration.

TASK

Divide into four groups.

Each group will produce a pamphlet to explain the political beliefs and aims of one group of Tsarist opponents, with reasons why the readers should support them and not one of the other opposition parties.

Group One will produce a pamphlet for the Social Revolutionary Party, designed to be read out to peasant communities.

Group Two will produce a Menshevik pamphlet for distribution to factory workers.

Group Three will produce a Bolshevik pamphlet, also aimed at factory workers.

Group Four will produce a Liberal pamphlet which explains why Russia needs a constitution and a different type of government.

When all the pamphlets have been completed, hold a class discussion about the respective merits, or otherwise, of the various political solutions which the Tsar's opponents were proposing.

Opposition to Tsardom

There had always been opponents of the ideology of autocratic Tsardom. As the nineteenth century progressed, those people in Russia who wanted changes in the way that Russia was ruled looked at what was happening in countries such as Britain. Did political change result in chaos or disaster, they asked, or was it not the case that liberal, reforming countries were the strongest economic and military powers in the world? They looked at backward Russia, ruled by the autocratic Tsar and his closed group of selected, loyal ministers, who appeared to them to be both incompetent and corrupt. The great mass of the Russian people were kept in poverty and deprivation. The Tsar's critics asked: was it not clear that Russia had to change?

As the century wore on, the political opponents of autocratic Tsardom increased in number. Most of them wanted to limit the Tsar's authority. Some of them sought to remove the Tsar's authority completely. This latter group, called revolutionaries, only appeared in numbers in the second half of the reign of Alexander II. Those who wanted the Tsar to remain, but with limitations on his authority, had a longer history. For example, the Decembrists of 1825 (referred to on page 24 in Issue 1) wished to bring into Russia a constitution which would establish limits on the Tsar's authority, state the rights of the people, and bring into being some form of elected government. These were things which existed in many western European states such as Britain. The Decembrists failed, but their aims continued to be sought by others in Russia. The people who worked to establish such aims were referred to generally as Liberals.

Faced with uncompromising Tsars who wished to retain their authority intact, Russia's Liberals made little headway. Gradually, the revolutionaries began making their presence felt in Russia. These revolutionary groups believed that the only way to oppose Tsardom was to destroy it. They had very definite visions of what they wished to put in place instead of Tsarist control of Russia. One group, the Populists, believed that Russia's future lay with a society which would grow out of the peasant village communities in the empire. Another group, the Marxists, believed in a pre-ordained historical process which made political revolution inevitable: from that political revolution would emerge an industrial nation run by the workers. These groups of revolutionaries, and others like them, were declared illegal in Russia, so they had to operate as an underground resistance to Tsardom.

Populism

The first revolutionary ideology in Russia which tried to win mass support was Populism. The Populists wanted to build a society which would be based upon Russian peasant village values.

Underlying Populism was the belief that Russia's culture was superior to all other cultures, her peasants were innately good and that, once the evil of serfdom was finally removed from the land, and once peasant villages were left in control of their own destinies, a new order would evolve naturally in Russia.

Figure 3.2 shows a typical Russian peasant village, or 'obshchina'. The standard of living in such a village was very low. What the Populists saw of merit in the 'obshchina' was concerned with the qualities of the peasants themselves.

Fig 3.2   A village or obshchina near Borispol in the region of Kiev.

Populist ideology was developed by intellectuals such as Alexander Herzen and admired by the great Russian writers such as Leo Tolstoy, Dostoyevsky and Turgenev. In *War and Peace*, written between 1861 and 1865, but based upon the invasion of Russia by the armies of Napoleon Bonaparte in 1812, Tolstoy describes a meeting between Pierre, a character based upon Tolstoy himself, and the peasant Platon Karateyev. Notice how the clever, educated Pierre is made to realise that true virtue and wisdom lie with the simple peasant:

> 'In the shed, where Pierre spent four weeks, there were twenty-three soldiers, three officers and two civilian functionaries, all prisoners like himself. Pierre remembered them afterwards as misty figures, except Platon Karateyev, who for ever remained in his mind as a most vivid and precious memory, and the very personification of all that was Russian... His face, in spite of a multitude of curving wrinkles, held an expression of innocence and youth; his voice had an agreeable sing-song note... His physical strength and agility during the first period of his imprisonment were such that he seemed not to know what fatigue or sickness meant... He knew how to do everything, not particularly well but not badly either. He could bake, sew, carpenter and cobble boots. He was always busy, and only at night allowed himself to indulge in conversation, which he loved, and singing... He sang not as a trained singer does who knows he is being listened to, but like the birds...'

(Leo Tolstoy, *War and Peace*)

This extract is representatives of the idealistic way that Populists regarded the Russian peasants.

Populist ideology grew in influence throughout the 1860s. The intellectuals behind it were of the educated middle and upper classes. Their problem was how to develop a plan of action which would allow their vision of a perfect Russia to develop. Between 1873 and 1874, a curious event occurred. Thousands of educated Populists decided to 'Go to the People' – to descend upon the remote peasant villages, to participate in the 'true' life of the Russian peasant, and to begin to 'educate' the peasants so that they would rise against the Tsar and establish a Populist state. The result of the 'Going to the People' movement was a disastrous failure. Often Populists were arrested with the active co-operation of the peasants whom they wished to prepare for revolution. Some Populists were physically attacked and beaten up. The Populists soon realised that Russia's peasants were very set in their ways and were not responsive to intellectual revolutionary arguments. Clearly the Populists needed to review their tactics.

Some Populists, such as the group in St Petersburg, lost faith in the idea that revolution would come from the peasants. They switched their efforts to the industrial workers and their ideas to those of Karl Marx (see page 66).

Other groups remained confident in the peasants and tried a different approach. One such group, which rose to prominence, was 'Land and Freedom', which appeared at the end of 1876. 'Land and Freedom' remained committed to the idea that revolutionaries should work amongst the peasants, gaining their confidence and educating them in such a way as to convince them that revolution was necessary and could be achieved by mass peasant support. Members of the 'Land and Freedom' group dressed in peasant clothes and became in every respect like peasants. Many of them took part in a second 'Going to the People' movement, settling in remote villages and doing vital jobs. Some became village doctors, or teachers, or skilled workmen. They helped the peasants in their daily lives, while at the same time organising peasant resistance to Tsarist officials and landlords. Although 'Land and Freedom' seemed to make significant headway in individual villages, and was of great assistance in practical ways to the peasants concerned, it soon became clear that there was little realistic hope that a peasant revolution would occur.

By 1879 'Land and Freedom' had ceased to exist. The Populists had yet again failed to achieve anything of note. In place of the earnest efforts of the early Populists, a new desperation was beginning to appear. Terrorism was now being advocated as the only way of forcing concessions from the Tsar. In April 1879 an attempt was made on the life of Alexander II. It failed. A new group emerged which believed that Populist ambitions could only make headway by an active campaign of political terrorism. This group was called the 'People's Will'. On 1 March 1881, members of the 'People's Will' carried out the act which it believed would force Tsarism to make concessions: they assassinated Alexander II. Figure 3.3 is an artist's impression of the terrorist bomb exploding and fatally wounding the Tsar. As already noted, instead of the hoped-for political revolution, this atrocity ended the attempts at liberal reform by Alexander II and ushered in a new régime of reaction under Tsar Alexander III.

The Populists were the originators of the revolutionary terrorism which plagued Russia during the reigns of the last two Tsars. In the 1880s, under Alexander III's strict régime, and because of a sense of failure in the minds of the Populists themselves, order of a sort was restored to Russia. Revolutionary terrorism, however, was never far away. For example, in 1887 a revolutionary Populist called Alexander Ulyanov and his colleagues plotted the assassination of Alexander III. They were caught and Ulyanov and four of his accomplices were hanged. Ulyanov's younger brother, Vladimir, swore vengeance on the Tsarist régime. In 1900 Vladimir Ulyanov adopted the name by which he became famous: Lenin.

The next surge of Populist activity occurred in the 1890s in response to the social changes which occurred because of the industrialisation process which will be examined in Issue 4. Populists saw the revolutionary potential of the new industrial workforce. Most of the new factory workers were really rural peasants who, despite working most of the time in the towns, continued to maintain contact with their villages. For example, they often left the towns at harvest time and returned to their

Fig 3.3   An artist's view of the assassination of Tsar Alexander ll in March 1881.

villages. Thousands of these people, crammed together in the poor quarters of St Petersburg and Moscow, were ready prey for revolutionaries. The Populists saw the potential of broadening the base of their revolutionary programme to include both peasants and industrial workers. They reasoned that both of these groups had a similar vested interest in bringing about the destruction of Tsardom.

The man who developed the new Populist strategy was Victor Chernov. In 1901 Chernov became leader of a new political party which had evolved from the Populists, but which took into account the changes which industrialisation had brought to Russia. This new party was called the Social Revolutionary Party.

Chernov believed that the Social Revolutionaries should adopt a positive approach to solving the most immediate problems of the poor. He proposed that Social Revolutionaries should be working to achieve tangible benefits for the peasants and for the industrial workers, such as land rights for the peasants, and better wages and conditions in factories for the workers. However, other Social Revolutionaries wanted to continue the kind of terrorism begun by the 'People's Will'. This terrorist group gained most attention in the early years of Social Revolutionary activity because of the huge scale of their campaign. Between 1901 and 1905 they carried out over 2000 political assassinations. Divisions appeared in the ranks of the Social Revolutionaries because of these different approaches, but in general they continued to have a lot of support from the peasants.

Marxism

Marxism takes its name from Karl Marx, a German of Jewish origin (see Figure 3.4). When Marx was a law student in the University of Berlin in Prussia, he became interested in philosophy, and especially in the ideas of the philosopher Hegel. Hegel wanted to discover how mankind could be truly free. He proposed that people lived in an unnecessary state of what he called alienation, because they saw each other only as rivals or enemies. Hegel proposed that if the barriers between people could be broken down, all mankind could be liberated in mind and spirit. From such a liberation would develop an ideal society.

Marx developed Hegel's idea by looking at European industrial societies and by asking whether the source of alienation which stopped people being truly free was the economic relationship between them. By 'economic relationship', Marx was referring to the way that, for example; rich people owned factories and made profits, while poor people worked for the rich for wages. This was the line of thought which lay behind Marx's future philosophy. He developed it further, not in Prussia, but in France and Britain.

By the 1840s Marx had been forced by the Prussian authorities to move to Paris: the Prussians saw him as a political troublemaker. In Paris he came into contact with active French Socialists. The 1840s were a time of economic depression all over Europe and the poor of Paris were in desperate straits. This mass of industrial poor, which Marx called the 'proletariat', owned nothing other than their ability to sell their labour at the going rate when there was work available. In the 1840s there was little work. As a result, the proletariat lived desperate lives of poverty and starvation. They could see the small élite group of people who owned things, including the places in which they might find work, living in great comfort amidst their despair. Marx saw in the despair of the proletariat a way forward to a different type of society. He believed that the urban poor of Paris were the same as the proletariat the world over. Properly organised and under the right conditions, the proletariat could rise in revolution, all over the world, to usher in a new type of society.

This might seem all very commendable, but how precisely was the mass of the proletariat supposed to bring about the change to society which Marx envisaged? Marx's key texts provided his answer. In February 1848 Marx and his friend Frederick Engels produced and published their most famous work, the *Communist Manifesto*. Later in 1848 Marx moved from Paris to London. He lived the rest of his life there. Britain was the world's industrial leader, and Marx could see at first hand the effects of advanced industrialisation. In 1867 he published the first part of his most extensive work, a book called *Capital*. *Capital* elaborated at great length on the themes outlined in the *Communist Manifesto*.

In the *Communist Manifesto*, Marx begins with an analysis of

Fig 3.4 A Russian postage stamp commemorating Karl Marx.

human social development. He explains that, at every stage in history, people are divided into 'classes' : a small, élite 'class' and a numerically much greater 'class' who are under the control of the élite:

> 'The history of all hitherto existing society is the history of class struggles. Freeman and slave, patrician and plebeian, lord and serf, guild-master and journeyman, in a word oppressor and oppressed . . .'

(Marx and Engels, *Communist Manifesto*)

According to Marx, each of these forms of society eventually breaks down because of economic reasons, and a new form of society emerges. Industrialisation brought about the collapse of feudal society, that is to say a social order of lords and serfs, and replaced it with a 'capitalist' society – a social order of capitalists, whom Marx referred to as the 'bourgeoisie', and the workers or 'proletariat'. In a capitalist society, the class distinction between the small élite of 'oppressors' and the mass of the 'oppressed' remained, albeit in a different form from in feudal society. According to Marx, 'capitalist society' made it very easy to distinguish between the classes:

> 'Our epoch [age], the epoch of the bourgeoisie, possesses . . .
> this distinctive feature: it has simplified the class antagonisms.
> Society as a whole is more and more splitting up into two
> great hostile camps, into two great classes directly facing
> each other: Bourgeoisie and Proletariat.'
> (Marx and Engels, *Communist Manifesto*)

In his book *Capital*, Marx agreed with other economists about what 'capital' actually was: it was all the requirements of production except labour. In other words, 'capital' was things such as factories, machines and raw materials. 'Capitalists', according to Marx, pay their workers the lowest wages that they can to ensure that they make as big a profit as possible. Then they use most of this profit to invest in even more capital, to hire even more workers at the cheapest possible rate. Great wealth is gradually created, but it lies in the hands of the capitalists. The workers, or proletariat, become more and more alienated from the process as it continues: their lives become drudgery; they become 'wage slaves'. Furthermore, in their rush to maximise profits, capitalists will engage in inhuman practices, such as using child labour, taking risks with people's lives by refusing to take safety precautions, and so on. After all, the capitalist seeks only to make as much profit as possible from his workers, and this means that he will not pay for any benefits for his workforce.

Capital is extensively filled with Marx's own descriptions of horrific factory conditions in mid-nineteenth-century Britain. Undoubtedly there were numerous examples of dreadful workplaces and abuses of labour for Marx to refer to, and he was scathing in his criticisms. Capitalism, declared Marx, was 'dripping from head to foot, from every pore, with blood and dirt'.

But a triumphant message emerged from Marx's text. He declared that capitalism had to collapse, because it was fatally flawed. It contained within its own mechanism the seeds of its own destruction. Not only that, but from the collapse of capitalism would emerge a new society, capable of using capital wisely and establishing the conditions whereby the spirit of mankind would prosper. Why was this?

According to Marx, capitalists would continue to minimise wages and maximise profits for investment, but eventually they would be in an impossible position. Profits could be made only if people bought the goods that the capitalists were producing. But these same people who were required to buy the goods were the proletariat – from whom the capitalists, by paying the minimum wages possible, were removing the ability to purchase the goods produced in the factories. What would happen then was that powerful capitalists, in response to falling sales and, hence falling profits, would undercut their rivals. This would put smaller capitalist businessmen out of business, until eventually only a handful of capitalists would hold all the means of production, and the mass of the people would have no means of buying what was produced. Economic collapse would occur and revolution would develop.

There could be only one winner of this revolution: the great mass of the proletariat. The proletariat would then take over the means of production – the factories, machines and so forth – and use their control of capital to form a different type of society. That would mean producing goods to meet the needs of the people themselves, not to make profits for a small number of capitalists. Marx coined the slogan which fitted in with this vision: 'From each according to his ability; to each according to his needs'. Alienation, the state of mankind first identified by Hegel, would be removed, because labour would be at one with tasks it was performing. Mankind would develop in harmony, each person at peace within himself and in his relations with his neighbours.

This was the vision which Marx saw. It seemed to him to promise an attractive future for all mankind. In addition – and this was one reason why Marxism became so popular – the Marxist world was one which the process of history had already pre-ordained would inevitably come into existence.

How relevant was Marxism to Russia?

Marx had developed a very attractive theory: what was desirable on moral or ethical grounds, the true liberation of the human spirit, *had* to happen because of the nature of the historical process and because of the inherent contradictions in capitalist industrialisation. However, his theory clearly suggested that only after a society had industrialised could the revolution occur from which a Communist society could emerge. In other words, a society had to move from the 'Feudal' phase of development to the 'Capitalist' phase. The problem for Russian Marxists was quite simply that Russia was not an industrialised nation. Indeed serfdom, which was recognisably feudal, had been abolished in Russia only in 1861. Russian industry was still in its infancy thirty years later. When Marx completed the first part of *Capital* in 1867, the entire work of over eight hundred pages contained only three fleeting references to Russia. The first two could easily be overlooked, so insignificant were they. The following is the sole mention of Russia of any length in *Capital*:

'Mr Redgrave gives full details as to the Russian cotton

factories, the data having been supplied to him by an English manager who until recently was at work in Russia. On Russian soil, where infamies are rife, the horrors of the early days of the Russian factory system are still in full bloom. The managers are, of course, English, for the native Russian capitalist is incompetent in this domain. Despite overwork, which is carried on without pause by day and by night, and despite the scandalous underpayment of the workers, Russian factory production is only able to maintain a precarious existence thanks to the prohibition of foreign competition.'

(Karl Marx, *Capital*)

This solitary reference to Russia points to a primitive economy, dependent on foreign capital and expertise to continue in its 'precarious existence'. Marx saw no possibility of the proletarian revolution occurring in Russia. He expected it to develop in Britain or Germany, the most advanced industrial nations in Europe. The implication of Marxist theory for Russia was that Russia would have to go through with mass industrialisation before a Marxist revolution could occur. Of course, for Russian Populists, the idea of industrialisation was repellent. Populists and Socialists in Russia read Marx's vivid descriptions of the horrors of the industrial cities of Britain, Germany and France. They wanted something different for Russia. They wanted to retain the distinctly Russian peasant village, with its innately virtuous people, and to develop a Communist society out of it. They wished to protect the Russian peasants from the evils of industrialisation.

Yet Russian Populists and Socialists were impressed by Marxist theory, and attracted by the idea that the revolution which they longed for would, according to Marx, inevitably happen. They began a correspondence with Marx, designed to answer one central question: was it possible for Russia to have a 'Marxist' revolution without having to industrialise?

At first Marx was adamant that the logic of history decreed that industrialisation was a necessary evil before the proletarian revolution could develop. Gradually, however, he changed. This may well have been because the revolution which he had so confidently been predicting would occur in Britain or Germany had failed to materialise. Russia, with all its problems, seemed to hold more promise for Marx. In the preface to the Russian edition of the *Communist Manifesto* of 1882, he wrote:

'The Communist Manifesto had as its object the proclamation of the inevitably impending dissolution of modern bourgeois property. But in Russia we find, face to face with the rapidly developing capitalist swindle and bourgeois landed property, just beginning to develop, more than half the land owned in common with the peasants. Now, the question is: can the Russian 'obshchina'... pass directly to the higher form of communist common ownership? Or, on the contrary, must it first pass through the same process of dissolution as constitutes the historical evolution of the West?

The only answer to that possible today is this: if the Russian Revolution becomes the signal for a proletarian revolution in the West, so that both complement each other, the present Russian common ownership of land may serve as the starting point for a communist development.'

(Marx and Engels, *Communist Manifesto*)

This was encouraging for Russian Populists and Socialists. It seemed, from this preface, that Marx was suggesting a way whereby a proletarian revolution could develop in Russia without Russia having to industrialise. However, in the 1890s, as we shall see in Issue 4, Russia embarked upon a massive programme of industrialisation and, for many Russian Marxists, this clearly suggested that the capitalist phase of historical evolution had begun in Russia and that the inevitable Marxist revolution was only a matter of time in coming. Others were not so sure. Divisions of opinion remained. Similarly, differences developed about how the revolution should be carried through in Russia.

It is to those differences, and to the revolutionaries who expressed them in Russia, that we now turn.

Fig 3.5   Georgi Plekhanov.

From Marxism to Leninism

Marx died in 1883. By then, his ideas had gained a solid foothold in Russia. The man who rose to the fore in adapting Marxist ideas into a policy of action for Russia was Vladimir Ilyich Ulyanov, later known as Lenin.

Ulyanov was born in Simbirsk on the River Volga in April 1870. When his older brother, Alexander, was hanged in 1887 for participating in a plot to assassinate the Tsar, Vladimir Ulyanov became committed to revolutionary politics.

Ulyanov was a student at that time, although he had just been expelled from Kazan University for participating in disorders, and he first became interested in Marxist ideas in 1888. He moved to St Petersburg to study law, and graduated in 1891. By 1893 he had joined a revolutionary group called 'Stariki' which was promoting Marxist ideas amongst the ranks of the growing industrial workforce.

Marxist ideas in Russia owed their origins to Georgi Plekhanov (see Figure 3.5), who knew Marx, had translated the *Communist Manifesto* into Russian, and had become known as the 'Father of Russian Marxism'. Ulyanov met Plekhanov in Salzburg in 1895. Plekhanov recognised in him an energetic man of action, and encouraged him in his endeavours.

Like many prominent revolutionaries, Ulyanov was eventually arrested by the Tsarist authorities and was exiled to eastern Siberia

Fig 3.6   Ulyanov (Lenin) sitting with a group of revolutionaries in St Petersburg in 1897. He is easily recognisable because of his baldness.

in 1897. Figure 3.6 shows Ulyanov with a group of revolutionaries in St Petersburg shortly before his arrest. In Siberia, Ulyanov plotted how to bring about the overthrow of Tsarism and the implementation of the Marxist revolution. It seemed to him that Communists and other opponents of the Tsar were too easily suppressed by efficient Tsarist agents. While he was in exile considering a future plan of action, a Marxist Party called the 'All-Russian Social Democratic Party', referred to as the 'Social Democrats', was formed in 1898. When he was released from exile, Ulyanov went to Germany, and with the help of friends he produced a Marxist newspaper which was to be smuggled into Russia. It was called *Iskra*, meaning 'The Spark'. Ulyanov began using the name pen-name 'Lenin' in 1900. In *Iskra*, Lenin promoted his ideas on how the Marxist revolution in Russia would come about.

Lenin's ideas were both distinctive and controversial. The first issue of *Iskra* contained the following telling insight into Lenin's ideology:

'If we have a strongly organised party, a single strike may grow into a political demonstration, into a political victory over the régime. If we have a strongly organised party, a rebellion in a single locality may spread into a victorious revolution.'

(*Iskra*, 1898)

This idea – of the strongly organised party acting as the vanguard of the revolution – became the basis of Lenin's revolutionary ideology. The revolutionary party would seize power and establish what Lenin called the 'dictatorship of the proletariat', which would remove capitalist opposition, socialise the Russian economy, and prepare for the transition to a truly Communist state along Marxist lines.

These ideas alarmed many Social Democrats, who did not trust this new direction in which he was taking Marxist theory. Most Social Democrats regarded themselves as true Marxists. Marx had predicted the inevitable collapse of capitalism and the coming into being of the Communist state. He had not included any kind of advance guard hurrying on the process. Now Lenin was proposing such a group. His opponents disagreed with him. They believed that Lenin's idea of a small revolutionary élite was potentially dangerous. They asked, should not the dictatorship of the proletariat come about from the efforts of all the workers, not just from a small élite party? Furthermore, didn't Marx say that the proletarian revolution could only occur at a precise point in historical evolution? Bearing these points in mind, what was the function of the revolutionary vanguard which Lenin wanted to set up? Who would control it once the revolution had occurred?

Lenin displayed an aspect of his personality which annoyed other Social Democrats. He appeared arrogant and opinionated; he was absolutely adamant that he was right and that everybody else was wrong. In 1902 he published a book called *What Is To Be Done?*. In it he emphasised the importance of the small revolutionary élite, well versed in Marxist ideology and in the techniques of bringing about revolution, who would lead the uneducated mass of the proletariat. He declared that it was vital to have the small revolutionary élite, working underground, as opposed to a mass party of all the workers who could easily be opposed by Tsarist agents. Lenin wrote:

> 'If we begin with the solid foundation of a strong organisation of revolutionaries, we can guarantee the stability of the movement as a whole and carry out the aims of both Social Democracy and of trade unionism. If, however, we begin with a wide workers' association, supposed to be most accessible to the masses, when as a matter of fact it will be most accessible to the gendarmes and will make the revolutionaries most accessible to the police, we shall achieve the aims neither of Social Democracy nor of trade unionism.'
>
> (Lenin, *What Is To Be Done?*, 1902)

Lenin's idea of a revolutionary élite never found universal favour amongst Russian Marxists. In 1903 a Social Democratic Party Congress was held. Brussels was the chosen venue, but the presence of police spies resulted in the Congress being switched to London. The task for the delegates was to put together a constitution for the Social Democratic Party which would be acceptable to all the members, and to agree on a programme of action. Although Lenin did not win every vote at the conference, he won the most important issues. The programme of the Social Democrats followed the Leninist line. However, many delegates continued to be very suspicious of the consequences of Lenin's idea that the revolution should be led from above. At the 1903 Congress, these delegates were in the minority, 'menshinstvo' in Russian, and they became known thereafter as the 'Mensheviks'. The majority, or 'bolshinstvo', became known as the 'Bolsheviks'.

Within months of the 1903 Congress, most Social Democrats had turned against Lenin's ideas. Some, like Akimov, asked a vital question: wasn't Lenin simply seeking to replace Tsarist autocratic authority not with a 'dictatorship of the proletariat' as he was suggesting, but with a 'dictatorship *over* the proletariat'? Lenin would not compromise with other Social Democrats. As a result, the mood within the Social Democrats turned against him – to such an extent that he was becoming isolated within the party. Curiously, however, his faction continued to be called the Bolsheviks, and the opposition to him still referred to themselves as the Mensheviks even though, clearly, the Mensheviks had come to represent the majority opinion of the Social Democrats.

Lenin thereafter remained uncompromising. His ideology, called 'Leninism' or 'Bolshevism', presented a practical way forward for opponents of Tsarism. All that was required was the opportunity to put it into action. Although Lenin and the Bolsheviks later rose to dominate the Russian Revolution, they appeared to be a fringe group of political extremists right up until 1917. At the beginning of that year, there were fewer that 20,000 Bolsheviks in Russia. Lenin's ideology, however, gave them purpose, strength and direction at a time when these qualities seemed to be non-existent amongst the other political groups.

Here is a brief summary of the essential differences between the Mensheviks and the Bolsheviks:

Mensheviks

The Mensheviks believed that the process of history was as Karl Marx had explained. They thought that Russia was still a feudal society gradually changing to an industrial society. Russia had still to have its capitalist stage of development before it was ready to have the revolution of the proletariat. While awaiting the inevitable arrival of the revolution of the proletariat, they thought that they should help the workers to improve their lives in the meantime, by assisting with trade union activities for example. They believed that the Social Democratic Party should be a broad-based party, open to all, with free discussion, elections to the leadership, and links to other opposition groups to the Tsar.

Bolsheviks

The Bolsheviks believed that it was not necessary to wait for full-blown capitalism to be established and then to collapse in Russia.

Properly directed revolutionary activity could make the proletarian revolution happen. They believed in a small, tightly controlled, élite party of professional revolutionaries, whose task was to foment revolution wherever possible, to overthrow Tsarism, and to establish the dictatorship of the proletariat who would oversee the revolution from above. They were opposed to any deals with other political parties, and even to helping with trade union activities, which they thought would unnecessarily delay the revolution by providing short-term solutions to the workers' problems. They believed that revolutionaries had a vested interest in the workers' conditions becoming worse.

The Bolsheviks and the Mensheviks were united in their opinion that Tsarist authority should be removed. Figure 3.7 is a postcard published in 1901. By using a wedding cake as a model, the Social Democrats give their view of Russian society. Look at the Tsar and the Tsarina seated at the top of the cake. But notice how, from

Fig 3.7   A postcard published by the Social Democratic Party in 1901.

within the ranks of the group at the bottom, on the left-hand side of the picture, activists are breaking away, encouraging others to join them. This is how the Marxist revolutionaries saw themselves, breaking away, waving the flag of liberty, and toppling the whole structure. As Marxists, they were convinced that it was only a matter of time before this would happen.

Liberalism

It must be emphasised that the majority of the opponents of Tsarist authority in Russia before 1917 were not Social Revolutionaries or Social Democrats: they were Liberals. The term 'Liberal', in the context of Russia before 1917, does not refer to a political party as such. Russian Liberals came from many different sources and had different ideas about what they wanted for Russia. Broadly speaking, however, they had a common aim: they wanted an end to autocratic Tsarist authority, but not an end to Tsarism. What the most outspoken of them wished for was that the Tsar should become a monarch with limited powers operating within a political system where there was a representative parliament and a constitution by which the people's rights were established. In other words, they wanted Russia to have a constitutional monarchy similar to that in Britain. This, they hoped, would remove the threat of revolution from Russia and allow for a peaceful transformation into a modern state.

Probably the decisive moment in the development of Russian Liberalism as a political force was when the Tsar Liberator, Alexander II, allowed the setting up of the zemstva in 1863. These zemstva (see page 32) were dominated by educated members of the landed gentry who employed large numbers of educated people – teachers, lawyers, doctors and so forth – to carry out all the administrative tasks in the countryside. So this was an important group of people who were active in the day-to-day running of Russia. They were educated and aware of the deficiencies in the Tsarist empire and keen to promote alternative ways of doing things. When Russia's cities began to grow because of industrialisation, especially in the 1890s, zemstvo influence in them grew as well.

A different group of critics of Tsarist autocratic authority also began to appear in numbers in cities such as St Petersburg and Moscow. These were the businessmen and financiers who were worried about Russia's economic backwardness, or the urban lawyers, teachers and doctors who were educated and aware of the shortcomings of the autocracy and wanted change.

Alexander III, as already noted, wanted to keep the zemstva which he had inherited from his father under Tsarist control; so he attempted to use his administrators to muzzle zemstva activities. In July 1889, for example, he replaced local zemstva justices of the peace with representatives of his own bureaucracy. In the following year he passed further administrative controls over the zemstva. These were the first, clear steps taken by Alexander III to remove the local powers which the zemstva possessed and to transfer those powers to Tsarist agents. Zemstva representatives were too perceptive not to be aware of what the Tsar was attempting to do, and they protested. They emphasised the historical role of the landed gentry in looking after the well-being of the peasantry. Their pleas fell on deaf ears. When Alexander III died, however, the zemstva hoped for a return to the ways of the Alexander II, the Tsar Liberator. They drew up an appeal to present to the new Tsar, Nicholas II, pledging their loyalty but requesting a return to their former status. Nicholas II's reply was a crushing blow to them:

'I am aware of late that, in some zemstvo assemblies, have been heard voices of persons who have been carried away by senseless dreams of the participation of zemstvo representatives in the affairs of internal administration. Let it be known to all that I, while devoting all my energies to the good of the people, shall maintain the principle of autocracy just as firmly and unflinchingly as did my unforgettable father.'

This Tsarist statement, delivered in a speech on 17 January 1895, shattered any illusions which the zemstva, and all Russian Liberals, might have held about the successor to Alexander III. It was a turning point in the development of Russian Liberalism. Many formerly moderate zemstva representatives joined with the radical elements within the zemstva; they abandoned political moderation and became active opponents of Tsarist autocracy.

Their spokesman was Peter Struve, a former Social Democrat. Struve drew up an open letter to present to the Tsar. He openly deplored the way that Nicholas II has dismissed the appeal made to him by the zemstva and warned the Tsar that because of this mistake Tsarist authority would soon collapse. Struve declared that Tsarist autocracy was out of touch with Russia's requirements and had become totally discredited:

'... your unfortunate expression ['senseless dreams'] is no mere reactionary blunder; it reflects a whole system. The Russian people will realise perfectly well that in your speech of 17th January you were the mouthpiece not of an ideal autocratic power whose holder you consider yourself to be, but of a bureaucracy jealously guarding its omnipotence. Now, instead of words promising a real and active union between the Tsar and his people ... [the autocracy] ... is digging its own grave, and sooner or later, but in any case in the near future, it will fall under the onrush of the living forces of the public.'

(Quoted in P. B. Struve, *My Contacts with Rodichev*, 1933–34)

Copies of Struve's letter were delivered to all the provincial zemstva and were well received.

By 1900 a Russian Liberal movement, as opposed to a series of totally unrelated groups who opposed Tsarist autocracy but who were not revolutionary, was in existence. Central to it were the zemstva, with their influential core of respectable landed gentry. But the Liberal movement included a wide range of groups whose common purpose was to bring about a change to the bureaucratic police régime which Tsarism had come to represent.

Of course, there were many disagreements within the ranks of the Liberals. For example, many of the old-fashioned landed gentry of the zemstva lived uneasily with a political movement which was designed to bring about the end of Tsarist autocracy, albeit not the end of Tsarism. Moreover, Struve had at one time been involved with the Social Democrats and he continued to refer to himself as a 'Legal Marxist', by which he meant that he believed in Marx's analysis of the process of history, but not in terrorism and violent revolution. When Struve used his editorship of the Liberal newspaper *Osvobozhdenie* to advocate a Russian constitution, thereby directly challenging the Tsar's authority, this proved to be too much for most of the gentry. The Tsar's Minister of the Interior, Plehve, successfully drew them away from Struve's Liberalism with promises of greater involvement in Russia's administration. Undeterred, Struve allied with prominent Liberals such as Professor Paul Milyukov and the lawyer Rodichev to develop a distinctive group of Liberals whose task would be to push for two main aims: a constitution and a democratic system of government for Russia. This was a further radical step with which many of the old gentry could not agree.

Despite the many divisions of opinion, Russian Liberals were evident in numbers in the early years of the twentieth century. They were in legal political groupings with determined views about how the political control of Russia should be changed. They were without any real political power, but they were in a position to take advantage of any weaknesses in Tsarist authority.

The national minorities and the politics of opposition

As noted in Issue 2, many of the empire's national minorities took great exception to Russification and sought to break away from Tsarist authority. The leaders of these minorities were understandably very interested in the development of the various political groups in opposition to the Tsar's authority. This was partly because they were interested in any challenge to Tsarist authority which might successfully overturn the autocracy and thus allow the national minorities to break free. In some cases, it was also because they agreed with the political outlook of one of the groups: in other words, as well as being nationalists, they were also Liberals, or Social Revolutionaries, or Social Democrats. But the essential question for the nationalists remained: how best could they achieve national self-determination? In this context, their response to the Tsar's political opponents was coloured by how those political opponents proposed to tackle the nationalities question.

Struve's brand of Liberalism seemed to hold promise for the national minorities. Personal and civil liberties were emphasised as being the cornerstones of Russian Liberalism. Shortly after the first edition of *Osvobozhdenie* in 1902, Struve and Rodichev established a Union of Liberation, with the aim of uniting those whose politics were broadly consistent with the editorial line of *Osvobozhdenie*. Rodichev later said of the Union of Liberation: 'This was not a party, it was a union of people of different tendencies who were drawn together by one object, the achievement of emancipation.' When the Union's first programme was adopted in St Petersburg in 1904, a key clause in that programme was the acknowledgement of the right of self-determination of Russia's national minorities.

This kind of endorsement meant that those nationalist activists who sought self-determination could live comfortably with Struve's Liberalism. Many of them were Liberal in political outlook in any case. When, as we shall see in Issues 4 and 5, political concessions were granted by the Tsar in 1905, many national minority representatives voted with Russian Liberal representatives in the parliament or Duma which was set up. Equally, however, many did not. This was because their politics lay more in line with those of the revolutionary parties. One might note, for example, the thirty Muslim representatives who were elected in 1905; most co-operated with the Liberals, but six Muslims formed a separate Labour Group. The politics of this Muslim Labour group were broadly in sympathy with those of the Social Revolutionaries – but the six Muslims emphasised that they remained a distinctly independent representation.

Clearly there existed in the minds of many nationalists a division of interests. They might favour the political aims of groups from different parts of the empire, but their prime ambition was to achieve national self-determination. This was certainly the case where a national minority of the empire lived in numbers on its own territory.

A very different situation existed for other national minorities, such as the Jews, who did not have any part of the empire which was recognisably a Jewish homeland. In such circumstances, it was natural that Jewish revolutionaries should merge with opponents of Tsarism from different ethnic backgrounds. To some extent, the same could be said of the Polish peoples within the empire.

The party which had most difficulty in coming to terms with nationalist opposition to Tsarism was the Social Democratic Party. Bolsheviks in particular were unsure how to respond. Marxism was an international creed. The concluding words of the *Communist Manifesto* are 'Workers of the World Unite'. Historian A. J. P. Taylor explains:

> 'Marx had laid down at the outset that all struggles were class struggles. Clearly this must also apply to struggles between nations. Therefore "in proportion as the antagonism between classes within the nation vanishes, the hostility of one nation to another will come to an end"...'
>
> (A. J. P. Taylor, *Introduction to the Communist Manifesto,*
> *Marx and Engels*, 1967)

According to Marx, nationalism was a by-product of the class struggle. With the coming of world revolution, nationalism would disappear. Lenin and the Bolsheviks believed this to be the case. They wanted to bring about a Socialist world without national divisions such as those which existed in the early twentieth century. As Marxists, they believed that the dissatisfaction of Russia's national minorities had more to do with 'class' considerations than with national ones. But national minority groups sympathetic to Social Democracy saw their problems as the result of *both* national oppression *and* 'class' oppression. Their numbers, and the problems that they caused for Tsarism, meant that Social Democrats had to respond to them in ways that satisfied them. However, once revolution had occurred in Russia in 1917, how to respond to the national minorities remained a problem for the revolutionaries – and one which they were never fully able to resolve. Perhaps A. J. P. Taylor's observation is worthy of consideration, and could apply to Lenin and the Bolsheviks as much as to Marx:

> 'The truth is that Marx had no clear grasp of nationalism, only a desire to discredit the champions of national freedom, who were his revolutionary rivals.'
>
> (A. J. P. Taylor, *Introduction to the Communist Manifesto,*
> *Marx and Engels*, 1967)

In the 1890s, when industrial workers began the kind of protests that Social Democrats had hoped for – strikes, protests and so forth – the main area of activity was St Petersburg and the central industrial area of the empire. But it was in the regions inhabited by non-Russian nationalities, mainly Poles and Jews, that the pace of activity for the country as a whole was set.

The Russian government's policy of anti-Semitism had helped to make educated Jews more aware of their national identity. Such Jews began to believe that the best way of protecting their interests would be the setting up of an independent Jewish movement, with the support of all Russia's Jews. In 1895 Martov, a prominent

Social Democrat who was Jewish, devised the idea of a Marxist Party which would adopt a recognisably Jewish policy. He suggested in a speech to Jewish Social Democrats that the Russian workers had shown no evidence so far that they would abandon anti-Semitism and bring in a state based upon the idea of international brotherhood. Martov said that Jews had their own interests to protect and that it was reasonable for them to set up an independent Marxist party, albeit one which would retain links with the Russian Social Democrats. He declared, 'The growth of national and class consciousness must go hand in hand.'

In October 1897 the organisation suggested by Martov was formed. It was called 'The General Union of Jewish Workers in Russia and Poland'. Thereafter it tended to be referred to as the 'Bund', from a Yiddish word. The Bund rapidly achieved a reputation for effective organisation and management. Its membership grew dramatically and, in the early years of the twentieth century, its success rate in winning what it set out to get from strikes was in the region of 90 per cent. Other Social Democrats were impressed by the Bund. Equally, they were worried by it. It seemed to them that one reason for Bund success was the disproportionately high numbers of skilled workmen, as opposed to unskilled labourers, in its ranks. Was this, they asked, a genuine party of the proletariat? Another cause for concern was the increasing tendency of Bund representatives to emphasise the Jewish question rather than the revolution. Social Democrats wondered whether Bund members were genuine comrades, or if they were just a group of heretics who should be weeded out.

Nationalism was an obvious threat to Tsarist authority. It had many strong adherents throughout the empire. However, for the ideological opponents of the Tsar, such as Marxist revolutionaries, nationalism also created problems. Nationalist activists were no less strong as opponents to Tsardom than political revolutionaries. Many of them did not hesitate to use the same extreme methods of terrorism. Often, their ambitions coincided with those of other political groups in Russia. But equally often there were differences. Nationalism, once again, was the great imponderable in the minds of those who wished to work out how Russia and the empire should be organised and controlled.

ESSAY

1. Were the solutions proposed by the Social Revolutionaries likely to solve the political problems of the Russian empire?

2. Were Russia's Social Democrats a unified Marxist party?

3. To what extent was Russian Liberalism the product of disillusionment with Tsarist rule?

4. Was nationalism within the Russian empire a help or a hindrance to the opponents of the Tsar?

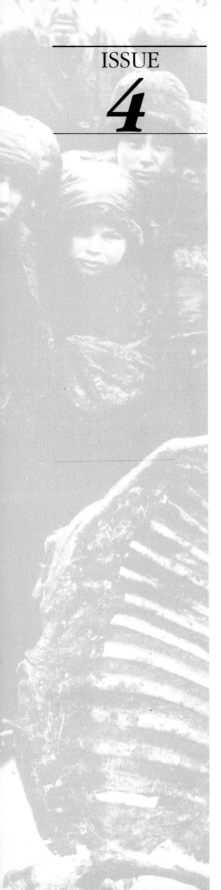

Why did Russia change?

During the 1890s Tsarist Russia began a massive programme of industrialisation. The Tsar and his government believed that this was necessary for Russia, but as a result great strains were placed on Russian society. The situation worsened when Russia went to war against Japan in 1904, and was defeated in 1905. Also in 1905, there was violent upheaval in St Petersburg. Unrest spread throughout the empire. The Tsar reluctantly agreed to allow Russia to have a constitution and a parliament, called the 'Duma'. In this chapter we shall be considering the following issues:

1. Why did Russia industrialise in the 1890s?
2. What were the effects of industrialisation in Russia?
3. How and why did the Duma come into being?

These issues raise questions about whether or not the *authority* of the Tsar was being eroded because of industrialisation and its effects on Russia and its people. Were the Tsar's people experiencing a change of *identity*? Were alternative *ideologies* to Orthodoxy, Autocracy and Nationality given new prominence because of the impact of industrialisation and war? How well equipped to deal with the empire's new problems was the new Tsar, Nicholas II?

TASK

It is January 1905. You are a factory worker in the Putilov steelworks in St Petersburg. You have heard that a march to the Tsar's Winter Palace is being organised. The purpose of this march is to bring the distress of the people directly to the Tsar's attention. Because you are one of the few factory workers who can write, you agree to draw up a summary of the grievances felt by you and your fellow workers, many of whom have recently come to St Petersburg from the countryside. You believe that the content of the document which you will produce, which will be approximately 1000 words long, will be reflected in the petition which will be presented to the Tsar.

Compose the message which you wish to have delivered to the Tsar, explaining how and why things have gone wrong for his people.

You should refer to:

1. living and working conditions in St Petersburg.
2. the situation in the countryside.
3. taxation and exports of food to pay for Russia's programme of industrialisation.
4. industrial unrest and the fear that workers are being drawn towards the revolutionaries.
5. the war against Japan.
6. your faith in the goodness of the Tsar, but your belief that the distress of his people is being hidden from him by corrupt officials.

Why did Russia want to industrialise?

As the nineteenth century moved towards its close, it was strikingly clear to Tsar Alexander III that the enormous Russian empire which he headed had failed to become one of the world's great powers. Historian Lionel Kochan comments on the dilemma facing the Tsar and his ministers:

'How could the empire continue to assert great power status . . . if its economy remained underdeveloped, its population illiterate, its agriculture unproductive . . . at a time when industrial development was constantly *widening* the gap that divided the great powers from the backward countries?'
(Lionel Kochan, *Russia in Revolution*, 1967)

Russia's internal problems were increasing in seriousness and this gave further urgency to the need for a change of direction for the empire. For example, the population was increasing dramatically (by over 90 per cent between 1860 and 1910). The emancipation of the serfs had failed to solve the problems of the countryside. Rural areas were overpopulated with landless peasants. Industry was so little developed that it could not give employment to more than a tiny fraction of the growing number of people.

It had not always seemed that Russia was destined to be economically backward. On the contrary, during the reign of Peter the Great (1682–1725), it appeared that Russia was set to become one of the great manufacturing nations of the world. Indeed, by the end of the eighteenth century, Russia was the world's leading producer of low-grade steel. A long-established 'domestic system' of textile production in Russia and the importation of the empire's first industrial spinning machine (to St Petersburg in 1798) seemed to be promising forerunners of mass production of cloth, the backbone of the British industrial revolution. In 1815 St Petersburg also produced Russia's first steamship. These developments should have placed Russia in a strong economic position in relation to the rest of Europe. But thereafter economic expansion stagnated. Following the Crimean War, Tsarist attempts to stimulate industrial development were only moderately successful. They paled into insignificance when compared with the dynamic advances being made by Britain and Germany in the second half of the nineteenth century. Why was this?

Several answers can be proposed. Firstly, Russia was severely lacking in capital: it had very few machines and factories, and very poor means of utilising the raw materials which were already present within the empire. Secondly, the empire's vital infrastructure – the system of roads, railways, canals, docks, and so on – was poorly developed. Thirdly, the labour force was largely unskilled and illiterate. Fourthly, the grinding poverty of the mass of the people meant that there was little or no market for manufactured goods in the empire, so there was little incentive to produce such goods. Fifthly, it seemed that the Russian outlook was opposed to industrialisation: the upper classes despised merchants and industrialists (the business classes are invariably ridiculed in the novels of writers such as Tolstoy and Turgenev), and revolutionaries such as the Populists saw the human cost of industrialisation as a great evil to be avoided.

Despite all these drawbacks, Alexander III decided that his empire had to industrialise on a massive scale. In 1892, two years before his death, he appointed as his Minister of Finance the man who would mastermind Russia's entry into the twentieth-century industrial world. His name was Sergei Yulievitch Witte.

Sergei Witte

Witte was born in 1849 in Tiflis, the capital of Georgia. He attended university at Odessa, where he specialised in mathematics. He was of minor noble rank. Following a successful academic career, he entered the service nobility, specialising in railway administration. As Russia's railways grew in importance, Witte's connections with other businessmen expanded, and he became widely recognised as a gifted, knowledgeable and reliable administrator. When the Tsar's government decided to create a new Railway Department in the Ministry of Finance, it came as no surprise that the man selected to lead it was Sergei Witte.

Witte was a great success from the start in his new office. In February 1892 he was appointed Minister of Communications. His main job was to oversee the completion of the trans-Siberian railway. He regarded this immense enterprise – a railway spanning the width of the empire from Moscow to Vladivostok, over a distance of some 6000 kilometres – as a vital project for the long-term economic development of Russia. The scale of the task was enormous, and in many ways it epitomised the massive job which the industrialisation of Russia entailed.

The route of the trans-Siberian railway is shown in Figure 4.1. Bear in mind that the railway had to cross the enormous distance from the Baltic to the Pacific, through remote and inhospitable areas of the empire. Think of the manpower and the materials such as iron and steel which were required from a nation whose industry was in its infancy. Consider the problems which this would entail, such as funding the venture.

Fig 4.1 Map showing the route of the trans-Siberian railway.

Despite all these obstacles, the project was completed in 1904. The benefits of the railway to Russia were immense. It provided easier access to vital raw materials. It opened up sparsely populated

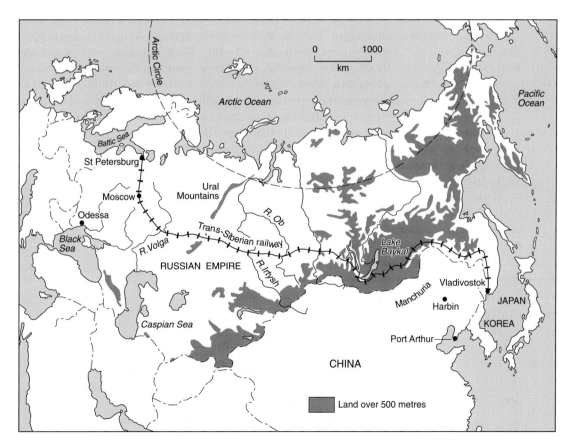

parts of the empire for resettlement from overpopulated areas and as a result increased Russia's food supply. It also had the effect of linking together the many different peoples of the empire more closely – and allowing a more rapid deployment of troops to areas where there were problems. So, although it was expensive to construct, the railway was a very important acquisition for Russia.

Six months after his appointment as Minister of Communications, Witte became the Tsar's Minister of Finance. By this time he had clearly found favour with Tsar Alexander III. This was no surprise because, as well as being a truly talented minister, Witte was also an uncompromising supporter of Tsarist authority. One reason for this was the personality of Alexander: Witte was subsequently to write in his memoirs that Alexander was a Tsar who stood above 'all selfish interests which prevail among ordinary mortals, above all the egoistical and material interests which so often corrupt the human heart'.

Witte appreciated the years of peace under Alexander III, which meant that the state's wealth was not squandered on wars which had been so much a feature of Russia's history. He and Alexander saw eye to eye on economic matters.

In his memoirs Witte recorded that 'Alexander III recognised that Russia could be made great only when it ceased being an exclusively agricultural country. A country without strongly developed industry could not be great.' Even on the specific point of the trans-Siberian railway, both men agreed that its construction should begin as soon as possible. Witte also fully appreciated the Tsar's desire to lead by example: the budget allocation for imperial court expenditure remained virtually constant, while every other government department was demanding more money. According to one historian, there was another important reason why Witte was such an enthusiastic supporter of Tsarist autocracy:

> 'But what perhaps endeared autocracy most to Witte – at least in the reign of Alexander III – was that under its firm protection a man could do a good job. Witte was an autocrat in his own right. Autocracy... favoured men of his type. What he wanted was a secure position from which to direct the affairs entrusted to him. Under Alexander III, the last Romanov who made his will felt throughout the government, he could do his job with the efficiency that comes from the possession of a delegated share of absolute power.'
>
> (Theodore H. von Laue, *Sergei Witte and the Industrialisation of Russia*, 1974)

Sadly Witte's time under Alexander III was not long. The Tsar died after an attack of nephritis (inflammation of the kidneys) in 1894. He was only forty-nine years old. He was a strong-willed and authoritative Tsar capable of living up to the role which he had inherited, and his premature death was a great loss to the supporters of autocracy.

Tsar Nicholas II

Figure 4.2 shows the new Tsar, Nicholas II. Nicholas Alexandrovich was twenty-six years old when his father died. When he learned that he was to become Tsar, he wept and declared himself not ready for the responsibility. Witte believed Nicholas to be recognisably more intelligent than his father, and fairly well educated, but the new Tsar's interests lay primarily in hunting, opera and socialising. He married a German princess, Alix of Hesse-Darmstadt, who took the Russian name of Alexandra Feodorovna, in November 1894, and when his children were born, his main preoccupation became his family. The much-recorded contemporary observation of Nicholas II – that he was not fit to run a village post-office, never mind the Tsarist empire – may well have been an unfair assessment. But it would be accurate to say that he was neither as strong nor as able a man as his father.

Fig 4.2
Tsar Nicholas II.

Nicholas was emphatically a Russian patriot. He was fascinated by the past history of the empire and was convinced of the merit of absolute Tsarist authority. His love of Russian ways was reflected in his observation that his least favourite ancestor was Peter the Great because despite Peter's 'great merits...he had too much admiration for European culture.' He determined that his reign would be that of an old-style Russian Tsar. He was convinced of the love and support which the vast majority of the people of the empire held for him, the 'Tsar-Batyushka' – the 'Little Father Tsar'. He was required to do his duty and would do so, and he planned eventually to pass on intact the autocratic power which he had inherited.

These might appear honourable and admirable ambitions. What was rather less honourable and admirable about Nicholas's personality was his preparedness to sanction quite brutal responses to challenges to his authority. He apparently believed that the vast majority of his people – the 'good people' – supported him and his autocratic power. Accordingly, if the few troublemakers who rebelled against him suffered floggings and executions, then they received their just deserts. Nicholas often recorded how he 'read with satisfaction' the details of his officers' inhuman treatment of strikers, rioters and dissidents. He always defended the actions of his officers and occasionally bestowed generous praise upon them.

But Nicholas had inherited his autocratic power at a time of enormous stress within the empire. As the situation evolved during the remaining years of Tsarist autocracy, wisdom decreed that at certain times the nature of the Tsar's role within the empire required adjustment. Nicholas, however, was stubbornly opposed to any concessions which would reduce his autocratic authority, only yielding when it seemed apparent that the alternative was violent revolution. In this he was energetically supported by Alexandra, who constantly reminded him of his unchallengeable, God-given, authority.

Nicholas's problems lay in the future. For the new Tsar, that future appeared bright when, to the accompaniment of cheering crowds, his coronation ceremony was held in Moscow in May 1896. This was the first coronation ceremony ever to be photographed. Nicholas had deliberately chosen Moscow and not St Petersburg for the ceremony, because it represented the old ways of old Russia, not the European modernity of a newer and, to his way of thinking, less attractive era. The lavishly arranged ceremony emphasised the close union between the Tsar, his state and the Church. Figure 4.3 shows the coronation procession. The enormous and enthusiastic crowds who turned out to cheer the Tsar seemed to symbolise a promising beginning to a new reign.

Fig 4.3   Nicholas ll's coronation procession in Moscow.

Witte as Minister of Finance

A startling reminder of the urgency of Russia's plight greeted Witte when he took office as Minister of Finance. The worst famine of the century, induced by drought and the resulting crop failures, caused nearly half a million peasants to die from hunger between 1891 and 1892. During his years as Minister of Finance, and then as Prime Minister, Witte worked towards a solution to the problems of the peasants. Indeed, his proposals pre-empted the work of the other great peasant-reforming figure of the pre-war period, Stolypin, of whom much will later be said (see page 115). Witte was in advance of Stolypin in promoting the ideas of annulling the redemption payments for peasants (see page 28) and of breaking up the inefficient peasant communes which so retarded agricultural development and played into the hands of revolutionaries. But the peasant question was, in Witte's eyes, just one of Russia's many problems, and as such would itself be removed in part by successful industrialisation.

Witte appreciated from the beginning that Russia lacked the capital and the expertise with which to lay down the extensive industrial base which he envisaged. He required an arrangement with a developed western power. As we saw in Issue 2 on page 44, common anxieties about developments in Germany under the new Kaiser Wilhelm II drew Russia and France closer together, and in 1894 an agreement was reached. The terms of the understanding required that both parties should work together in matters of common interest. Twenty years later, in 1914, Russia and France did unite to engage Germany and Austria-Hungary in war. But in 1894 the first item on the agenda was the development of Russia with French loans, capital and expertise. France saw nothing but merit in the arrangement: it would result in her having influence in Russia, the loans would be repaid with interest, and the money would be being used to make her ally stronger.

French capital alone did not finance Russia's industrial development. Other countries, such as Belgium and Britain, were convinced by Witte and the Tsar that Russia would be a good country in which to invest, to build factories, and to make loans. But of course the bulk of the investment in Russia's industrialisation programme came from within Russia itself. Between 1894 and 1902, almost 70 per cent of Tsarist government expenditure was directed towards the economy. Central to the whole programme was the railway system, the rapid expansion of which greatly stimulated the iron and coal industries. The Tsar's Treasury placed orders with Russian manufacturers, even though the materials could have been imported from nations such as Britain for less than half the price paid. The following table outlines the scale of railway development:

Railway development in Russia, 1881–1913
(in kilometres)

1881	21,228
1891	31,219
1900	53,234
1913	70,156

Other areas of the Russian economy grew equally impressively. The textile industry, long-established but in a lacklustre state before the 1890s, developed rapidly around St Petersburg. Essential raw materials, such as coal and iron ore, were mined relentlessly. The oilfields around Baku were vastly expanded. Accompanying all this industrial growth, the service industries – banks and financial institutions – grew rapidly. Specialist schools and polytechnics were formed in order to provide the skilled personnel required by an advancing industrial nation.

In his book *Sergei Witte and the Industrialisation of Russia*, T. H. von Laue has calculated that, if total production in Russia were set at an index figure of 100 in 1913, the relevant figure for 1892 was 31 and in 1904, after Witte's dismissal, it was 64. In other words, Russia's total industrial output *doubled* in the years during which Witte was Minister of Finance.

This was the positive side of the Witte years. There was also a negative side. Firstly, and most pressingly, developments on such a scale had to be paid for. Witte and the Tsar believed that eventually the benefits of industrialisation would be felt by the Russian people and would be reflected in a higher standard of living for everybody. In the short term, though, while capital was being built up, both the peasants and the rapidly growing industrial working class would be required to work hard for low wages and to pay high taxes. As most of these people lived very hard impoverished lives in any case, the extra demands imposed on them were liable to drive them to breaking point. At times both the peasants and the town workers faced intolerable pressures because of rapid industrialisation. Here are some of the reasons why:

Exports

Every year under Witte, Russia exported more than it imported so that enough money could be accumulated to pay for the foreign loans which were so essential to the programme of industrialisation. One key commodity which was exported in vast amounts was grain – and this occurred in a country which had so recently experienced a horrible famine and which lived in permanent fear of another one. There were massive grain exports which left from Odessa on the Black Sea. In 1897 famine returned, and stayed until 1899. Yet still the exports of grain continued. Figure 4.4 (on page 92) shows starving people from the Volga region during one the famines in the 1890s.

Living conditions in the industrial cities

Food shortages also affected the industrial workforce, but this was only one of their problems. In Russia's industrial cities, the worst social effects of early industrialisation had arrived with a vengeance. St Petersburg had a million factory workers and their families by 1900. Father Georgi Gapon, who later played a leading role in the events of 'Bloody Sunday' (see page 99), described their existence as follows:

'The normal working day ... is eleven and a half hour of work, exclusive of mealtimes. But ... manufacturers have received permission to work overtime, so that the average day is longer than minimally allowed by law – fourteen or fifteen hours. I often watched the crowds of poorly clad and emaciated figures of men and girls returning from the [cotton] mills. It was a

Fig 4.4   Starving people from the Volga region during a famine in the 1890s.

heart-rending sight. The grey faces seemed dead, or relieved only by eyes blazing with the rage of desperate revolt. Why do they agree to work overtime? They have to do so because they are paid by the piece and the rate is extremely low. Returning home exhausted and resentful after his long day's labour, the workman sees the sad faces of his wife and hungry children in their squalid corner where they are packed like herrings.'

(G. Gapon, *The Story of My Life*, 1905)

90 per cent of Russia's industrial workers were peasants, who returned to their villages at every opportunity. In many cases, their living accommodation in the cities consisted of wooden beds set one alongside another in factory-owned dormitories with primitive facilities. Even as late as 1910, 10 per cent of St Petersburg's population deserted the city at harvest time to return to their villages. When unemployment was high, most workers stayed permanently in their villages. Gradually, however, some towns, and St Petersburg in particular, were building up an industrial labour force which had no rural connections. This was the group which the Marxist revolutionaries regarded as being most likely to respond to their message.

The impact of industrialisation on ideology, identity and authority

From the statistics and sources referred to, it seems clear that Witte's programme was bringing about impressive results, but was placing great stress on Russian society. In addition, rapid industrialisation was altering the identity of Tsarist Russia and the identities of many of its people.

The revolutionaries in Russia responded to Russian industrialisation in different ways. Many Social Revolutionaries were dismayed that the Russian peasants were being sacrificed to the process of industrialisation, despite all the efforts made on their behalf. Furthermore, they viewed what was happening as part of a process which would ultimately destroy the innate goodness of the Russian peasant on which they wished to build a new Russia.

Other Social Revolutionaries saw the distress of Russia's urban workers as an ideal breeding ground for developing much greater, active opposition to the Tsar.

The Social Democrats, as followers of Marx's theory of historical development, believed that what was happening in the 1890s was the beginning of the transformation of Russia from the feudal stage in its development to the capitalist stage. They took considerable satisfaction from the belief that the next stage in Russia's historical development would be the collapse of capitalism in Russia and the revolution which would lead to the setting up of a socialist state. Social Democrats worked tirelessly amongst the factory workers in Russia's cities, especially in St Petersburg and Moscow, to prepare 'the proletariat' for the revolution.

The question for the Tsar and his ministers was whether they could continue to exert autocratic control over an industrialising Russia in the same way that they had done over a backward, agricultural Russia. The Tsar and his ministers had for some time been aware of some of the potential problems which the growing generation of industrial workers might present for them. As we shall see, as early as the 1880s, Tsar Alexander III had passed legislation designed to give some protection to the workers, thus emphasising his continuing authority over their well-being. But unrest, strikes and violence were clear indicators that not enough was being done. No Tsarist initiative had developed throughout the 1890s to exert authority over workers' organisations, such as unions. All that had been passed was an outright ban on the activities of such organisations. This drove the desperate workers towards extremism and towards support for revolutionaries. The Tsar and his advisers realised belatedly that they should be attempting something rather more positive so that the workers would not be driven into the revolutionaries' camp.

The first real attempt by Tsarist officials to bring factory workers under closer control and supervision was devised by Sergei Zubatov, as described below. This attempt shows how the Tsarist autocracy tried to use old ways to deal with new problems. Its failure was an indication to those in authority that their ability to control every aspect of Russian life was becoming more difficult to exercise. Lenin's observation was chillingly accurate:

'Revolution lies where the masses are. Not where there are hundreds, or thousands, but where there are hundreds of thousands.'

The labour problem and Zubatov's attempt to tackle it

With low wages, slum housing, rigid factory discipline and few effective safety precautions in industry, the workers understandably were seeking something better. However, the authority of the Tsar backed Witte uncompromisingly, and most of the ways by which the workers could pressurise their employers into making improvements were barred to them. Striking was illegal. Any attempt by the workforce to improve its position was sure to be a breach of some law. A few early attempted strikes failed to achieve anything of note, partly because the workers were passive and subservient, and partly because they were frightened of being dismissed and deprived of their means of livelihood.

As the industrialisation programme developed, however, the influence of the revolutionaries came to be felt more and more. They educated the workers on how to organise themselves and how to arrange strikes more effectively. In 1896 and 1897 Lenin and the Bolsheviks organised strikes of the St Petersburg textile workers and won a maximum working day of eleven and a half hours. During these strikes the Bolsheviks established for the first time workers' strike committees, called 'soviets'.

The response of those in authority was predictable. As the number of strikes grew, Witte recruited more men into the police in an attempt to keep the strikers in check. He did not hesitate to call in the army to suppress strikers, and the number of times when this desperate measure proved necessary increased dramatically. Army units were used to combat strikers fifty times in 1899, but over 500 times in 1902. This heavy-handed approach was not universally approved by the Tsar's ministers. The Ministry of the Interior, which often disagreed with Witte's Ministry of Finance, favoured a more subtle approach. This was attempted in 1901 under the guidance of the Head of the Moscow Security Police, General Sergei Zubatov.

Zubatov was convinced that the Tsarist autocracy had to do something to remove the appeal of the revolutionaries. He devised a scheme whereby the Tsarist state would control the workers' organisations. Workers' trade unions would be allowed to operate under police control. This might seem an astonishing proposition, but it was a measure totally consistent with the Tsarist autocracy's desire to exert its authority over every aspect of Russian life. Russia's programme of industrialisation had been state-controlled and the Tsar saw as part of that control the need to look after the requirements of the workers.

Protective legislation had been passed for the benefits of Russia's workers even before Witte's appointment as Minister of Finance. In June 1886, legislation affecting wage rates, medical assistance, food prices and so forth was introduced by Tsar Alexander III. Factory inspection was catered for. In addition, a large number of public holidays were allowed, usually in celebration of Orthodox Christian feast-days. The principle was clearly established that the Tsar was continuing to exert his paternal authority over his people. Unions and strikes might be banned, but an appeal to the goodness of the Tsar to help his people often brought some kind of positive response.

The Tsar's approach caused much resentment in the minds of Russia's merchants and businessmen who protested that Russia's economic development was being held back by government interference. Witte tended to sympathise with them, but his opponents in the Ministry of the Interior, mainly members of the old nobility who saw it as their duty to protect the vulnerable and to avoid public disorder if at all possible, were equally adamant in their views. The attitude of the Ministry of the Interior was that strikes were illegal and undesirable, but understandable. Rather than resorting to forcible suppression, they saw it as the duty of the Tsar's ministers to remove the causes of the dissatisfaction which had led to the strikes in the first place.

This was the background to the Zubatov initiative. It was an attempt to extend Tsarist influence to the industrial workforce in such a way that the attraction of those who sought to destroy the Tsar's authority – that is the revolutionaries – would be removed. Officially-sanctioned trade unions, operating with the Tsar's blessing, were to be a sign that, once again, the wishes of businessmen were to take second place to the Tsar's desire that his people be looked after.

Initially, it seemed that Zubatov had considerable success. His 'police socialism' adopted many of the methods of the revolutionaries. The 'Zubatov Unions' held meetings, discussion groups and lectures. Their purpose was to advocate a series of non-revolutionary methods of tackling the workers' economic problems. Social clubs were set up and plans were devised whereby workers' welfare schemes could be financed. All this seemed to be very commendable: the workers, apparently, were responding positively to the Zubatov unions. But the scale of the Zubatov movement began to worry the industrialists. When the Zubatov unions used their organisation to participate actively in mass strikes in the south of Russia in 1903, Zubatov was dismissed and the experiment branded a failure.

The collapse of the Zubatov scheme was a clear indication that the labour problem was not going to be controlled in the way that the Tsar and his ministers had hoped for. The twentieth century in the Tsar's empire began with many of the symptoms of a society in crisis: assassinations, strikes and rioting. It seemed that the policy of industrialisation, which both Alexander III and Nicholas II had believed to be so vital for the survival of the Russian empire, was beginning to appear as a double-edged sword. At times Russia's cities were becoming uncontrollable.

Witte's period in charge of Russian industrialisation came to an end in August 1903. His policies had so completely dominated the previous decade that other ministers of the Tsar were clamouring for a change of emphasis in how the empire was run.

The Witte years had transformed the nature of Tsarist Russia. The positive side of this transformation was the gigantic stride taken towards making Russia a strong, modern state. The negative side was the social cost involved in the process.

The 1905 Revolution
War with Japan and new demands in Russia

There were many problems for Tsar Nicholas II and his government as the twentieth century began. Russia's big cities, especially St Petersburg and Moscow, were experiencing great distress because of the effects of industrialisation. Violent strikes occurred in 1902 and 1903. Troops were readily used to restore order, but the scale of the striking, and the leading role adopted by the revolutionaries, meant that the situation seemed at times to be getting beyond control. While this was happening in Russia's cities, peasant riots caused by food shortages were widespread in the countryside. To make things worse, high-profile assassinations were taking place with worrying regularity. The Minister of Education, Bogolepov, was killed in 1901, and in 1902 Sipyagin, the Minister of the Interior, met a similar fate. This was the situation in Russia when war began with Japan in February 1904.

Russia and Japan had had long-standing arguments about territory and trading concessions in China. These disagreements increased considerably when Witte began the construction of the trans-Siberian railway. Witte expected that the tremendous investment in the railway would pay dividends to Russia in a variety of ways. For example, Witte believed that Russia would make great profits from freight charges as trade was opened up between Europe and the Far East. Russian naval strategists were also interested in the development: they were looking for a naval base on the Pacific which could be used throughout the year (as Vladivostok was ice-bound in winter), and they were attracted to the plan to take the trans-Siberian railway through northern Manchuria. This eventually occurred. Treaties signed with China in 1896 allowed the trans-Siberian railway to join Vladivostok with Siberia by the shortest route, which meant passing through northern Manchuria; they also gave Russia a naval base in Manchuria at Port Arthur for a period of twenty-five years. Port Arthur was linked to the trans-Siberian railway by a south Manchurian railway. Encouraged by these developments, Russia's naval commanders asked for more. They now sought a base in Korea which would establish a link between Port Arthur and Vladivostok. The barrier to such a link was Japan, which controlled the Tsushima Straits and had its own ambitions for the territories in which Russia was establishing such a strong presence. Figure 4.5 shows the area in question.

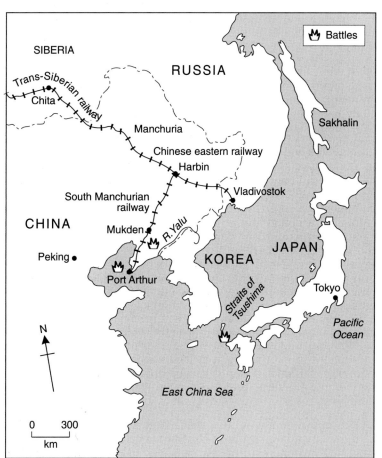

Fig 4.5 Map showing areas of conflict between Russia and Japan.

Japan had long viewed China's extensive territories as an area in which to solve Japanese over-population and as a source of raw materials. In 1894 the Japanese had seized the very territories which Russia was now expanding into, but had been compelled to withdraw by Russia, France and Germany. The involvement of these powers in the affairs of China were a reflection of the weakness of China and the watchfulness of all the Great Powers to ensure that they gained as much as they could from the situation. In 1899 there was a Chinese reaction to the involvement in their affairs by outsiders. This 'Boxer Rebellion', as it was called, was put down by the foreign powers, including Russia, which moved troops into Manchuria. When the Boxer Rebellion was crushed, Russia showed a marked reluctance to remove these troops. The Japanese were of the opinion that Russia was deviously taking control of Manchuria. By 1904 the Russian troops were still in place and the Japanese had had enough of Russian policy in the Far East. Japan attacked Port Arthur in early February and the Tsar responded immediately with Russia's war declaration.

At first the Tsar and his advisers were not too worried about the war with Japan. They expected to win. They assumed that with a population three times the size of that of Japan and with the resources of a huge empire they would defeat the Japanese. Moreover, they thought that a victorious war would rally the nation behind the Tsar, and act as a much-needed diversion from the problems at home. Unfortunately for them, their optimism was ill-founded. The war with Japan was fought on the eastern side of the Russian empire, remote from reinforcements of men and supplies. Russia's European-based fleets, which were desperately needed in the Pacific, had tremendous problems in escaping from their bases. The Black Sea fleet had been forbidden by a European treaty, the Straits Convention of 1841, to enter the Mediterranean. The Baltic fleet had to sail around Europe, Africa and Asia. Moreover, Japan proved to be a competent naval and military adversary which managed to deal with everything that the Russians could throw against them.

The war became a nightmare for the Tsarist autocracy. Instead of being a diversion from the problems in Russia, it added immeasurably to them. War disasters had the effect of triggering off protests on an even larger scale than before. As early as April 1904, a defeat at the Yalu River, with the loss of the lives of 2000 soldiers – many of whom had been conscripted from the national minorities – led to considerable nationalist hostility. In Finland, Bobrikov, the Governor, was assassinated. An event of much greater significance was when Plehve, the unpopular Minister of the Interior who so much embodied the spirit of the Tsar's government, became the victim of a Social Revolutionary's bomb.

Faced with a disastrous war and with collapsing social order at home, the Tsar and his government were being pressurised into a change of direction. Plehve's successor, Mirsky, actually held discussions with zemstva representatives about establishing some kind of consultative process by which the Tsar and his government would be placed more directly in contact with the people. But other powerful ministers immediately stepped in to curb what they saw as an unwelcome development. The political opponents of the Tsar and his government then arranged their own conference in Paris in September 1904 to discuss a way forward for Russia. There they organised what became known as the 'Paris Bloc' of opponents to Tsarist autocracy.

The Paris Bloc contained Liberals, Social Revolutionaries, Social Democrats and Nationalists. Their aims were carefully worded to appeal to all strands of the political opposition and included the removal of autocracy, national self-determination, and a democratically elected government.

The delegate who had represented Struve's group of Liberals in Paris, Paul Milyukov, began arranging 'revolutionary banquets' in St Petersburg. These 'revolutionary banquets' were in imitation of gatherings which had preceded the 1848 revolution in France. Moscow and Kiev followed St Petersburg's lead. At the banquets, influential members of the intelligentsia openly declared their support for a constitution for Russia. Some zemstvo representatives agreed with this demand; others, usually the old-fashioned landed gentry, did not. However, the dissatisfied groups found adequate common ground to put together a series of resolutions to present to the Tsar. Mirsky agreed to give the Tsar their requests.

The Tsar's response was uninspiring. A few token concessions were granted, such as a reduction in the amount of press censorship and a slight increase in the powers of the zemstva. More importantly, however, the Tsar indicated his displeasure to the zemstva in a communiqué on 14 December. They, and other organisations, were ordered 'not to go outside their proper sphere and not to examine questions for the study of which they have been given no legal rights'.

If the Tsar assumed that the political opposition would disappear following his rejection of their suggestions, he was mistaken. Within a few weeks, he was facing his greatest crisis yet within his empire.

Bloody Sunday

The biggest disaster of the war with Japan occurred on 2 January 1905: Port Arthur fell to the Japanese. The campaign to defend it had cost over 17,000 lives. The Tsar was now actively seeking a way of getting out of the calamitous war from which he and his advisers had expected so much. No immediate means of escape was evident. Meanwhile, an even more pressing problem was developing on his doorstep. This, coupled with the background of war disaster, was to place an intolerable pressure on the autocracy.

On 9 January 1905, a huge demonstration took place in

St Petersburg. It involved 200,000 people, at the head of whom was an Orthodox priest, Father Georgi Gapon.

Father Gapon first came to prominence in St Petersburg during the time of the Zubatov police unions. Zubatov had wished to include religious discussion on the agenda for the meetings of his societies, believing that such discussion would add to the appeal of the Tsar as the head of the Orthodox Church. Gapon was recommended to Zubatov as a young, trustworthy priest, popular with the representatives of the factory workers, who could become part of the police union scheme. His church agreed that he should take part, provided that he kept purely to religious matters.

Gapon, however, was appalled by the living and working conditions of the poor, and he became more and more involved with union activity. According to his autobiography, *The Story of My Life*, he decided in May 1903 to continue collaborating with Zubatov, but to take over the running of the St Petersburg Zubatov union through a secret committee which would exploit its police contacts, win over all the workforce, and establish a plan of action to improve the workers' conditions.

In February 1904 Gapon, with official authorisation, formed the 'Assembly of Russian Factory Workers of St Petersburg'. This Assembly adopted Zubatov methods designed to give it a broad appeal. It had its own clubhouses, where dances and concerts were held. It had a sickness scheme and a retirement scheme. By the end of 1904, it had a membership of many thousands. In January 1905 the opportunity for the Assembly to test its strength appeared. Three prominent members of the Assembly were dismissed from employment in the giant Putilov steelworks in St Petersburg, many of whose workers were members. A strike was called and the entire workforce of 13,000 responded to the call. Gapon, at the head of affairs, demanded the reinstatement of the sacked men and a considerable improvement in the working conditions of all the workforce before a return to work could even be contemplated. Over the next three days, other factories came out on strike in support. By 8 January, less than a week after the fall of Port Arthur to the Japanese, over 100,000 workers in St Petersburg were on strike and the city was at a standstill.

The response of the Tsar and his government was predictable. Large numbers of troops were brought in and were placed to guard essential services, such as gasworks and electricity generating stations. The Tsar's Winter Palace was extensively guarded. These precautions were an ominous foreboding of what was to come.

Gapon decided that the most effective way forward for the workers in St Petersburg was to make a direct appeal to the Tsar himself, who was believed to be in residence at the Winter Palace. This immediately found favour with the people whom he represented. The idea that the Tsar, the 'Little Father', would respond to the desperate plight of his people once their distress was made known to him was not as ridiculous as it might seem. There was an enduring notion amongst Russia's peasants and industrial workers that the Tsar, the godlike leader of Holy Mother Russia, was being kept in ignorance of his people's plight by his corrupt ministers, who shielded him from the truth for their own purposes. Once he saw such a demonstration, what else could he do but respond to his people, seeing for the first time their hunger and distress?

A lengthy petition was drawn up for presentation to the Tsar. Here is an extract from it:

'Oh Sire! We working men of St Petersburg, our wives and children, and our parents, helpless and aged men and women, have come to you, our ruler, in quest of justice and protection. We are beggars, we are oppressed and overburdened with work; we are insulted, we are not regarded as human beings, but are treated as slaves who must suffer their bitter lot in silence. We have suffered but are driven further and further into the abyss of poverty, injustice and ignorance; we are strangled by despotism and tyranny, so that we can breath no longer... Our patience is at an end... Break down the walls between yourself and your people... Let the election of members to the constituent assembly take place in conditions of universal, secret and equal suffrage... This is our chief request; upon it all else depends.'

(Quoted in L. Kochan, *Russia in Revolution*, 1967)

On Sunday, 9 January, the massed crowds of St Petersburg and their families, about 200,000 people, began their march to the Winter Palace. The people were dressed in their Sunday clothes, and the march was deliberately made to look like a religious procession: Father Gapon led it, hymns were sung, and portraits of the Tsar were carried by his hopeful people. Figure 4.6 was taken during the procession. Notice how the portrait of the Tsar is prominently displayed.

Fig 4.6   Part of the procession on the way to the Winter Palace in St Petersburg on 9 January 1905.

A contemporary newspaper report describes what happened next:

'Joining in the stream of the working men, I proceeded in the direction of the Winter Palace... The first trouble began at 11 o'clock, when the military tried to turn back some thousand of strikers at one of the bridges... The Cossacks at first used their knouts, then the flat of their sabres, and finally they fired. The strikers in the front ranks fell on to their knees and implored the Cossacks to let them pass, protesting that they had no hostile intentions. They refused, however, to be intimidated by blank cartridges, and orders were given to load with ball.

The passions of the mob broke loose like a bursting dam. The people, seeing the dead and dying carried away in all directions, the snow on the streets and pavements covered with blood, cried aloud for vengeance. Meanwhile, the situation at the Palace was becoming momentarily worse. The troops were reported to be unable to control the vast masses which were constantly surging forward. Reinforcements were sent and at 2 o'clock here also the order was given to fire. Men, women and children fell at each volley, and were carried away in ambulances, sledges and carts...'

(*The Weekly Times*, 27 January 1905, quoted in R. W. Breach, *Documents and Descriptions in European History 1815–1939*, 1964)

Fig 4.7   The Tsar's troops turning their guns on the crowd in front of the Winter Palace.

Figure 4.7 shows troops turning their guns on the crowd outside the Winter Palace. As events turned out, the Tsar himself was not even in the Palace. He recorded his response to news of the events in his diary:

'A dreadful day. Serious disorders took place in Petersburg when the workers tried to get to the Winter Palace. The troops were forced to fire in several parts of the city and there are many killed and wounded. Lord, how painful and sad this is. Mama arrived from city just in time for mass. The family lunched together. I went for a walk with Michael. Mama stayed overnight.'
(Quoted in Marc Ferro, *Nicholas II: the Last of the Tsars*, 1991)

The setting up of the Duma

The reverberations of the massacre on Bloody Sunday were felt throughout Russia. Strikes, peasant uprisings, and nationalist revolts became commonplace. Meanwhile, the disasters of the war with Japan continued to plague the autocracy. In May 1905 the Baltic fleet, the last hope of a change in fortunes, was destroyed in the Tsushima Straits (see Figure 4.5). The Americans offered to put together a peace package which was signed on 6 August at Portsmouth in New Hamphire. There could be no hiding from the fact that Russia had suffered a humiliating defeat.

Strikes and unrest were now clearly getting out of hand. The Tsarist authorities felt that they should take some precautionary measures, such as the censorship of critical pamphlets (see Figure 4.8).

Fig 4.8 Soldiers searching a train at a station for illegal literature in 1905.

The beleaguered Tsar, faced with a now irrepressible surge in demand for a change in the way that the empire was governed, eventually agreed to the setting up of a consultative assembly. The importance of the word 'consultative' should not be overlooked: the proposed assembly might 'consult' the Tsar, but the Tsar would be under no obligation to respond to its wishes. But it was a start. Zemstvo representatives, industrialists, and even some of his ministers had succeeded in convincing Nicholas that he could no longer continue to rule by force alone.

The first plan of the Tsar for this consultative assembly, called the Duma, was that it could be set up or dissolved as and when he wished. Furthermore, membership was to be denied to industrial workers and to members of the intelligentsia – the intellectuals who were most prominent in challenging the Tsar's authority and in proposing different ways for Russia to be governed.

Once people had realised the true nature of the Duma, they made their displeasure known: strikes and rioting, which had been on the wane, returned with a vengeance. So bad was the situation that the Minister for Agriculture was asked to devise a plan by which the soldiers in the now-finished war with Japan would be given land in Siberia on which to settle: the Tsar's government was afraid that the embittered soldiers would join the revolutionaries and overthrow the state!

Tsar Nicholas appeared at this stage to have a stark choice: either he could resort to outright brutality and establish a military dictatorship; or he could grant a constitution acceptable to most of his people. He decided on the latter course of action, and on 17 October 1905 he issued a set of decrees which subsequently became known as the October Manifesto.

The Manifesto appeared to be a considerable concession. It provided for basic liberties, such as the freedom of the press and the right to form associations. It extended the electorate of the Duma to include those groups previously overlooked. It increased the scope of the Duma itself: the Duma was no longer merely consultative, that is with the power only to suggest measures for the government to consider – it could now propose legislation. A pledge was made that a constitutional charter, formalising the extensive changes to the way in which Russia's citizens were governed, would be drawn up in the near future.

It seemed that those who wanted Russia to have a constitution had won what they had been seeking. It seemed that the authority of the Tsar had been successfully challenged. But had the process by which these concessions had apparently been won destroyed for all time a vital source of the Tsar's authority: the faith, trust and love of his people? One biographer of Nicholas II believes so:

'Bloody Sunday put an end to the myth of the Tsar-Batyushka, the "Little Father" Tsar, the loving father from whom nothing but good could come. For a long time the people had thought

that the nobles had kept them apart from their Tsar, turning him into someone who could no longer be approached or even spoken to. But the day was bound to arrive when Tsar and people would at last be able to understand one another...
Yet when the people had come, with banners flying, to pray and speak to their beloved Tsar, his soldiers had replied with bullets... Bloody Sunday was an explosive revelation...
Bloody Sunday snapped the "sacred bond" which had united the people with their Tsar – the people upon whom Nicholas founded his faith and the legitimacy of his rule.'

(Marc Ferro, *Nicholas II: the Last of the Tsars*, 1991)

ESSAY

1. Why did Tsarist Russia embark upon a programme of industrialisation in the 1890s and how successful was it by 1903?

2. Was Russian industrialisation in the 1890s a triumph for the economy but a disaster for the autocracy?

3. Assess the view that 'Nicholas II's most notable achievement up to 1905 was losing the affection of his people'.

4. How important a factor in bringing about the 1905 revolution was the Russo-Japanese war?

The Duma and the Stolypin reforms

Between 1906 and 1914 the Tsar and his government worked alongside the representative parliament called the Duma. Many people in Russia believed that the October Manifesto and the setting up of the Duma meant that Russia had a political system which would allow changes to take place. For that to happen would require a Duma with real political power. The most important Tsarist minister of the period, Petr Stolypin, tried to work with the Duma to remove the tensions within the Russian empire and to bring stable government. In this chapter the following issues will be considered:

1. How much authority did the Duma really have?
2. How did Stolypin try to solve the empire's problems?
3. Were Stolypin and the Duma successful?

By investigating these problems, we will develop our understanding of the concepts: ideology, identity and authority. The October Manifesto seemed to be a major concession by the Tsar. His *authority* was surely diminished if he were required to accept the Duma. But would the Duma amount to anything of substance? Was there a change in *ideology* which allowed a representative parliamentary system to implement successfully vital changes affecting the *identity* of the different peoples within the empire?

TASK

As you work through Issue 5, prepare notes which will enable you to complete the following exercise.

You are a journalist employed by a British newspaper in 1911. You are required to write an obituary of Petr Arkadievich Stolypin, who has recently been assassinated. You would assume that your readers have a broad understanding of the situation in Russia, but you would expect that few of them would have heard very much about Stolypin and his reforms. Your obituary, therefore, should include a brief survey of Tsarist Russia's problems in the early twentieth century so that Stolypin and his years in office may be placed in proper perspective. Your final comments should include observations about the significance of the death of Stolypin. How great a loss is he to Russia? Should his successor carry on with his reforms? What might be the consequences for the Tsar if the Stolypin programme is brought to an end?

Your completed article should be about 800–1000 words in length.

Attitudes towards the Duma

Many historians believe that Russia's experiment with the Duma was an unfortunate failure. They feel that, had the October Manifesto been given proper support from all sides, and had the Duma been allowed to work more effectively, then Russia might have been transformed to such an extent that the 1917 Revolution could have been avoided:

> 'The October Manifesto provided a framework within which the Russian state and Russian society should have found it possible to reduce the tension dividing them. This it failed to accomplish. A constitutional régime can function properly only if government and opposition accept the rules of the game: in Russia, neither the monarchy nor the intelligentsia was prepared to do so. Each regarded the new order as an obstacle, a deviation from the country's true system, which for the monarchy was autocracy and for the intelligentsia, a democratic republic. As a result, the constitutional interlude, while not without achievements, was largely wasted – a missed opportunity which would not recur.'
>
> (R. Pipes, *The Russian Revolution 1899–1919*, 1990)

Fig 5.1 Voters in St Petersburg participating in the election of delegates to the Duma in early 1906.

Figure 5.1 shows voters in St Petersburg participating in the election of delegates to the Duma. The expectations of voters such as these were high. They believed that they were participating in a

process which would create a representative parliament with real power to bring about change in Russia. However, even before elections to the Duma were held, there were differences of opinion about what it actually was and what the nature of its authority should be. The delegates who were subsequently elected could refer to the clause in the October Manifesto which stated that, in future, no law could be passed in Russia without Duma approval. That seemed to pledge a considerable degree of authority to the Duma.

In April 1906 the constitutional charter promised by the October Manifesto finally appeared. Notably, it was not called a constitution. Indeed the word 'constitution' did not appear in it at any stage. Instead it was called the Fundamental Laws. The implication was that the Tsar was allowing no more than an amendment to the Fundamental Laws which were already in existence – that is to say the Fundamental Laws which asserted his autocratic power.

The debate with the Tsar over one point contained in the amended Fundamental Laws gives a clear indication of his apparently changed attitude towards the October Manifesto.

The point in question concerned what would replace Article One of the Fundamental Laws: 'The Emperor of all the Russias is an autocratic and unlimited monarch. God himself commands that this supreme power be obeyed, out of conscience as well as fear.' This article had remained virtually unchanged since the time of Peter the Great. But, clearly, some kind of rewording was required if it were to appear that the Duma was a representative assembly with any real power. Eventually, a text was agreed upon. It read:

'The Tsar of all Russia possesses supreme autocratic power. He is to be obeyed not out of fear but as a matter of duty, in accordance with divine decree.'

The vital substitution is of the word 'supreme' for the word 'unlimited'.

But two things are of particular significance in how this change came about. Firstly, there was the extreme reluctance of the Tsar to make any kind of concession at all. The following is an extract from the minutes of the meeting held to discuss the issue:

'[The Tsar]: "Let us look at this Article . . . I am filled with doubt. Have I the right, before my ancestors, to alter the limits they bequeathed to me? . . . I am, believe me, sincere when I tell you that if I were convinced that Russia wanted me to abdicate my autocratic powers, I would do that, for the country's good. But I am not convinced that this is so . . ." '
(Marc Ferro, *Nicholas II: the Last of the Tsars*, 1991)

Eventually, the Tsar was persuaded to accept the new Article One, but the concession was a reluctant one.

The second point of significance – and this goes some way towards explaining why the Tsar did accept the amendment to

Article One – was the retention of the word 'autocratic' in the revised version. The simple fact of the matter was that there *were* no limits to the power of an autocratic monarch, therefore the inclusion of the word 'unlimited' in the Fundamental Laws was unnecessary in any case. The Tsar had accepted a change in wording. He had not accepted any reduction in his authority.

There already existed clear evidence that the Tsar was in no mood to make real concessions to the Duma. On 8 March 1906, a month prior to the debate about the content of the Fundamental Laws, the Tsar felt confident enough to publish the budgetary rules. These declared that army, navy, and Imperial Court expenditure were outside any control of the Duma. Thus, by the time of the publication of the redrafted Fundamental Laws, it had become clear that the Duma was to be bereft of any authority. The Fundamental Laws emphasised the minimal role which the Duma was to play. The Duma was to be little more than a chamber for discussion. The President of the Duma might approach the Prime Minister, another minister, or even report to the Tsar – but none of these individuals was required to act in response to the wishes of the Duma.

The Tsar apparently regarded the Duma, not as a parliament capable of passing laws, but as a body of elected representatives who could offer advice. He declared to his Minister of War:

'I created the Duma, not to be directed by it, but to be advised.'
(G. A. Hosking, *The Russian Constitutional Experiment*, 1973)

The Tsar also considered it his right to remove what he had 'created' if it did not fit in with his purposes. This attitude of the Tsar seems strangely at odds with the attitude shown at the time of the 1905 crisis. Apparently, this came about because the Tsar became convinced that the concessions which he had felt forced to grant did not really reflect the wishes of his people. As early as 27 October 1905, he had begun to have second thoughts. In a letter to his mother, he wrote:

'In the first days after the manifesto, the bad elements strongly raised their heads, but then a strong reaction set in, and the whole mass of loyal people came alive... It is startling with what unanimity and suddenness this happened in all the cities of Russia and Siberia.'
(Quoted in Andrew Marshall Verner, *Nicholas II and the Role of the Autocrat during the First Russian Revolution, 1904–1907*, 1986)

This was the first of several references to the 'loyal people' who were willing Nicholas to restore order. As the experiment with the Duma continued, the Tsar became more and more convinced that the vast majority of his people favoured a continuation of

Orthodoxy, Autocracy and Nationality. According to Andrew Marshall Verner, he reached that conclusion because of an organised campaign:

> 'The Tsar's new-found resolve to see autocracy maintained coincided not only with the waning of revolutionary danger and the restoration of order, but with a growing stream of loyal addresses and audience requests . . . . the overwhelming majority of these petitions came from peasants . . . All the messages affirmed the peasants' love and devotion to their Tsar and to little mother Russia; they denounced the . . . traitors' attempts to limit the Tsar's autocratic power . . . Again and again, peasants called on Nicholas not to deliver them and Russia into other, non-Orthodox hands, but to remain the defender of the Orthodox faith, a Tsar in the fullness of his powers . . .
>
> 'What the Tsar did not say, nor realised presumably, was that these loyal sentiments very definitely were the result of a massive and well-co-ordinated campaign by local clergy, landowners, or government officials.'

This was the background to official attitudes towards the Duma. In such a situation, those delegates who had hoped that the Duma would allow far-reaching changes to be made were being far too optimistic.

As a final indication of the Tsar's attitude towards the Duma, he refused outright to set foot inside their meeting place at the Tauride Palace. Instead, from the beginning, he was only prepared to receive Duma deputies in the Winter Palace.

The main political groupings and the Duma

The delegates elected to the Duma represented a range of political outlooks.

The Liberals

The Russian Liberals were split into two factions. These were the Octobrists and the Kadets.

The Octobrists accepted the October Manifesto and the Duma as being the political concession which they had been seeking from the Tsarist autocracy. They were the minority group of the Liberal Constitutionalists and were dominated by the moderates of the zemstva and by the business class. Their main spokesman was Guchkov.

The Kadets, a shortened form of 'Konstitudo-demokratich-eskaya', were prepared to work with the Duma, but wished to push for a Duma with significantly greater powers. For example, they wanted the Duma to redraft the Fundamental Laws, and they sought to pass measures for land reform. Prominent spokesmen for the Kadets were Struve and Milyukov.

The Social Revolutionary Party

At its first full conference in Finland in January 1906, the Social Revolutionary Party continued to endorse terrorism as a legitimate weapon in the struggle against Tsarist authority. This did not appeal to all those present. A faction broke away and became the People's Socialist Party. Whilst the Social Revolutionaries agreed to boycott the elections for the Duma, the People's Socialist Party decided to put up candidates for election. These candidates included peasants. They became known as the Trudoviks, from 'Trudovaya Gruppa', meaning 'Labour Group'. One member of this group who was later to emerge as a figure of considerable significance was Alexander Kerensky.

The Social Democrats

The attitude of the Social Democrats to the Duma was mixed. Mensheviks and Bolsheviks attended a congress in Stockholm in April 1906. The broad opinion of both groups was that the Duma elections should be boycotted. They believed that participating in the Duma would divert attention from the revolutionary struggle. But some individual Social Democrats had already decided to stand for election to the Duma, and an agreement was reached in Stockholm that they could form a Social Democratic faction in the Duma as long as they agreed to being directed by the party leadership.

Nationalists

Nationalists included representatives of the extreme Union of the Russian People (see page 57), as well as delegates from the minority nationalities. The members of the Union of the Russian People were amongst the most right-wing elements in the Duma. Mostly they were land-owning nobles from border areas who felt directly threatened by the minority nationalist movements. They had a strong vested interest in opposing any break-up of the empire. At odds with them were the minority nationalist groups who objected to what they saw as the excesses of Russification and who sought greater autonomy for their respective provinces.

The first Duma

Tsar Nicholas II presided over the opening ceremony of the first Duma which was held in the throne room of the Winter Palace in St Petersburg. The magnificence of the Imperial Palace was an astounding spectacle for many of the Tsar's impoverished subjects. Count Kokovtsov, the Minister of Finance, later described the scene which he attended:

> 'St George's Hall, the throne room, presented a queer spectacle at this moment, and I believe its walls had never before witnessed such a scene. The entire right side of the room was filled with uniformed people, members of the State Council, and, further on, the Tsar's retinue. The left side was crowded with the members of the Duma, a small number of whom had appeared in full dress, while the overwhelming majority, occupying the first places near the throne, were dressed as if intentionally in workers' blouses and cotton shirts, and behind them was a crowd of peasants in the most varied costumes, some in national dress, and a multitude of representatives of the clergy.
> (Quoted in Marc Ferro, *Nicholas II: the Last of the Tsars*, 1991)

Also present was V. Gurko, who believed that he could detect strong hostility during the proceedings:

> 'Naively believing that the people's representatives, many of whom were peasants, would be awed by the splendour of the imperial court, the ladies of the imperial family had worn nearly all their jewels . . . This oriental method of impressing upon spectators a reverence for the bearers of supreme power was quite unsuited to the occasion. What it did achieve was to set in juxtaposition the boundless imperial luxury and the poverty of the people. The demagogues did not fail to comment upon this ominous contrast.'
> (Marc Ferro)

The Tsar greeted the assembled delegates in the following way:

> 'With ardent faith in the radiant future of Russia, I greet in you those best men whom I ordered my beloved subjects to choose from their midst . . . May this day be henceforth remembered as the day of the rebirth of the moral fibre of the Russian land, the day of the rebirth of her best forces.'
> (T. Riha, 'Constitutional Developments in Russia', in T. Stavrou (ed.), *Russia under the last Tsar*, 1969)

This apparently optimistic address having been delivered, and the rest of the formalities having been dispensed with, the Duma representatives prepared for their opening session, which was held in the Tauride Palace on 10 May 1906. Figure 5.2 shows the religious service which marked this occasion.

Fig 5.2 The religious service which marked the opening of the first Duma in May 1906.

Political classification of the various members of the Duma is difficult, one reason being that many of the 200 or so peasant representatives were not members of any political party. The biggest single group was of Kadets, with 179 seats. The Octobrists had at least 32 seats and the Social Democrats, mainly Mensheviks, had 18. Of the rest, the dozen or so minority national groups had about 60 seats: their delegates were dressed in traditional clothing. The Union of the Russian People had about 100. Those peasant deputies who declared a political affiliation were mainly Trudoviks: they numbered 94. Altogether there were some twenty-six different political groupings, as well as the national groups.

Figures 5.3 and 5.4 show groups of Duma representatives. You can get some idea of the many types of delegates who attended the first Duma from these photographs. One observer noted:

'It would be difficult to imagine a more picturesque gathering. Each man wore the costume of his class. The country gentry and the Intelligents dressed very simply, but there were Russian priests with long beards and hair, a Roman Catholic bishop in skull-cap lined with red, finely accoutred Cossacks from the Caucasus, Bashkirs and Buryats in strange and tinselled Asiatic dress, Polish peasants in the brilliant and martial costumes of

Fig 5.3 and 5.4   Groups of Duma representatives.

their people, and a whole mass of staid, bearded, and top-booted peasants.'

(B. Pares, *Russia and Reform*, 1907)

Such a diversity of political identities in a newly established representative assembly with no real authority of substance led to a confused situation. In fact, the opening session proved to be pandemonium. Speaker after speaker rose to demand changes which would have led to the overthrow of the state. Such demands were absolutely futile and only served to discredit the Duma.

Nicholas II tolerated the situation for a mere three months. Then, clearly displaying how lacking in any real authority the Duma was, the Tsar declared in July 1906 that it was dissolved. Troops were sent in to occupy the Tauride Palace, where the Duma met.

Nicholas decreed that a new Duma would be assembled in February 1907. By the terms of the October Manifesto, the Tsar was legally obliged to give dates for new elections. Nicholas decided to ignore this: elections for a new Duma would be held when the Tsar decided that they should be held. Such was the reality of the authority of the Duma and of the binding nature of the October Manifesto. It seemed that the 1905 Revolution had already been forgotten and that the authority of the Tsar was absolutely intact.

Some of the Tsar's advisers, however, were of the opinion that the extensive problems within the Russian empire needed to be tackled and that a properly organised Duma was a vital part of the government machinery needed to do the work. They suggested that the 1905 Revolution was a warning which should not be ignored. Tsarism, they believed, had to adapt to the changing situation which Russia found itself in. The Duma could be made to work and should be made to work. The most outspoken Tsarist Minister who thought these things was Stolypin.

Petr Arkadievich Stolypin (1862–1911)

Figure 5.5 shows Stolypin in about 1900.

Stolypin has become of great interest to historians of the Russian Revolution. Some historians believe that the reforms which he supervised between 1906 and 1911 were the beginnings of a programme of change in Russia which, had it been allowed to continue, would have enabled the empire to avoid the Revolution of 1917. Leonard Schapiro comments about Stolypin:

'Probably no other figure in the modern history of Russia has aroused so much controversy. By the left, he is generally dismissed as a savage butcher who hanged peasants and workers... To the extreme right he became an odious figure, whose policy of reform and attempt to work with the Duma, or parliament, were a threat to the sacred principle of autocracy... For his many admirers he has posthumously become the wisest statesman that Russia ever had, who could, had he been given time, have saved Russia from war and revolution, and have effected a peaceful transformation of the country on moderate and modern lines.'

(L. Schapiro, *Russian Studies*, 1986)

Fig 5.5   Stoylpin in about 1900.

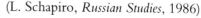

Stolypin was the son of a landowner. He became notorious as governor of the province of Saratov. His uncompromisingly brutal punishment of peasant revolutionaries was already legendary when, on the day of the opening session of the first Duma, he was appointed as Minister of the Interior.

He was the creator of a distinctive line of approach to the problems of Russia. He wanted to develop serf emancipation beyond the limitations of the Act passed by Alexander II so that there would be established millions of independent peasants, removed from the commune and set up as individual, legally protected owners of their land. He was convinced that revolution remained a great threat in Russia and that the best hope of averting that revolution lay with the real emancipation of the mass of naturally conservative Russian peasants. Once they were secure on their own land, they would be loyal to the Tsar and fearful for themselves of the consequences of revolution. Stolypin reasoned that this mass of land-owning peasants would view revolutionaries as a threat to their own property rights and would therefore not engage in the mass rioting which usually coincided with disturbances in the cities.

Once social stability had been established, Stolypin would begin the process of political reforms which would bring stability to the empire and remove the appeal of the revolutionaries:

> 'Stolypin's aim was to preserve the authority of Tsarism by introducing reforms that would strengthen its social and public base. Convinced that the socio-economic and educational advancement of the nation had to precede major political reforms, he sought to reconcile public opinion and government by minor reforms and to remove certain out-of-date practices that were incompatible with the spirit of the times. His political motto was "first pacification, then reforms".'
>
> (Ben-Cion Pinchuk, *The Octobrists in the Third Duma, 1907–1912*, 1974)

Stolypin rose to be President of the Council of Ministers, or Prime Minister, following the collapse of the first Duma. In keeping with his uncompromising approach to revolutionaries, he came down heavily on armed peasant insurrectionists who were protesting about the Duma. He was certainly encouraged to be harsh at this time: a Social Revolutionary bomb blew up his house, gravely injuring his daughter although missing him. Twenty-seven people were killed in the incident. The harshness of the Stolypin response can be gauged from the term which was used for the hangman's noose: 'Stolypin's Necktie'. This was extensively used in the months up until April 1907. Field courts-martial set up by Stolypin carried through a recorded 683 death sentences. While this was going on, Stolypin was attempting to get prominent Octobrists to join his ministry, thereby forging a link between the government and the Duma. The attempt failed, but

Stolypin was undeterred, and he arranged to hold elections for a second Duma in February 1907.

He presented the second Duma with a wide-ranging series of reforms, the purpose of which was to remove what he identified as the prime areas of social discontent. He was convinced that for the Tsar and the government to respond negatively to the failure of the first Duma, and to the acts of terrorism which continued to plague the empire (there were 3000 deaths caused by terrorist activities in 1907 alone) would be a fatal error.

The second Duma was offered improvements in the workers' conditions, and the reform of civil rights, of policing, of local government, and so forth. The Duma's response was aggressively non-co-operative. Like the first Duma, it was not prepared to work with the Tsar's government in the way that the Tsar's government required. Its fate was therefore clear. Like the first Duma, it was dissolved. The Tsar issued the decree on 3 June 1907.

Stolypin's solution to the lack of co-operation by the Duma was simple: if a Duma elected under one set of rules was not prepared to work in the way that he wanted, he would implement another set of rules whereby the kind of Duma which he required would come into being. He was consistent in his opinion that the Duma had to be made to work:

> 'He accepted the Duma as a permanent feature of the régime. He realised that with a suitable composition, the Duma could be of help in achieving his goals; its abolition, he thought, could be fatal to Tsarism. He certainly rejected the idea of returning to pre-1905 absolutism. "One should not even talk about a return to absolutism," he told Peter B. Struve in 1907.'
>
> (Ben-Cion Pinchuk)

The key to the process by which Stolypin could get his kind of Duma was a greatly restricted franchise. This was a further violation of the October Manifesto. For that matter, it was a violation of the Fundamental Laws of 1906. To Stolypin, that was incidental. He had his eye on what he believed to be Russia's solution, and he had every intention of putting his plan into action. Using autocratic means and supported by the Tsar, he prepared for the setting up of a third Duma, a Duma which would operate according to his wishes.

The third Duma

By greatly reducing the franchise and by altering the process of election (the required law was passed on 3 June 1907), Stolypin created a Duma with which he believed he could work. The third Duma was dominated by delegates of a much more conservative outlook than those of its predecessors. The largest group was of

Octobrists, who had more than twice as many seats as the Kadets. However, their 154 seats fell short of the required overall majority of 222 seats. This being the case, the Octobrists had to seek the support of other groups to get their propositions passed by the Duma.

Among the minority representations, the Social Democrats had 12 seats. A small representation of Independent Nationalists were heavily outnumbered by right-wing Russian Nationalists, who had 76 seats, and were predominantly gentry landowners from the western border provinces of the empire. Their great fear was that the empire might split because of the activities of the nationalist movements in Poland, in the Baltic provinces, and in the Ukraine. Their attitude was of uncompromising support for the Tsarist empire and of rigid Russian nationalist control, by any means necessary, of the disturbed provinces. They discovered a ready ally in Stolypin, partly because Stolypin agreed with them, partly because their numbers meant that they and the Octobrists could form a working majority.

The other combination which could form a working majority was of Octobrists and Kadets. Stolypin, therefore, had to retain the support of the Octobrists, but he could vary the contents of his programme, appealing either to the Russian Nationalists or to the Kadets, and he could thus still claim majority Duma support. In such circumstances, a 'hung' Duma was a most useful arrangement for Stolypin.

The third Duma could hardly be called representative. The enormous restrictions on the franchise allowed rich landowners and businessmen to dominate, and the identity of the delegates in the Duma and the policies which they were prepared to promote clearly reflected this. However, it would be wrong to see the third Duma as being no more than a front for what was in reality a re-established autocracy: the Duma was not without a degree of authority, although that might not have appeared to be the case.

Too much had changed in Russia for the old autocracy to be restored. Stolypin was acutely aware of the situation. He could manipulate the way that the Duma was elected in order to ensure that opposition parties were denied access to the Duma, but the widespread support which these parties had from many of the peoples of the empire was plainly evident to him. Opposition parties were still legally entitled to form, to hold meetings, and to participate in the Duma if elected. Censorship was relaxed and the expression of opinion of any persuasion was freely allowed as long as it was not regarded as incitement to violence or to revolutionary insurrection. These concessions had been granted by the autocracy because it had been forced to realise that outright suppression of opposition did little good and possibly much harm.

Perhaps the most important source of Duma authority lay in the minds of the Duma representatives themselves. They were not prepared to be servile. An early incident in the life of the third

Duma clearly emphasised this. In preparation for the state opening of the Duma, right-wing representatives, mainly the Russian Nationalists and a minority of the Octobrists, declared their wish that the Tsar should be addressed as 'Autocrat of all the Russias'. Their motion was defeated by 212 votes to 146. Despite this unpromising beginning, the initial relationship between Stolypin and Guchkov, the leader of the Octobrists, was positive. They appeared to be able to work together. Guchkov clearly shared Stolypin's vision of a way ahead which would lead to a new stability for Russia. In 1907, at a meeting of zemstvo representatives, he declared, 'If we are now witnessing the last convulsions of the revolution – and it is undoubtedly coming to an end – then it is to this man that we owe it.'

The Stolypin reforms

The peasants

Essential to the Stolypin programme was the establishment of social stability through the setting up of a large, land-owning peasantry. Stolypin declared to the third Duma in November 1907:

> 'As long as the peasant is poor, does not possess individual landed property, and is held in force within the vice of the commune, he will remain a slave, and no written law will give him the benefits of civil liberty . . . The small landed proprietor . . . will introduce into the village culture, enlightenment, and prosperity. Only then will paper freedom be transferred into real freedom.'
>
> (Quoted in J. Walkin, *The Rise of Democracy in Pre-Revolutionary Russia*, 1962)

Stolypin recognised that peasant dissatisfaction and unrest was caused mainly by disillusionment with the terms of the 1861 emancipation. Of particular importance was the issue of redemption payments. The mass peasant revolts of 1902 and the violent risings of 1905 and 1906 had clearly emphasised that the time had long arrived for an energetic government response to the problem. The autocracy at first attempted brutal repression – and Stolypin, it will be recollected, was an active participant in the process. What convinced the Tsarist autocracy of the need for a more subtle approach was the great peasant support for Kadet candidates for the first Duma. Either the Tsar would have to respond to his peasant peoples more sympathetically or clearly he would lose their support altogether.

In November 1905 redemption payments had been abolished. This destroyed the legal ties which held the peasant communes together. It was not until six months after this that Stolypin became Minister of the Interior. Thus, a vital step in the Stolypin programme pre-empted Stolypin himself.

Stolypin's first major piece of legislation affecting the peasants was the law of 9 November 1906. Any householder in a commune where there had been no redistribution of land since 1882 could apply to become owner of all the land in his possession. Further concessions were granted to householders on land where there had been a more recent redistribution. The peasant with adequate initiative could therefore become a private landowner through a simple procedure.

This was the base on which Stolypin continued to build in the years of his involvement with the third Duma. Further laws were passed in June 1910 and in May 1911 to facilitate further the development of independent peasants. The complexities associated with amalgamating strips of land to the satisfaction of the new peasant landowners were tackled by later laws. The practical problems involved were approached by land organisation commissions.

In effect Stolypin was carrying through a huge, state-supervised enclosure movement in the Russian empire. He wanted to set up millions of independent farms owned by peasant farmers. He hoped that the social spin-off would be greater political stability and the removal of the threat of revolution. In the stable social environment which would result, he could then tackle Russia's political problems. The completion of the process would be the ushering in of a modern, constitutional Tsarist state, able to take its place in the developed world.

Stolypin saw the reforms affecting the peasantry as economically advisable as well as politically desirable. The Russian countryside was virtually bankrupt, and the empire, with all its resources, could scarcely feed itself. Stolypin believed that peasant proprietors would be keen to produce extra food to sell for profit. A new prosperity, from which everyone would benefit, would descend upon the Russian countryside. An additional bonus, Stolypin believed, would be the sweeping away of the remnants of the old rural gentry who had become little more than of nuisance value to the empire.

Russia's peasants appear to have responded well to Stolypin's measures, although precise figures are almost impossible to gauge. As a result of conflicting evidence, historians often disagree about what was actually happening in the Russian countryside during the Stolypin years. Hugh Seton-Watson, in *The Russian Empire, 1801–1917*, suggests that by 1915 about seven million peasant households, roughly half the total in Russia, held their land under hereditary private tenure. Moreover he contends that a considerable amount of buying and selling of land was taking place. This occurred between peasants: some chose to sell out and move elsewhere. Stolypin also used a Peasant Land Bank, transferring millions of acres of state land to peasant ownership by means of a loan system at low rates of interest. Another means of providing peasants with land was to move them from overpopulated European Russia to underpopulated Siberia. As many as five million peasants may have been resettled in this way before the First World War.

R.B. McKean, in *The Russian Constitutional Monarchy, 1907–1917*, paints a much bleaker picture. He suggests that the process whereby peasants set up independent households was an uneven one. Take-up was considerable between 1908 and 1910, but thereafter the number of applications declined steadily. By 1915 not many more than 100,000 households had set up independently outside the commune. Most of the 'enclosing' which occurred consisted of strips of land being consolidated into enclosed plots by the commune, not by individual peasants. This 'enclosure' was to allow different methods of agriculture and was not a response to official encouragement to break up the commune. Russia's age-old peasant habits of communal co-opera-tion in subsistence agriculture were intensely difficult to break down. McKean suggests that Stolypin was out of touch with the reality of the Russian peasant outlook and that therefore his strategy was doomed from the beginning.

McKean and Seton-Watson are agreed, however, that peasant disturbances were much less in evidence after 1906. Possibly the removal of restrictions on peasant movement from the communes was one reason for this. Alarmingly, though, Russian agriculture remained unable to produce the kind of surplus food which would see the populace adequately catered for in times of distress. Both McKean and Seton-Watson reach similar conclusions about the impact of the Stolypin rural reforms:

'The agrarian reforms stood little chance of developing a conservative capitalist peasantry. In the absence of class struggle in the Marxist sense in the countryside and in the face of peasant belief in collective ownership of land, the premises of the Stolypin legislation are false.'

(R.B. MacKean, *The Russian Constitutional Monarchy, 1907–1917*, 1977)

'The extravagant claims made by some on his [Stolypin's] behalf, that he was a statesman of genius who placed Russia on the way to a peaceful happy future from which she was diverted only by a war forced on her by others, may be discounted...'

(H. Seton-Watson, *The Russian Empire, 1801–1917*, 1967)

Other historians are not so convinced. H.T. Willets observes:

'No study at once comprehensive and impartial has been made of the social and economic effects of Stolypin's reconstruction.

It is, however, noteworthy that his more balanced critics were willing to concede him a measure of success . . . The liberal A.A. Kauffman was . . . ready to recognise the soundness of Stolypin's political calculations. "In the rising class of small proprietors," he wrote, "a conservative class was being created . . . If Stolypin's successors had been given a little more time . . . who knows, it is very likely that the possibility of a decisive political overturn would have been averted for a long time, or that the overturn would have taken another direction." '

(Katkov (ed.), *Russia Enters the Twentieth Century*, 1971)

The cities

The attempted transformation of the countryside was only one aspect of Stolypin's work. He and his successors in the third and fourth Dumas also sought to bring peace to Russia's cities. The industrial workforce between 1907 and 1912 – the Stolypin Duma years – was relatively subdued.

A new surge of industrial activity had occurred after 1907, partly fuelled by a rearmament programme made necessary by the disastrous war against Japan and by the developing tensions in Europe. Work was created. St Petersburg's large engineering firms benefited in particular. The St Petersburg industrial workforce grew by over a third, to almost a quarter of a million, during these years. But the city could not cope with an expansion of this scale. Incoming factory workers had no choice but to squeeze into the existing shanty dwellings which had been thrown up beside the factories. Conditions were deplorable.

Trade unions were made legal in March 1906, but their activities were severely restricted. One thing they were barred from doing was accumulating strike funds. With no strike funds, the unions could not provide relief for striking members. Realising that long-term strikes were not a feasible option for the unions, the industrialists simply refused to negotiate with them. This meant that the unions were impotent, and an impression of industrial calm existed. However, what happened was what Zubatov had tried to combat some years previously: the workforce became attracted to political struggle – and this played directly into the hands of the revolutionaries.

The collective frustrations of the workforce finally found expression in April 1912. In the Lena goldfields in eastern Siberia, Tsarist troops fired on 5000 striking miners, killing over 200 of them and wounding many more. Figure 5.6 shows widows and their children standing beside the memorial to the victims. The majority of the representatives in the Duma protested vigorously, and public opinion was inflamed when Makarov, the Minister of the Interior, publicly defended the action taken by the troops. Eventually a Commission of Enquiry was sent out to the Lena

Fig 5.6 Widows and children standing beside the memorial to the victims of the Lena goldfield massacre in 1912.

goldfields. The dreadful conditions in which the miners lived and worked were duly recorded. Vague promises of improvements did nothing to appease the Russian workers, and after Lena, strikes became much more numerous all over the country. The centre of activity was St Petersburg, which in 1914 provided over half of all the recorded strikes.

Much of this striking had become recognisably political. Lenin's Bolsheviks were quick to seize the initiative. In April 1912 they published their newspaper, called *Pravda* ('Truth'). Bolshevik deputies were returned in six seats in the elections to the fourth Duma. Of the seventeen unions operating in St Petersburg, fourteen could express an allegience to the Bolsheviks by the middle of 1914.

These events clearly indicate that the Stolypin initiative had had no discernible impact on the industrial workforce. The relative calm which had existed during the Stolypin years was coincidental, and was not a positive response from factory workers.

Many of the new, young industial workers were not prepared to await any initiative from Lenin (who was in exile). Following a shooting of strikers at the Putilov works in July 1914, young Bolsheviks put up revolutionary barricades, despite warnings from the leadership. This was a disorganised attempt at revolution which was rapidly suppressed. It does, however, reinforce the view that by the time that Russia went to war in 1914, the problems of the empire had been far from resolved by the Stolypin years and their aftermath.

The national minorities

The policy of Russification had continued following the accession of Nicholas II. The Stolypin years saw no respite. Stolypin was a Russian nationalist in outlook, and as such he was a vehement opponent of those who wished to break away from the empire. He was perfectly prepared to accept the distinctive identities of peoples within the empire – as long as those same peoples were prepared to accept that their identity was primarily Russian. For Stolypin, distinctive national characteristics were fine as long as they were manifested in local folklore or its equivalent. On the other hand, he viewed nationalist ideology as promoted by active Polish or Finnish or Ukranian national activists as a pretext for the unacceptable activities of a minority of troublemakers.

The Russian Nationalists in the Duma were enthusiastic supporters of Stolypin's attempt to kill off the efforts of Poles, Finns and Ukranians to achieve any kind of independence. Stolypin used the tactic of introducing into these areas allegedly democratic reforms, which were in reality anti-nationalist policies. For example, in Poland he extended the zemstva representation in the western provinces, but manipulated the franchise in such a way as to remove Polish national influence. He established a new Ukranian province, Kholm, out of former Polish provinces, thus reducing Polish territory. He introduced new municipal councils in Polish cities, but again the nature of the limited franchise placed power in Russian hands.

Ukranian nationalists were dismissed from positions of influence. They were denounced by Stolypin as unrepresentative elements of the intelligentsia. The Finnish Diet was reduced to little more than a provincial assembly. Jews and Muslims were never allowed to feel at ease in the empire. Russification, endorsed by the Tsar and pursued by Stolypin and his successors, was anti-Jewish and anti-Muslim. In 1910, the Kazan representative in the Duma complained that Russian Muslims – some twenty million of them – were being unfairly treated by those who associated Russification with missionary Christianity. While Russian Muslims were prepared to accept what he defined as 'Russian civil culture', they were not prepared to renounce their own ideology and identity as expressed by nationality, religion or culture.

The Stolypin years featured at best a holding operation on the issue of the national minorities.

The achievements of the third Duma

In 1912 Mackenzie Wallace wrote of the Duma:

> 'No one now imagines, as many imagined in 1906, when the first Duma was opened, that it is possible to cure, in the short space of a few weeks, by the indignant denunciations and untried statesmanship of four or five hundred national representatives, the administrative and political evils from which Russia has been suffering for centuries.'
>
> (D. Mackenzie Wallace, 'Looking back over forty years', in *Russian Review No 1*, 1912)

Mackenzie Wallace went on to suggest that the Duma was continuing to be a representative assembly from which a more effective form of governing the Russian empire might eventually evolve. Prominent Duma members, such as Milyukov, expressed the opinion that the more radical Duma members were continuing to seek a Duma with much greater powers, but '...so long as Russia has a legislative chamber...the Russian Opposition will remain His Majesty's Opposition, and not opposition to His Majesty'. The Duma did have successes, and many people in Russia continued to believe that it was a body from which more change could come.

One area of considerable achievement by the Duma was in the sphere of education. The Tsarist Ministry of Education was more interested in promoting propaganda than in providing Russia with the educated workforce which a developing economy required. Stolypin, however, was very keen to improve Russian education. He believed that ignorance lay behind much of Russia's social and political distress, and that an uneducated population could not provide Russia with the skilled workforce which her economy needed. Educational improvement was an essential dimension to the Stolypin programme. In the Duma years before the First World War, annual expenditure on education quadrupled. The literacy level in Russia had been below 30 per cent at the turn of the century, but was over 40 per cent in 1914.

The Duma was also increasing the extent of its say in controlling Russia's budget: at the beginning of the third Duma, it controlled 53 per cent of Russia's government expenditure, but by 1912 this figure had risen to 62 per cent. And Duma influence was also becoming very marked in the areas of defence and foreign policy. The leader of the Octobrists, Guchkov, was savagely critical of Russia's military situation after the 1905 defeat by the Japanese, and actually raised more funding for military expenditure than the military commanders managed to spend. All these subtle and understated extensions of Duma activity clearly indicate a parliamentary body which, though limited in authority, was expanding the scope of its activities in an impressive manner.

The speculation which has developed about the Duma and about Stolypin's reforms tends to revolve around the suggestion that, had Stolypin been allowed to continue his work and had Russia not become involved in the First World War, then the Revolution of 1917 might not have occurred. Instead, Russia's constitutional experiment would gradually have allowed a transformation of the empire into a modern state with a working parliamentary system headed by a constitutional monarchy.

However, it is the case that the Stolypin programme was regarded with great suspicion by the Tsar and by many of his closest advisers. They remained stubbornly convinced of the merits of Orthodoxy, Autocracy and Nationality. They looked on with dismay at the developing influence of the Duma in state affairs. By 1911 Stolypin's time as Prime Minister was already running out. His preparedness to bypass the Duma to get what he wanted meant that he also had many enemies there. Guchkov, the leader of the Octobrists, had bitterly fallen out with Stolypin when Stolypin, with Tsarist support, pushed through legislation affecting the structure of the zemstva in the western provinces despite Duma opposition. The co-operation between Stolypin and the Octobrists, which had been so vital in allowing the Stolypin programme to take off in the early years of the third Duma, was now over.

Subject to Tsarist court intrigue, confronted with powerful enemies, and having lost the support of the Octobrists, Stolypin's days in office were probably numbered in any case when the assassin's bullet struck.

The end of Stolypin

Stolypin's assassination in 1911 by a revolutionary terrorist is described in a letter written by Tsar Nicholas II to his mother:

> 'We had just left our box during the second intermission, since it was very hot in the theatre. Suddenly we heard two noises, as if something had fallen on the floor . . . To the right I saw a group of officers and other people dragging someone. Some ladies screamed, and opposite me in the orchestra stood Stolypin. He slowly turned to face me and with his left hand blessed the air. Only then did I notice that he was pale and that there was blood on his hand and tunic. He quietly sat down on his chair and began to unbutton his tunic . . . Poor Stolypin suffered greatly that night, and was given morphine often . . .

'On September 6, at 9:00 a.m. . . . I learned of Stolypin's death. I went to the hospital immediately, and a requiem was held in my presence.'

(Quoted in V. V. Shulgin, *The Years: Memoirs of a Member of the Russian Duma, 1906–1917*, 1925)

A fourth Duma was formed in 1912. To Stolypin's successor, Kokovtsov, Tsar Nicholas offered the following advice: 'Don't follow the example of Petr Arkadievich, who tried to overthrow me.' This is further proof that the Tsar had lost faith in Stolypin. In 1917 Guchkov observed, albeit with the benefit of hindsight:

'But even before the physical death of Stolypin, I had lost faith in the possibility of a peaceful evolution of Russia. As Stolypin was gradually dying politically it became increasingly clear to me that Russia would be forced . . .to follow a different road – a road of violent change that would sever the ties with the past, that Russia would drift along the shoreless seas of political and social searching, without compass or rudder.'

(Ben-Cion Pinchuk, *The Octobrists in the Third Duma, 1907–1912*, 1974)

If the Stolypin programme did at any stage offer the possibility of a peaceful transition to a different kind of Tsarist empire, then that possibility had already ended by the time of his assassination. The 'different road' referred to by Guchkov was already beckoning in 1914.

ESSAY

1. 'In reality, the October Manifesto detracted nothing from the authority of Tsar Nicholas II.' Discuss.

2. To what extent did Stolypin's reforms solve the problems of the Russian countryside?

3. How accurate would it be to suggest that Stolypin had some success with Russia's peasant problem but only failure elsewhere?

4. Is it accurate to suggest that 'The years of the Duma were years of much talk and little action'?

Why did the Revolution of February 1917 occur?

In 1914 Russia entered the First World War. The Russians believed that they would win. The Tsar and his ministers believed that a victorious war would rally the people behind them. This did not happen. Russia had a disastrous war, and in February 1917 the Tsar and his government were overthrown. The following issues need to be considered:

1. What problems did Russia have during the First World War?
2. What caused the Revolution of February 1917?

These issues require us to question how the *authority* of the Tsar had disintegrated by 1917. Was a system of government based upon Tsarist *ideology* found wanting in Russia's greatest hour of need? Were the Russian people now prepared to assert their desire for a new *identity*, as citizens of a nation governed by their own representatives? Did revolutionary *ideology* lie behind the February 1917 Revolution, or was it caused by a more spontaneous sequence of events?

TASK

It is January 1917. You are a Russian soldier on the Eastern Front (see Figure 6.3). At the start of the war, you were an enthusiastic patriot. Your sister, who is a Petrograd factory worker and a supporter of the Social Democrats, saw things differently from you at that time.

You decide to write a letter to your sister in Petrograd. A friend who is due for a period of leave has agreed to deliver this letter: the letter will therefore not pass through the censors' hands, so you can be as open as you wish in describing your feelings.

In the letter you discuss openly your disillusionment about the war and your concern about your sister's welfare. You acknowledge that, the way that things have turned out, she was right in 1914 and you were wrong. You now begin to see merit in the activities and the attitudes displayed by the Social Democrats.

As you work through Issue 6, make notes which will enable you to comment on:

1. your initial enthusiasm for the war.
2. the reasons why you have become disillusioned:
a. the way in which Russian lives are wasted.
b. the lack of facilities for the wounded.
c. the deficiencies in equipment.
d. the fact that there seems to be no end of the war in sight.
3. your loss of faith in the Tsar and his ministers.
4. your awareness of the situation in Petrograd (food shortages, unrest, and so on) and your anxiety about your sister.
5. your thoughts about what must happen to improve your situation: has it become necessary to have a revolution and to establish a new government for Russia?

Then use your notes to write an appropriate letter 1200–1500 words long.

Russia and the First World War

Archduke Franz Ferdinand, the heir to the throne of the Austrian Empire, was assassinated in Sarajevo on 28 June 1914. When Austria decided to use the assassination as a pretext for declaring war on Serbia, the Tsar, who was regarded as the protector of the Orthodox Slav peoples, felt compelled to support the Serbs. The mobilisation of the Russian armies which began as a result of the Tsar's determination to stand by the Serbs set in motion the sequence of events which saw Europe's two 'Armed Camps' become embroiled in war.

One of Russia's early actions when hostilities broke out was to change the name of St Petersburg to Petrograd. It was believed that St Petersburg was too Germanic a name for the first city of a nation at war with the Germans.

The war was greeted with enthusiasm in Russia. Meriel Buchanan, the daughter of the British Ambassador to Russia, described some of the scenes which she witnessed in Petrograd as the Tsar's people rallied behind Mother Russia in the summer of 1914:

> 'The processions in the streets carrying the emperor's portrait . . . the bands everywhere playing the National Anthem . . . the long unending lines of khaki-clad figures who marched away, singing and cheering: tall, bronzed men with honest, open faces, with childlike eyes, and a trusting faith in the little father, and a sure and certain hope that the saints would protect them and bring them safely back to their villages . . . Those first days of war! How full we were with enthusiasm, of the conviction that we were fighting in a just and holy cause, for the freedom and betterment of the world! Swept away by the general stir of excitement, we dreamt dreams of triumph and victory! The Russian Steam-Roller! The British Navy! The French Guns! The war would be over by Christmas . . .'
>
> (Meriel Buchanan, *Dissolution of an Empire*, 1932)

Scenes such as this were in evidence all over Europe. The participating nations were involved in grand alliances which seemed to have awesome power, and each nation and its people believed that they were fighting a just war which they would win.

Moreover, few of those going off to the front had had any experience of war. The terrible destructive capacity of the weapons which had been developed had never fully been displayed, and certainly not to them. There was also the general assumption that the war would be won quickly: that it truly *would* be 'over by Christmas'. Figure 6.1 is an early propaganda postcard published in Russia. The Russian soldier is contemptuously punishing the German Kaiser, while the tiny figure of Emperor Franz Joseph of Austria attempts to flee from a similar fate.

The reality of war soon dispelled these optimistic notions and images.

Once the campaign had begun in earnest, some of Russia's fundamental weaknesses rapidly became clear. Her allies looked confidently towards a decisive contribution from the apparently limitless manpower of the Russian empire: the 'Steam-Roller' referred to by Meriel Buchanan would surely sweep over everything on the Eastern Front. There were, however, enormous obstacles to be overcome before the 'Steam-Roller' could be put to effective use.

For a start, Russia's geographical size and location created immense problems. Russia was effectively cut off from her major allies, France and Britain. Her Baltic fleet was closed in by Germany, and her Black Sea fleet was locked out of the Mediterranean by Turkey. One possible point of access, the port of Archangel in the extreme north of the empire, was ice-bound for half the year, and even during the other half was remote from

Хоть одѣтъ ты и по формѣ
Получай на по платформѣ,
А чтобъ не былъ ты кремнемъ,
Проучу тебя ремнемъ.
А союзнику убогу
Прищемлю я больно ногу,
Чтобы долго помнилъ шельма,
Что страдаетъ за Вильгельма.

Fig 6.1   An early propaganda postcard published in Russia in 1914.

centres of population and from the soldiers at the front. Entry could be made at the other end of the empire, for example through Vladivostok when *it* was not ice-bound, but this entailed a journey half-way round the world.

This geographical disadvantage was such a severe blow to Russia because of her other major weakness: the inability of her economy and administration to equip adequately the soldiers fighting at the front. Russia *did* have enormous manpower: the army's strength in 1914 was in the region of one and a half million men, with a further three million in reserve; by January 1917, some fourteen million men had been mobilised. All these were required to fight in barbaric campaigns, the dominant characteristic of which was trench warfare. Russia's manufacturing capacity was unable to keep them supplied even with boots and the most basic armaments. As early as December 1914, over two million of the six million men who had been mobilised did not have rifles. In campaigns during the crisis summer of 1915, only one man in three carried a rifle when going 'over the top': the other two carried sticks – the instruction being that they pick up the rifle of a wounded or dead compatriot who had fallen under the machine-gun and artillery barrage of the enemy! In some areas of the front, men were rationed to five rounds of ammunition a day. The Tsar wrote from the front to the Empress:

[2 December 1914]   'The only great and serious difficulty for our army is again the lack of ammunition. Because of that our troops are obliged, while fighting, to be cautious and to economise. This means that the burden of fighting falls on the infantry. As a result our losses are enormous. Some army corps have been reduced to divisions, brigades to companies, et cetera . . .'

[7 July 1915]   'Again that cursed question of shortage of artillery and rifle ammunition – it stands in the way of energetic advance. If we should have three days of serious fighting we might run out of ammunition altogether.'

(Quoted in A.F. Golder, *Documents of Russian History*, 1927)

The Tsar sought to participate actively in Russia's war effort. Figure 6.2 shows him displaying a holy ikon to his troops and blessing them before they went into battle. The loyalty and faith displayed by the soldiers were soon to be sorely tested. The nature of the combat which developed during the Great War meant that Russia's greatest strength, her manpower, could never be a decisive force in determining the outcome of the war. Once the lines of the trenches were established, defensive weapons dominated the war, because weapons such as machine-guns, mortars and heavy artillery, and the use of barbed-wire fences, made it virtually impossible to advance on enemy positions without suffering appalling losses.

Fig 6.2   Tsar Nicholas II displaying a holy icon to his troops and blessing them before they went into battle.

Because of the shortages of equipment just described, it is not surprising that the first campaigns involving the Russian troops proved to be disastrous. Figure 6.3 shows a map of the Eastern Front from 1914 to 1916. Russia invaded the East Prussian part of Germany in August 1914. The aim was to provide some relief for her allies, who were suffering onslaught on the Western Front as the Germans put their war strategy, the Schlieffen Plan – which was designed to crush France in six weeks – into action. The German commanders in the east, Hindenburg and Ludendorff, responded by shifting two army corps from the west – an action which undoubtedly weakened the Germans' ability to carry the Schlieffen Plan through to a successful conclusion. France was saved; but the cost to Russia was a crushing defeat at the Battle of Tannenberg, where over 100,000 troops were captured. Figure 6.4 shows some of these troops being herded off by the Germans.

Shortly afterwards, a further Russian setback in the region of the Masurian Lakes resulted in Russian troops being pushed back out of German territory.

The First World War, wherever it was fought, rapidly became a war of immobility. Trench networks, heavily reinforced with murderous defensive weaponry, became impossible to break down. This did not stop the generals from attempting to break

Fig 6.3   Map showing the
Eastern Front from 1914
to 1916.

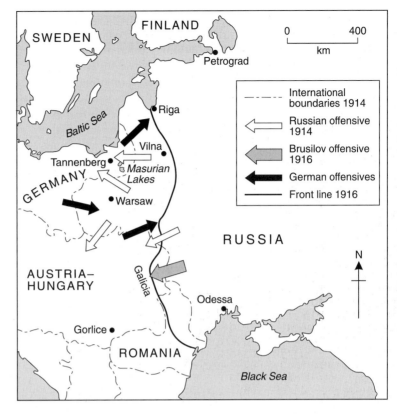

Fig 6.4   Troops who had
been captured during the
Battle of Tannenberg being
taken away by the
Germans.

them. On all fronts, a futile slaughter occurred over the years of the war. But Russia's losses were very much greater than those of any other participant. Furthermore, the way in which Russian lives were thrown away was particularly objectionable to Russians. The Battle of Tannenberg, urged on Russia by France and Britain, gave an early indication to the Russians that their allies were quite prepared to sanction great Russian manpower losses in order to take some of the strain off themselves on the Western Front. To the Russian soldiers, it rapidly became clear that they were little better than cannon-fodder, even in the minds of many of their own officers. After the war, General Hindenburg, a key German commander on the Eastern Front, wrote:

> 'In the Great War ledger, the page on which the Russian losses were written has been torn out. No one knows the figure. Five or eight millions? We, too, have no idea. All we know is that sometimes in our battles with the Russians we had to remove the mounds of enemy corpses from before our trenches in order to get a clear field of fire against fresh assaulting waves. Imagination may try to reconstruct the figure of their losses, but an accurate calculation will remain forever a vain thing.'
> (Quoted in Gwyneth Hughes and Simon Welfare, *Red Empire*, 1990)

Divisions within Russia: the case of the war wounded

The wounded suffered horribly from Russia's lack of preparedness for the war. Hospital facilities were often primitive or non-existent. Part of the reason for that was bureaucratic suspicion and intrigue, most notably by Tsarist ministers and administrators. These Tsarist officials were of the opinion that Duma representatives would use the war as a way of increasing their role in Russia's administration. The Tsar's ministers were vehemently opposed to the Duma and the zemstva expanding the scope of their activities within the empire, irrespective of the circumstances. They placed barriers to frustrate Duma and zemstva representatives, even though the sufferers in the process were Russian soldiers. One could take an example to illustrate this. The President of the Duma, Rodzianko, visited Poland in the early weeks of the war, because he wanted to find out about the facilities provided for wounded men. He had to go to Poland because he found himself not being allowed to see wounded men in Russia itself:

> 'At this time, my wife was patroness of the Elizabeth Society [the Red Cross Organisation] and it was reported to her that . . . trains passed the field units of her society, stopping sometimes at the stations, but that those in charge would not allow the sisters to enter the cars. There was a certain amount

of rivalry between the Ministry of War and the Red Cross. Each acted independently of the other and there was no co-ordination . . .'

In Poland, Rodzianko saw the reality of Russian medical provision for the wounded:

'Soon after my arrival at Warsaw in November 1914, I had a call from Vyrubov, who asked me to go with him to the Warsaw–Vienna station where there were about eighteen thousand men, wounded in the battles near Lodz and Berezina. There I saw a frightful scene. On the floor, without even a bedding of straw, in mud and slush, lay innumerable wounded, whose pitiful groans and cries filled the air. "For God's sake, get them to attend to us. No one has looked after our wounds for five days."

It should be said that after these bloody battles the wounded were thrown into freight cars without order, and thrown out at this station without attention . . .'

(Quoted in A.F. Golder)

Figure 6.5 shows what was classified as a Russian field hospital in Lithuania in February 1915.

The zemstva and city councils in Russia had quickly taken the initiative to deal with the problem of the war wounded. During the early weeks of the war, they had formed 'All Russian Unions'. And the Duma, within days of the beginning of hostilities, had appointed a provisional committee to deal with the affairs of all victims of the war. As early as October 1914, the 'All Russian Unions' had provided over 100,000 hospital beds in preparation for the returning wounded.

Fig 6.5   A Russian field hospital at Suvalki in Lithuania after a battle in February 1915.

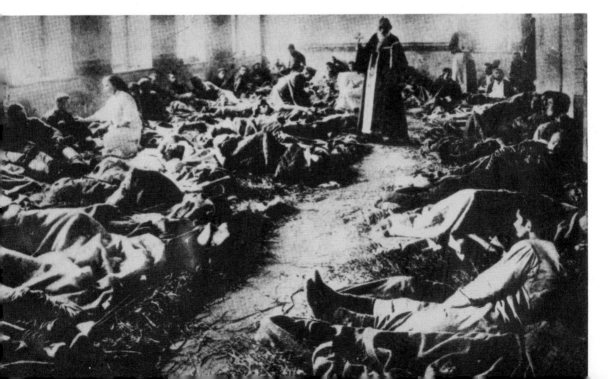

Clearly, the facilities prepared for the wounded by those in authority were totally inadequate, and contrasted most unfavourably with the provisions made by the Duma, the zemstva and the city councils.

Representatives of the Duma, the zemstva and the city councils were becoming much more outspoken in their criticism of the Tsar's government as the war progressed and Russia's fortunes retrogressed. By 1915, the conduct of every aspect of the handling of the war by the Tsar's ministers was under constant damning appraisal. The response of the Tsar's ministers was to continue to view these critics as a threat to the authority of the Tsar's government and to attempt to cut them off from proceedings.

Court intrigues at a time of crisis

In 1915 Russia's position in the war deteriorated rapidly. Austria and Germany decided to turn their attention more energetically towards Russia, and an offensive at Gorlice in Galicia on 2 May 1915 was a great success for them. Many Russian soldiers had no weapons whatsoever in this battle. The Germans and Austrians pushed on throughout the summer, taking approximately a million prisoners in the process.

Such was the scale of these disasters for Russia that the whole military strategy of the empire came under review. The Commander-in-Chief, Grand Duke Nikolay Nicholayevich, was replaced. Such a high-ranking figure could only be replaced by one of even higher rank: Russia's new Commander-in-Chief was Tsar Nicholas II. This decision was to prove a serious error of judgement by the Tsar. Thereafter, he was directly and personally responsible for Russia's performance in the war.

When the Tsar became Russia's Commander-in-Chief in 1915, his active role at the front meant that he was effectively passing over control of the empire to his wife, Alexandra. She had never been popular in Russia: her Protestant Germanic background and her uncompromising support for autocracy did not endear her to many of the subjects of the empire. Her active participation in discrediting those of the Tsar's ministers with whom she disagreed was another source of her unpopularity in the minds of many influential people in Russia. She was regarded generally with suspicion and distrust, and a further source of unease about her and about the Tsarist court in general was the apparent hold which the mysterious 'monk' Rasputin seemed to have over Tsar Nicholas and his family.

To understand the influence of Rasputin, it is necessary to appreciate the condition of the Tsar's son, Alexis, who was born in 1904, and was the heir to the Russian empire. The Tsar and Tsarina already had four daughters, but the birth of the long-awaited son was an event of great joy for them. Very soon, however, they learnt that Alexis suffered from haemophilia.

Fig 6.6   A contemporary cartoon entitled 'The Russian royal house'.

Alexandra, whose family had a record of passing on the disease, was heartbroken. Much of her alleged coldness and aloofness, which caused unfavourable comment about her, stemmed from this time.

The condition of Alexis was regarded as being incurable. The implication – that Nicholas II would not have the successor he believed the empire required – was kept hidden. Attempts to conceal this truth resulted in the Tsar and his family becoming progressively more remote and detached. Into this situation came Rasputin, introduced to Alexandra by one of her ladies as a mystic with remarkable powers. Alexandra allowed Rasputin to examine Alexis. The experiment was an apparent success. Rasputin had the ability, probably through hypnotism, to control the disease which, at times, threatened the life of Alexis. His presence at court thereafter became a necessity for the Tsar and Alexandra.

Having achieved royal favour, Rasputin began to create his own following within the Tsar's court. Much of his 'mysticism' seemed to revolve around questionable antics, usually in the company of many of the court ladies. Scandalous rumours began to appear about Rasputin, spread eagerly by the many enemies whom he rapidly accumulated. It was believed, with some justification, that Rasputin's hold over the Romanovs meant that he had influence far beyond the care of Alexis. It was said that Rasputin was influencing Alexandra and, ultimately, Nicholas, in the selection of ministers. It was suggested that the wives of ambitious husbands were courting Rasputin to assist in the career prospects of their menfolk. Court life at the best of times could be petty and vindictive, filled with jealousies and intrigue. The extra element of Rasputin played havoc with what order existed in the Tsar's court. Figure 6.6 is a contemporary cartoon entitled 'The Russian royal house'. It is typical of much press speculation about Rasputin and his hold over the Tsar and Tsarina.

While this was going on in the Tsar's court, the conflicts and suspicions between the Tsar's ministers and others engaged in the war effort continued. Organisations such as the Duma, the zemstva and city councils were honestly attempting to contribute in positive and humane ways, but continued to find themselves up against the blocking tactics of ministers and bureaucrats. Meanwhile, Russian soldiers were deprived of the most basic equipment and were suffering horribly when wounded because of inadequate hospitals and medication.

Criticism of the performance of the Tsar's government became more outspoken. Prominent opponents of the autocracy formed a 'Progressive Bloc' to urge reform of the way that Russia's war effort was organised. They met on 7 September 1915, and attached their signatures to a list of demands:

'The undersigned representatives of factions and groups of the State Council and State Duma, activated by the conviction that

only a strong, firm and active authority can lead the fatherland to victory, and that such an authority can be only that which rests upon popular confidence and is capable of organizing the active cooperation of all citizens, have arrived at the unanimous conclusion that the most important and essential object of creating such an authority cannot be attained without . . .
1. The formation of a united government . . .
2. Decisive change in the methods of administration . . .

(Quoted in A.F. Golder)

The other demands included the release of political prisoners; concessions to Poles, Finns and Jews; and free trade union activities. The Tsar and his government could only interpret such demands as a challenge to their authority and a vindication of the mistrust with which they had always viewed the Duma and the zemstva. Their response was to adjourn the Duma. Prime Minister Goremykin issued the instruction on 15 September 1915.

Within days, the Congress of Representatives of the Provincial Zemstva met in Moscow. Prince George Lvov, the respected moderate liberal, addressed the meeting:

'. . . it is not the Government, but the people, that is fighting the war. The Government may hold itself aloof from the people, but we shall be only still more confirmed in our conviction that the organization of victory is possible only through full union of Government and people, through their legal representatives, and we regard it as indispensible to have the work of the State Duma resumed as soon as possible . . . the Russian people is determined to prosecute the war to final victory . . . But fatal obstacles in the path of final victory . . . are still here: the irresponsibility of the Government, and its lack of real contact with the people . . . In the place of the present Government, there should be summoned persons possessing the confidence of the nation . . .'

(Quoted in A.F. Golder)

This was the situation of court intrigue, mistrust and political turmoil in Russia's political life at a time when the empire was involved in a desperate war for survival.

The changes in government personnel perhaps provide an indication of the political uncertainty: in the first two years of the war, Russia had four Prime Ministers, three Foreign Ministers, three Defence Ministers, and six Ministers of the Interior. In January 1916, Goremykin was replaced by Sturmer, a man who was almost seventy, who suffered from ill-health, and who had clearly been promoted through favouritism. His main task was not to bring stability to the government so that the war could be fought to a successful conclusion: it was to keep in order the Duma, the zemstva and city councils, and anyone else who might be seen as a threat to the authority of the Tsar and his government.

The situation of the people in Russia and the empire

Russia's war had a profound effect on every aspect of the life of the empire. Obviously, those parts of the empire in which the war was actually fought, for example Poland and the western provinces, experienced the most acute distress. As Russian Poland was a reluctant part of the Tsar's empire, the dreadful experience of invasion and war could only serve to worsen the problems which were already there. One peculiarity of Poland's situation was that the division of Polish territories meant that there were Poles fighting on either side. The demands of the war also created great stress in the parts of the empire remote from European Russia. For example, a situation of brutal civil strife occurred in Turkestan in 1916 (see page 140).

To the rear, behind the fronts, Russia's cities were acutely affected by the war. There were many reasons for this. The sheer scale of the demand for men for the army meant a considerable reduction in the size of the labour force in both the towns and the countryside. In some rural areas, about half of all the able-bodied men were conscripted. As much of the countryside had been overpopulated in any case, this did not have too detrimental an effect on the ability to produce grain. The problem thereafter lay in getting the grain to where it was really needed – the cities.

There were two main reasons for grain shortages. Firstly, Russia's railway system had reached breaking-point. During the early period of the war, the retreat from Poland and the western provinces meant that a key section of the railway network, stretching from north to south, had been lost. Much of what remained of the railway link in this area had been taken over for military purposes. The demands of the armies were colossal. Meeting these demands was often achieved at the cost of allowing cities such as Moscow and Petrograd to go short. By early 1916, less than half the required food supplies were reaching Russia's cities. This problem was made all the greater because the cities continued to grow rapidly during the war. The extra production required for the war effort was one reason for this. The other was the influx of refugees from Poland and the western provinces after 1914. Russia's urban population grew by almost a quarter, from 22 million to 28 million, between the start of the war and the Revolution in February 1917. The facilities to cope with this growing population simply did not exist. Employment was usually available in heavy industry, but high inflation caused by the government's habit of printing banknotes to buy its way out of problems meant that the workers were paid very little in real terms. Food shortages and the resulting high prices added to the process whereby workers were kept desperately impoverished.

The second reason for grain shortages was the fact that the

peasants felt no incentive to deliver their grain to Russia's cities in any case. The reason was that the paper money which they received in exchange could not be used to buy anything which the peasants wanted. Russia's factories were churning out goods for the war, not consumer goods such as clothes, shoes, and utensils which the peasants wanted to buy. The few consumer goods which were produced were so expensive because of scarcity that even inflated food prices meant little to the peasants. The peasants did not waste or destroy their surplus food. They simply relaxed into old-style self-sufficiency and refused to produce extra food to sell.

Another headache for the Tsar and his government was the response of nationalist dissidents to the war. We can consider the case of Poland, some of whose problems have already been referred to. Even before hostilities began in 1914, a Polish Nationalist, Josef Pilsudski, had been preparing a secret Polish army with the aim of securing Polish independence. Pilsudski contacted the Austrians, offering his soldiers to assist them in the event of a war against Russia. The Tsar and his government had the foresight to comprehend that a loyal Poland was vital once war broke out: on 14 August 1914, Grand Duke Nicholay Nicholayevich, then Commander-in-Chief, issued a decree promising that Poland would be reunited and self-governing within the Russian empire once the Tsar's army had won the war. This secured the support of most Poles for Russia's war effort, but Pilsudski was unimpressed. His soldiers formed 'Polish Legions' which operated under Austrian command in southern Poland. Some of Pilsudski's best officers formed the 'Polish Military Operation', a secret force which operated behind Russian lines. This was the kind of extra complexity which the Tsar and his government could well have done without – especially as there were Polish soldiers under Tsarist command.

Poland was caught squarely between both warring factions. Poles were attached to both armies. Clearly, there was the opportunity for either side to win the diplomatic initiative over Poland with, it was assumed, full Polish support as the prize. In 1916 Germany and Austria, who by then occupied much of Poland, declared their intention of establishing a Polish kingdom. A few days later, they announced the existence of a Polish army – which was to be placed, in the meantime, under their command. Russia responded in kind, referring rather vaguely to the possibility of full Polish independence after the war and pointedly establishing separate, purely Polish, divisions out of their armies.

A very different nationality problem appeared in Central Asia in the second half of 1916. In Turkestan, simmering resentment about the growing numbers of Russian settlers in the region finally brought forth a violent reaction. The catalyst, again, was the war situation. The Tsar's government devised a plan to mobilise almost half a million Muslims from the region and shift them to the rear of the war front to make up for labour deficiencies brought about by the demand for soldiers. The revolt which erupted as a result was violent and vicious in nature. Official estimates indicated some 3000 Russians were killed, but Muslim casualties, as the Tsar's government suppressed the dissidents, may well have numbered hundreds of thousands. Many other Muslims fled from the empire into China. This nationalist problem was remote from the action of the Great War and had very little effect on the political position in European Russia. But it was a further unwelcome complication for the Tsar and his ministers at a desperate time and its importance should not be overlooked.

1916 – an improvement in Russia's fortunes?

The 1916 campaigns of the Russian army were nothing like as disastrous as those of 1915. Indeed, the campaign which has become known as the Brusilov Offensive, between June and September 1916 (see Figure 6.3), was quite remarkably successful. This offensive, planned to coincide with the Anglo-French assaults on the Western Front, of which the Battle of the Somme was the centre-piece, appeared to present the possibility of a telling break-through against the Austrians. Russian forces did actually break through the Austrian lines in several places, capturing some 400,000 prisoners in the process. Brusilov had taken advantage of Austrian complacency by launching a wide offensive using all four of his armies over a wide front. The Austrians were routed. Brusilov then continued with an impressive advance over nearly one hundred kilometres – an astounding achievement in a war of stalemate. The cost in lives, however, was immense. Brusilov's one hundred kilometres were won with the loss of over a million Russian soldiers. The advance came to an abrupt end when faced with organised and determined German positions along the Carpathian Mountains. Moreover, the success of Brusilov in advancing at all meant that it became progressively more difficult to get supplies and reinforcements to him. Once again, the Eastern Front drifted into stagnation.

By this time the Russians were war-weary. Despite the apparent improvements, for example in the general supply situation and in the performance of the army, it was clearly the case that there was no end to the war in sight. At least two million Russian soldiers had been killed, four million wounded and a further two-and-a-half million taken prisoner-of-war. The countryside was in desolation and the major cities overcrowded and starved of essential supplies. The Tsar's government was regarded with derision by all but a few close supporters. One general, Krymov, openly told a Duma delegation that, 'The spirit of the army is such that news of a coup d'état would be welcomed with joy.'

A police report from Petrograd to the Minister of the Interior in October 1916 declared:

'The brilliant success of the offensive of General Brusilov in the spring of the present year and the current solution to the problem of supplying the troops proved convincingly that the task undertaken by the Government and the community has been fulfilled more than successfully. The question of the organisation of the army supply may be held to have been satisfactorily settled . . . But, on the other hand, the disintegration of the rear, that is of the whole country, which is now steadily increasing has today reached such monstrous and extreme form that is has begun to be a menace to the success obtained at the front, and in the very near future promises to throw the country into chaotic, spontaneous and catastrophic anarchy.'

(Quoted in R. Brown and C. Daniels, *Documents and Debates: 20th Century Europe*, 1981)

Police reports from Russia's cities were provided in response to a circular from the Minister of the Interior in 1915. They were to be delivered monthly. Their existence provides a clear indication of the state of anxiety of the Tsar's ministers. They had much to feel anxious about. Food shortages in Russian cities began to be acute in 1916. Output of grain had fallen by over 20 per cent since the start of the war, and the demands of the army were remorseless. The State Police Department reported at the time:

'If the populace thus far has not engaged in food riots, that does not mean that it is not going to do so in the near future. The exasperation of the people is growing in leaps and bounds. Every day, more of them demand, "Either give us food or stop the war." And they are amongst the most suitable element among which to conduct anti-government propaganda. They have nothing to lose from a disadvantageous peace. Just when the thing will happen and how it is hard to tell. But events of the greatest importance and fraught with the most dangerous consequences are most certainly close at hand.'

(Quoted in David Shub, *Lenin*, 1948)

One cause for celebration among critics of the régime occurred on 29 December 1916: a right-wing group, led by Prince Felix Yusupov, murdered Rasputin. Tsar Nicholas returned from the front and another ministerial reshuffle occurred.

Contemporary accounts show that Rasputin fought for his life and required a great deal of killing before he was finally thrown into the River Neva and disappeared under the ice. As 1916 drew to a close, the question was: could the Tsarist régime put up such a spirited fight to stay in power?

The February Revolution

Bread shortages, strikes and mutiny

The impending crisis predicted in the report of the State Police Department just given was not long in materialising. More and more police reports talked of people 'being on the edge of despair', especially in Petrograd. A British diplomat, Sir Henry Wilson, wrote from the city only days before the Revolution that 'It is as certain as anything can be that the Emperor and Empress are heading for a fall. Everyone – officers, merchants, ladies – talk openly of the absolute necessity of doing away with them.'

The ingredients for the February Revolution were all in place in Petrograd. First of all, there were 170,000 garrisoned soldiers sullenly awaiting the call to the front to fight an apparently hopeless war. The army had always been the reliable bulwark of Tsarist autocracy, able and willing to turn its arms against either foreign enemies or fellow Russians as the case required. The Tsar's soldiers did not hesitate to fire on the peaceful marchers in 1905 or on the striking Lena mine-workers in 1912. This, however, was a different army – an army of conscripted men fully attuned to what awaited them at the front, embittered by their experiences under the autocracy, cynical and lacking in motivation.

Then there were the ordinary people of Petrograd, whose position was described as follows in another police report:

'The proletariat of the capital is on the verge of despair . . . the mass of industrial workers are quite ready to let themselves go to the wildest excesses of a hunger riot . . . The prohibition of all labour meetings . . . the closing of trade unions, the prosecution of men taking an active part in the sick benefit funds, the suspension of labour newspapers, and so on, make the labour masses, led by the more advanced and already revolutionary-minded elements, assume an openly hostile attitude towards the government and protest with all the means at their disposal against the continuation of the war.'

(Quoted in M.T. Florinsky, *The End of the Russian Empire*, 1931)

Unrest began in response to the food shortages already referred to on page 139. By late January 1917 bread shortages in Petrograd were becoming acute and rationing was discussed. Rumours of impending shortages spread rapidly and queues immediately began appearing at bakeries and other food supply shops. Figure 6.7 shows one of the food queues in Petrograd in February 1917. Each day, women began queueing at dawn in temperatures well below zero to attempt to get bread. Scenes like the one shown in Figure 6.7 were commonplace. Shops soon ran out of supplies.

Fig 6.7   People queuing for bread in Petrograd in February 1917.

When this happened, the women often reverted to violence against the shops. The situation was clearly becoming unbearable.

The first disorders of note appeared on 23 February. Strikes broke out, at first dominated by women workers, and processions of protesters gathered in Petrograd. By the next day, the strikers numbered tens of thousands. This was the type of situation which the Tsar and his ministers had previously responded to by sending in the army. Indeed Nicholas sent a telegram to General Khabalov, District Commander of Petrograd, telling him to suppress the strikes, which were unacceptable at such a time of war. The Tsar clearly believed that the army would do his bidding. The conscript soldiers in Petrograd, however, had different ideas. The decisive moment of the February Revolution occurred on the 26th – that was when the Volonsky regiment mutinied. On 27 February, they killed their commanding officers and joined the strikers. All defence for the Tsar was removed at a stroke when the Petrograd soldiers, who were armed and trained, joined the protest against the autocracy.

Rodzianko, the President of the Duma, frantically telegraphed the Tsar just after midnight on 26 February. He urged Nicholas to oversee the creation of a government acceptable to the mass of the people:

'The situation is serious. The capital is in a state of anarchy. The Government is paralysed; the transport service is broken down; the food and fuel supplies are completely disorganised. Discontent is general and on the increase. There is wild shooting on the streets; troops are firing at each other. It is urgent that someone enjoying the confidence of the country be entrusted with the formation of a new Government. There must be no delay. Hesitation is fatal.'

Some hours later, Rodzianko, still awaiting the Tsar's response, pleaded:

'The situation is growing worse. Measures should be taken immediately, as tomorrow will be too late. The last hour has struck, when the fate of the country and dynasty is being decided.'

(Quoted in A.F. Golder)

The Tsar's response was to outlaw the Duma. Rodzianko and other Duma leaders, faced with the reality of impending social collapse and a Tsar who remained obstinate and unyielding, decided that their only course of action was to establish a provisional form of government, capable of restoring order to Russia. At the head of this government was Lvov, with the title 'Prime Minister and Minister of the Interior'. The cabinet, that is to say the key ministers of this provisional government, was composed mainly of Octobrists and Kadets. Amongst the most important of these were Milyukov, who was appointed as Minister of Foreign Affairs, and Guchkov, who became Minister of War. The Ministry of Justice went to the popular Alexander Kerensky. The Duma continued to operate meantime, with Rodzianko at its head.

In order to emphasise to the people that dramatic change would rapidly come about, the newspaper *Izvestiia* published the names of the new cabinet, described as the 'Provisional Executive Committee of the members of the Duma'. The report declared:

'The Cabinet will be guided in its actions by the following principles:
1. An immediate general amnesty for all political and religious offences . . .
2. Freedom of speech and press; freedom to form labour unions and to strike. These political liberties should be extended to the army in so far as war conditions permit.
3. Immediate preparations for the calling of a constituent assembly, elected by universal and secret vote, which shall

determine the form of government and draw up the
Constitution for the country.
4. Elections to be carried out on the basis of universal, direct,
equal, and secret suffrage.
5. The troops that have taken part in the revolutionary
movement shall not be disarmed or removed from
Petrograd ...'

(Quoted in A.F. Golder)

This report was a clear and unambiguous statement of intent. It
contained a succession of points which would have popular appeal.
Very importantly, it gave the Petrograd soldiers guarantees which
ensured that they would give their support to the Duma.

On the same evening that the report was published, Guchkov
led a deputation to the Tsar. Nicholas had attempted to return
from the front on 28 February, but had given up when information was relayed to him that the railway lines into Petrograd and
Moscow were being guarded by revolutionaries. He had taken
sanctuary in the Northern Front headquarters at Pskov. There,
Guchkov informed Nicholas that the purpose of his mission was to
accept the Tsar's resignation. An attempt was made over the next
twenty-four hours to secure the passage of the Tsarist title to
Nicholas's brother, but the arrangement, despite the qualified
support of Guchkov and Milyukov, was never a realistic proposition.

The Russian empire which had existed for centuries had
become a republic.

The speed of events had been bewildering. Kerensky later
wrote in his memoirs:

'Three days without any government whatsoever. An empire
with an army of over ten million men fighting at the front, and
in the throes of a great economic crisis, suddenly left, as it
were, at the mercy of the winds ... Those who did not witness
the early days of the Russian Revolution from its storm-centre
cannot imagine the extent of the collapse of the administrative
structure: it was a veritable catastrophe! ... Discipline, civic and
military, disappeared throughout the land ... The French
Revolution seems to me like a gradual evolution compared
with the lightning crash of the Russian monarchy ... There still
stood the outer shell of the empire, but within it every rivet,
every link had snapped. It was a terrifying moment!'

(Alexander Kerensky, *The Great Catastrophe*, 1927)

Where were the revolutionaries?

On first investigation, it would appear that revolutionaries were not a significant factor in the events of February 1917. Lenin, the Bolshevik leader, had been in exile in Switzerland during the course of the Great War. In January 1917 he informed an audience at a meeting in Zurich that, 'We of the older generation may not live to see the decisive battles of this coming revolution.' In Russia itself, Lenin was virtually unknown, except within the ranks of the professional revolutionaries and by their opponents within the Tsar's administration.

However, one should not be too dismissive of the Bolshevik influence in February 1917. In several ways which were to prove very important, Bolshevik groups had for years been active in Russia's major cities. Of particular significance was the way in which Bolshevik representatives had gained control of many workers' representational organisations, especially in Petrograd and Moscow. This began to happen in earnest following the Lena goldfield strike in 1912 which marked the end of the period of relative peace and stability following the 1905 revolution. In the elections to the fourth Duma held in 1912, Lenin had instructed Bolshevik candidates to stand. All six of Russia's major industrial cities saw the labour vote go to Bolshevik candidates. In the next two years, Bolshevik representatives systematically won over control of even more workers' organisations, especially in St Petersburg. There was a curious irony here: many of these organisations had been set up by Mensheviks who had moved away from supporting revolution and towards the idea of using trade union methods to improve the workers' conditions. By July 1914 the Bolsheviks could declare that they controlled fourteen of the eighteen trade unions in Petrograd and ten of the thirteen in Moscow. From this position of strength, the remaining Menshevik factions were systematically forced out of the few footholds they had retained.

When the war broke out in 1914, Lenin and the Bolsheviks were dismayed at the way in which the masses rallied to the Tsarist war effort. Nevertheless, the machinery by which the Bolsheviks might eventually take control of all the significant workers' organisations in Petrograd, such as the strike committees called 'soviets', was firmly in place by 1917. Most soviets throughout Russia were still dominated by Mensheviks, but it was the Petrograd Soviet which was to play the most vital role in 1917, and it was this soviet which had the highest number of active Bolshevik members. When the Petrograd garrison mutinied and joined the strikers, a 'Soviet of Workers' and Soldiers' Deputies' was rapidly formed. This Soviet's co-operation in the drawing-up of the political programme of the Provisional Committee of the Duma was regarded by Rodzianko, Lvov and the rest as vital. The Soviet declared that it would support the Duma if a number of pledges were made. These pledges were clearly the major part of the principles published in *Izvestiia* (see page 145).

The Bolsheviks, therefore, would not have been regarded as a major political force within Russian in February 1917, and certainly not by the Duma representatives who formed the Provisional Government. But they were placed in positions of strength and influence in the organisations of the workers – and now of the soldiers. What would happen if the Provisional Government failed to live up to its early promise?

In Switzerland, Lenin heard of the momentous events with astonished delight. Had his hour arrived at last?

ESSAY

1. Why was the Russian 'Steam-Roller' so ineffective during the First World War?
2. How accurate would it be to suggest that the Tsar and his ministers were more of a hindrance than a help to Russia's war effort?
3. Was government incompetence or military inadequacy more to blame for Russia's poor performance in the Great War?
4. To what extent was the February Revolution in Russia caused by her involvement in the First World War?

The Bolsheviks seize power

The new people in charge of the Russian empire called themselves the Provisional Government. Their time in power was brief. Within eight months, the Provisional Government had collapsed and the Bolsheviks had seized power. These issues will be considered in this chapter:

1. The Provisional Government and how it attempted to rule Russia.
2. The opposition which the Provisional Government faced.
3. The overthrow of the Provisional Government by Lenin and the Bolsheviks.

These areas of study and others related to them will allow us to investigate how much *authority* the Provisional Government really had. Did it operate through any recognisable *ideology* or did it simply seek to hold Russia together? Did it seek to offer a new *identity* to the peoples of the empire – the peasants, the workers, and the national minorities? How did Lenin and the Bolsheviks overthrow the Provisional Government with such apparent ease?

TASK

It is early October 1917. You are the editor of a newspaper in Petrograd. Your newspaper has been supportive of the Provisional Government, but you feel that the situation in Russia is such that you can no longer continue that support.

You express your opinions in a front page editorial headed, 'Should the Bolsheviks be given a chance?' In this editorial, you should comment on:

1. the 'Dual Authority' and how well it is working.

2. the handling of the war effort.
3. the situation in the towns.
4. the situation in the countryside.
5. the national minorities.
6. the July Days and the Kornilov Affair.
7. what the Bolsheviks are offering as an alternative.

As you are working through Issue 7, make notes which will allow you to write this editorial. When completed, it should be approximately 1200 words long.

The 'Dual Authority'

The Provisional Government and the concept of 'Dual Authority'

By adopting the name 'Provisional Government', Russia's new administration, headed by Prince George Lvov, accepted that it was a temporary form of authority which had been rushed into power following the collapse of Tsarism. Its only claim to legitimacy was that its members were people whom the voters had elected to the Duma. When Milyukov, the Minister of Foreign Affairs, read out the list of cabinet members appointed by the Provisional Government, one of the listening crowd called out, 'And who appointed you?'. The question was an incisive one. Milyukov had no satisfactory answer, nor had any of his cabinet colleagues, most of whom were Octobrists and Kadets. Lacking legitimate authority, there were only two ways by which the Provisional Government could survive for any length of time: either by winning popular support because of the way that it tackled Russia's problems; or by having an enforced authority established with military backing – that is, by becoming a dictatorship.

The Provisional Government believed that its job was to allow the empire to continue to function until a constitution could be drawn up and a government could be elected. In the interlude, the Provisional Government would act as an unelected authority, setting up the assembly which would draw up Russia's new constitution; running the Empire; and organising the war effort.

One major source of weakness in the Provisional Government was that other groups could claim that they too had played a part in overthrowing Tsardom and that they too were representative of large sections of the people. They therefore ought to be entitled to have some authority in deciding what should happen in Russia. The group which were most insistent in this respect were the soviets. In particular, the Petrograd Soviet rapidly made known its intention to be involved in the very heart of government. Soviets in other parts of Russia followed the Petrograd line; they wanted to make sure that the rights of workers and soldiers were being properly looked after by the Provisional Government.

The soviets were very clever in ensuring from the start that their influence would be brought to bear on the Provisional Government. This happened in the following way. On 1 March, two days after the first meeting of the Provisional Government, the Petrograd Soviet issued its 'Order Number One' in the newspaper *Izvestiia*. Order Number One was directed towards Russian soldiers:

> 'The Soviet of Workers' and Soldiers' Deputies has resolved:
> 1. In all companies, battalions, [etc.] . . . committees from the elected representatives of the lower ranks . . . shall be chosen immediately . . . .
> 4. The orders of the military commission of the State Duma shall be executed only in such cases as do not conflict with the orders and resolutions of the Soviet of Workers' and Soldiers' Deputies.
> 5. All kinds of arms, such as rifles, machine-guns, armoured automobiles, and others, must be kept at the disposal and under the control of the company and battalion committees, and in no case be turned over to officers, even at their demand.
> 6. In the ranks . . . soldiers must observe the strictest military discipline, but outside the service . . . soldiers cannot in any way be deprived of those rights which all citizens enjoy. In particular, standing at attention and compulsory saluting, when not on duty, is abolished.'
>
> (Quoted in A.F. Golder)

Notice the essential elements of Order Number One: the Petrograd Soviet was giving itself the power to veto military decisions passed by the Provisional Government; it was ensuring that all arms and ammunition would be controlled by soldiers who were members of the Soviet; and it was removing the power of the officer class to give orders to the soldiers except on the battlefield. Very neatly, and from the first hours of the Provisional Government coming into being, the Petrograd Soviet had recognised the need to control the army and had taken appropriate steps to do this. After 1 March 1917, the men in the Russian army, when not at the front, were under the control of the Petrograd Soviet. Order Number One was a very shrewd means of taking control of the army. Leon Trotsky, the leading revolutionary who later founded the Red Army, said that Order Number One was 'The only worthwhile document of the February Revolution'.

It is necessary to stress at this stage that the Petrograd Soviet and, later on, soviets throughout Russia were not opposed to the Provisional Government. The soviets were initially strike committees of workers. The February Revolution made their role in Russia much more political, but they were not seeking to challenge the Government. Kerensky emphasised this point in his memoirs: until Lenin's takeover in October 1917, soviet leaders, with the exception of Bolsheviks, accepted the Provisional Government and wanted to work with it. Indeed, both Kerensky and Milyukov later paid tribute to the enormous efforts made by the soviets to restore order and discipline to Russia's cities, notably Petrograd, when the collapse occurred on 27 February 1917.

Order Number One was conceived as part of the effort to keep the army under control and it was not regarded as at all ominous by Lvov and his ministers. Indeed, at a time of approaching anarchy, they were glad to see an authority which could bring order to the armed forces. The soviets, in the midst of ruin and disintegration, were the first and most effective support which the new government had amongst the masses. They were invaluable.

During the weeks following the February Revolution, the expansion of soviet influence throughout Russia was enormous. As there were no developed local political parties in Russian cities, the soviets were seen as the only organisations which represented the ordinary people. Their moderate, helpful approach towards the Provisional Government came about partly because most of the soviets were dominated by Mensheviks: Bolshevik influence was minimal. In April 1917 the first All-Russian Congress of Soviets took place. Out of the 1600 soviet deputies from all over Russia, only forty or so were Bolsheviks.

Despite its apparently weak position, the Provisional Government managed to complete an enormous programme of legislative changes for the empire within the first two months of its life. It declared a political amnesty for everyone; introduced trial by jury; abolished capital punishment and exile; and established independent law judges. It removed all discrimination based upon religion, nationality or class. It removed censorship. It established local government in rural areas, gave civilian rights to all soldiers, and introduced the eight-hour working day.

These were all entirely satisfactory measures to the mass of the people in Russia. The problem was that, unless the Provisional Government could do something about Russia's state of crisis, its new laws would mean virtually nothing. The Government had inherited a mass of problems from the Tsarist régime, chief amongst which was the increasingly unpopular war. In addition, the food supply to the towns was wholly inadequate and the peasants were clamouring for land. Industry was facing collapse. Faced with these problems, the Provisional Government continued to rely on the soviets, and in particular on the Petrograd Soviet. As early as 9 March the Minister of War, Guchkov, wrote:

> 'The Provisional Government has no real force at its disposal and its decrees are carried out only to the extent that it is permitted by the Soviet of Workers' and Soldiers' Deputies which has in its hands the most important elements of real power, such as the army, the railways, the post and telegraphs. It is possible to say flatly that the Provisional Government exists only as long as it is allowed by the Soviet of Workers' and Soldiers' Deputies. In particular, it is now possible to give only those orders which do not radically conflict with the orders of the above-named Soviet.'

(Quoted in A.F. Golder)

Out of this situation there developed what has become known as 'Dual Authority' between the Provisional Government and the soviets – in particular the Petrograd Soviet. Lvov declared his belief that neither could exist without the other; the soviets had 'power without authority' whilst the Provisional Government had 'authority without power'.

The reality of the relationship was somewhat different, as was soon to be seen. Real power as well as authority lay with the Petrograd Soviet, or more specifically with the intellectuals at its head – mainly the Mensheviks and the Social Revolutionaries. Why then did the Petrograd Soviet not simply assert that *it* was the real authority in Russia and that it would govern accordingly? There were several reasons for this.

Firstly, there existed a general attitude amongst government ministers and soviet deputies that a revolution had occurred and that Provisional Government and Soviet alike were now engaged in a common programme of much-needed reform: actual, tangible reforms were taking place, as has already been noted.

Secondly, after the frightening experiences of the February Revolution, there was a general sense of relief that some kind of order had been restored to Russia. If that order fell apart, the empire could collapse into anarchy.

There was also the question of ideology and how the events of February 1917 should be interpreted.

The Mensheviks, who dominated the soviets in early 1917, were Marxists who believed that the February 1917 Revolution marked the final transformation of Russia from its 'feudal' stage to its 'capitalist' stage. As such, it was part of the logical process of historical evolution as defined by Karl Marx. The Mensheviks therefore believed that for a limited historical period a government such as the Provisional Government had to be allowed to operate. Eventually, when the time was right, Russian capitalism would collapse, and Russia would move to the socialist phase of her development. This again was part of the clearly defined pattern of historical development recognised and explained by Karl Marx.

The Mensheviks recognised the problem which the Provisional Government was facing in February 1917: without mass support it could not survive. Menshevik-dominated soviets therefore agreed to enter into Dual Authority with the Provisional Government to allow it to fulfil its historical function. The understanding was always, of course, that eventually capitalism would collapse, that the Provisional Government or its successor would collapse with it, and that eventually a socialist form of society would appear in Russia.

This was the reality of Dual Authority. For the Provisional Government it meant dependence on the continued support of the soviets. For the soviets it meant supporting the Provisional Government until the conditions for the transfer to socialist society were in place.

Such a relationship could only be vulnerable, especially with the Bolsheviks awaiting their opportunity. Bolshevik ideology required the small revolutionary élite to seize power and to establish the 'dictatorship of the proletariat'. This was a clearly defined course of action. The Menshevik-dominated soviets and the vulnerable Provisional Government lacked the clear, authoritative sense of purpose and direction possessed by Lenin and the Bolsheviks, and this added further to the weakness of the Dual Authority.

Lenin and the Bolsheviks

The amnesty for all political prisoners granted by the Provisional Government meant that all dissidents were free to return from exile. Political activists sought to get to Petrograd as quickly as possible. Prominent Bolsheviks such as Stalin and Kamenev managed to reach Petrograd by late March. To Lenin's dismay, they began co-operating with the Provisional Government. Lenin was still exiled in Zurich. From there, in a series of dispatches which were called his *Letters From Afar*, he poured out scorn on the Provisional Government and urged the Bolsheviks not to comply with its regulations. He declared that the Provisional Government was a government of capitalists who had been running Russia economically before 1917. Now they had used the collapse of Tsarism to establish political control. Lenin insisted that the soviets were the real revolutionaries. The soviets, he declared, should shun the Provisional Government. They should get rid of the Menshevik idea that they had to support the Provisional Government to protect the developing revolution – an idea referred to as 'revolutionary defencism':

> 'He who says that the workers must *support* the new government in the interests of the struggle against Tsarist reaction . . . is a traitor to the workers, a traitor to the cause of the proletariat, to the cause of peace and freedom.'

Lenin attributed the success of the Provisional Government in coming to power at least in part to foreign intrigue designed to get Russia to continue the war:

> 'That the revolution succeeded so quickly and, seemingly . . . so radically is due to [firstly] . . . the conspiracy of the Anglo-French imperialists, who impelled Milyukov, Guchkov and Co. to seize power for the purpose of continuing the imperialist war . . .'
>
> (Lenin, *Collected Works*)

This point became one of Lenin's key themes when attacking the Provisional Government. He continually emphasised that the Great War was a war of capitalist imperialism, and that the Provisional Government was actively participating in a process by which millions of Russian workers were being slaughtered to make money for rich western businessmen.

Lenin urged the soviets to withdraw their support from the Provisional Government and to usher in a proletarian revolution:

'The proletariat cannot and must not support a war government . . . To fight reaction, to rebuff all possible and probable attempts by the Romanovs and their friends to restore the monarchy and muster a counter-revolutionary army, it is necessary not to support Guchkov and Co., but to organise, expand and strengthen a proletarian militia, to arm the people under the leadership of the workers.'

(Lenin, *Collected Works*)

Lenin produced five of these *Letters From Afar*. Their content gave a clear indication of what his approach would be once he returned to Russia. His problem was how to cross through German territory and join his fellow Bolsheviks to direct affairs. An unlikely ally appeared on the scene. When it became clear that the Provisional Government was going to continue fighting the war, the Germans hit upon the idea of smuggling Lenin into Petrograd in the hope that he and the Bolsheviks would use their influence to undermine the Russian army and eventually the Provisional Government. A 'sealed train' was arranged and appropriate passes were prepared for Lenin. A route was planned: north through Germany, across the Baltic into Sweden, north to Finland and then down into Petrograd (see Figure 7.1 on page 156).

This arrangement was controversial to say the least: it seemed that Lenin, without invitation from the Provisional Government or the Petrograd Soviet, had taken it upon himself to make a deal with Germany from which the Germans obviously hoped to benefit in their war against Russia. To his opponents, Lenin's behaviour was traitorous. Lenin's critics could point to the fact that he and his Bolsheviks had been receiving financial help from the Germans since the early days of the war because the Germans believed that Bolshevik-inspired unrest in Russia would operate to their advantage.

With this controversy still fresh, Lenin arrived at the Finland Station in Petrograd in April 1917. Within days, he had released his *April Theses* in which he outlined Bolshevik strategy for the immediate future:

'1) In our attitude towards the war, which under the new government of Lvov and Co. unquestionably remains on Russia's part a predatory imperialist war owing to the capitalist nature of that government, not the slightest concession to "revolutionary defencism" is permissible.

2) . . . the country is passing from the first stage of the revolution – which, owing to the insufficient class-consciousness and organisation of the proletariat, placed power

in the hands of the bourgeoisie – to its second stage, which must place power in the hands of the proletariat and the poorest sections of the peasants.

3) No support for the Provisional Government; the utter falsity of all its promises should be made clear ...'

(Lenin, Collected Works)

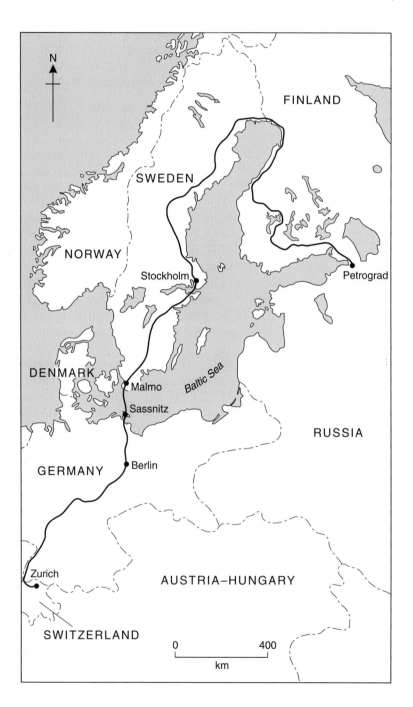

Fig 7.1   Map showing Lenin's return route from Zurich to Petrograd.

In his *April Theses*, Lenin went on to explain some of the things that the revolution should be working towards achieving, such as the nationalisation of all the land, the amalgamation of all banks, and the bringing of all production and distribution of goods under the control of the soviets. He went on to declare that Bolsheviks should make the break with other Social Democrats absolutely clear by giving their party a new name: the 'Communist Party'.

From writings such as the *Letters from Afar* and the *April Theses*, it is clear that Lenin's return to Petrograd meant the end of the conciliatory relationship between the Provisional Government and all the political groupings within the soviets. Lenin's approach was uncompromising. The Provisional Government, he persistently declared, was composed of the leftovers of discredited Tsarism. Gentry aristocrats such as Lvov and bourgeois intellectuals such as Milyukov should be swept away in Russia's real revolution. The real revolution was the revolution of the proletariat. The real source of authority in Russia should be the organs of the proletariat: the soviets. Soviets should work with the party of the proletariat, the Bolsheviks, to usher in the Communist Revolution.

Urgings such as these shattered any complacency which might have developed about the Dual Authority. The emphasis was being squarely shifted by Lenin on to the soviets and their right, their duty, to give the revolution a proper direction. This line of approach gradually led towards the key question of the late spring and summer of 1917: who should control the soviets, and to what end?

The Provisional Government and the war

The Provisional Government had little choice but to continue the war. There were two broad reasons for this. The first reason was to do with Russia's relations with her allies. Russia by 1917 had become dependent upon western allied assistance to survive. The empire was bankrupt. It was being kept afloat by injections of capital from abroad. One of the first groups of visitors to talk to the new Provisional Government consisted of foreign bankers who had provided this capital. They declared their intention to allow finance to continue to flow to the Provisional Government on the understanding that it would continue with the war effort. The Provisional Government had to agree, even though the sacrifices being required of Russia were enormous.

The second reason why the Provisional Government had to continue the war was the army itself. Russia in 1917 had nine million soldiers, armed and trained. They could not be disbanded while the empire was still at war, but they required a purpose, otherwise they would become a threat to government stability. Lenin and the Bolsheviks, in keeping with the strategy outlined in the *April Theses*, were constantly working in the midst of garrisoned soldiers. The Provisional Government was well aware of how dangerous the army might be if it were won over to Bolshevik persuasion. Kerensky later wrote of the army in 1917:

> 'To say to an army in the midst of war that under no circumstances would it be compelled to fight is tantamount to transforming the troops into a meaningless mob, useless, restless, irritable and therefore capable of all sorts of excesses. For this reason and to preserve the interior of the country . . . it was incumbent upon us . . . to make of it once more an army, i.e. to bring it back to the psychology of action, or of impending action.'
>
> (Alexander Kerensky, *The Catastrophe*, 1927)

The fronts where Russian soldiers were involved had come to a virtual standstill. It may seem strange that the Germans and Austrians were not taking full advantage of Russia's internal turmoil. They, however, believed that this was exactly what they were doing. The Germans in particular believed that by holding off from attacking the Russians, they would allow revolutionary propaganda to infiltrate the Russian army and encourage defeatism. The Germans believed that a separate peace with Russia could be concluded because of the anti-war sentiment of the revolutionary parties. They were prepared to sit back and allow events to follow their course.

Things did not work out in quite such an uncomplicated manner. Instead, differing attitudes towards the war became the cause of the first major disagreement between the Petrograd Soviet and the Provisional Government. Milyukov, the Foreign Minister, had despatched a memorandum to Russia's allies in late March, emphasising Russia's determination to honour her treaty obligations and to fight the war to a successful conclusion; he went as far as to say that the popular desire in Russia to win the war had increased since the Revolution. But when the text of this memorandum was made known to the soviets, popular outcry was immediate. Massive street protests involving thousands of soldiers developed. Fighting broke out between them and pro-Milyukov protesters, during which arms were used. By the end of April a crisis was developing, and the Provisional Government was seeking ways of placating the protesters by inviting more active involvement by the Petrograd Soviet in government decision-making. Milyukov and Guchkov, the Minister of War, were opposed to this. Both resigned in protest at what they believed to be the army's impending lack of ability to fight the war.

At first the Petrograd Soviet rejected the invitation to join in a coalition with the Provisional Government, believing that such a move would ultimately lead to it being discredited in the minds of the workers. Kerensky managed to persuade the Soviet that unless it joined the coalition, further unrest would surely come.

Eventually the Soviet agreed, the price being that the Provisional Government should work more energetically to achieve peace; should agree to accept soviet control over industry, labour and agrarian policy; and should push forward towards producing a constitution for Russia as quickly as possible. The soviets, in turn, agreed that a new military offensive should be launched in June 1917. They were apparently won over by the argument that a successful summer offensive might halt the disintegration of the army, rally the people behind the Provisional Government, and enhance the international prestige of revolutionary Russia. With this agreement established, a new cabinet of the Provisional Government emerged, containing six Socialists. The key change was at the Ministry of War, where Kerensky took over from Guchkov.

Kerensky was the up and coming figure in the Provisional Government. He applied great energy to the war effort in preparation for the June offensive. His approach was to encourage the soldiers by appealing to their revolutionary patriotism, while at the same time restoring power to the commanders in the field. General Brusilov, the hero of the 1916 offensive, was given the position of Commander-in-Chief.

Commanders were given the power to use force against men who disobeyed orders. But the soldiers' representation organisations were to continue to operate. Commissars were appointed to every army unit to act as intermediaries between the soldiers' organisations and the generals – and, in addition, to raise morale amongst the troops. Kerensky himself toured the front, making fiery speeches to the soldiers. Figure 7.2 shows Kerensky visiting troops at the front. He rapidly became known as the

Fig 7.2   Kerensky visiting the troops at the front.

'Persuader-in-Chief' because he was an effective orator and his speeches were usually well received. But the army had really lost the will to fight. In addition, its command structure had suffered fatally, despite Kerensky's attempts to restore discipline. Soviet interference, for example through documents such as Order Number One, had removed much of the ability of the officers to command the men.

With the Russian army in a state of impending disarray, the result of the June offensive was predictably disastrous. There were some initial areas of success, partly because of the low morale of the Austrian troops who were defending the positions in question. For example, the Commander of the South-Eastern Front, General Kornilov, broke through the Austrian lines on a thirty-kilometre front, taking over 10,000 prisoners in the process. However, the rapid transfer of German troops to vulnerable areas reversed the Russian advances, which were already stuttering to a halt because many of the troops were refusing to obey orders. Figure 7.3 shows Russian soldiers retreating in disarray in July 1917. The breakdown of discipline within the army was emphasised as it went into retreat. Desertion became rife.

Fig 7.3   Soldiers retreating in chaos after the failed offensive of June 1917.

Fig 7.4   A Russian soldier trying to stop his fellow-soldiers from deserting.

Figure 7.4 shows how some soldiers tried to oppose the deserters. But desertions were widespread, and bands of soldiers outwith the control of anyone became a blight on the areas through which they passed, as they stole, destroyed property and murdered at will.

Fig 7.5   Russian deserters returning home in 1917.

Fig 7.6   A political meeting held by troops at the front during the summer of 1917.

60,000 soldiers were killed outright in the fighting of the June offensive and the whole operation collapsed into an appalling shambles. A telegram from the front read:

> 'The majority of the units are in a state of ever-growing disintegration. There is already no question of authority and subordination. Persuasion and argument have lost force. They are answered with threats, sometimes with shooting. Some units leave their positions at will, not awaiting the approach of the enemy. There were cases when an order to move quickly for support was debated for hours at meetings, so that the support was delayed for days . . .'
>
> (*The Revolution of 1917*, Chronicle of Events Vol 3)

Figure 7.6 shows the kind of debate just referred to. An army could not be effectively organised when the authority of its commanding officers was being so obviously weakened.

After the failure of the June offensive, the hopes that success in the war would provide an escape from the developing crisis facing the Provisional Government and its supporters were dashed. The Russian army was becoming a greater threat to Russia than it was to the enemies of Russia. Some of the old-style generals seem to have derived a degree of malicious satisfaction from the absolute failure of the new-style revolutionary army. Kerensky's attempt to replace military obedience with revolutionary enthusiasm had patently failed, and Russia was rapidly approaching a situation of total collapse.

General Kornilov demanded that the June offensive should be ceased and that a different type of offensive should take its place:

against the political opponents at home who were destroying the ability of the army to function and who were undermining the authority of the Provisional Government. Facing criticism from all sides, Lvov felt unable to continue in office. Kerensky, perceived as the only man who could get a following from the Provisional Government, the soviets and the army, became Prime Minister. General Kornilov became Army Commander-in-Chief.

The situation outside Petrograd

The peasants

Since the peasant question had been of paramount importance for several decades preceding the February Revolution, it seems peculiar that the Russian countryside was hardly mentioned as the Provisional Government took form. Of course it took some time for news of the events in Petrograd and other cities to travel into the interior. Furthermore, most of the people who would have been most active once news did emerge were involved in fighting the war. As a result, the early response to the February Revolution in the countryside was one of deceptive calm. It did not take long for the calm to be broken.

The party which seemed to reflect the aspirations of Russia's peasants was the Social Revolutionary Party. The land programme of the Social Revolutionaries was to take all the lands held by the gentry and the Church, and to redistribute them through the peasant communes. Land belonging to small peasant landowners was to be left untouched. Social Revolutionaries were a significant presence in the first Provisional Government. So Russia's peasants now expected that the great landed estates of the gentry and the Church would be shared out amongst them.

The Provisional Government had to ensure that food supplies to the cities were maintained and it requested that the peasants be patient. It emphasised that the task of land redistribution was an enormous one. In late April 1917 it established the principle of land committees for each region which would work to put together effective legislation. Official 'commissars' were appointed. Peasants were asked for their co-operation: they were requested to 'wait peacefully'; peasants in the armed forces were assured that in their absence and without their participation no decision would be made regarding the land question.

By May 1917 little of significance had happened; but in that month, the leader of the Social Revolutionaries, Chernov, became Minister of Agriculture in the Coalition Government – that is to say the Provisional Government acting with the soviets, as agreed after the April crisis. A mood of keen anticipation developed amongst the peasants, more especially as Chernov declared his intention of making available 'all the land to the labouring people'. In truth, in many parts of the empire the 'labouring people' were already making the land available to themselves. Peasant committees seemed to appear out of nowhere after the February Revolution and they decided on the redistribution, not only of land, but also of livestock and agricultural implements in their areas. The government commissar in the province of Kovno complained:

> 'Never once was it said that they [the peasants] should turn to the district commissar... all the decisions... were put into effect without any participation at all of the district commissars...village committees removed the landowners, disposed of privately owned meadows, woods, pastures, etc., as if they were their own property... When the commissar tried to restrain the peasants from land seizures they shouted to him: "We elected you and if you don't go with us then we'll throw you out." '
>
> (Quoted in L. Kochan, *Russia in Revolution*, 1967)

By the summer of 1917, the situation throughout the countryside was getting totally out of control. Chernov's measures seemed to be adding to the chaos and, following a disagreement with Kerensky, he resigned. Thereafter Chernov, in his role as leader of the Social Revolutionaries, tried to embarrass Kerensky's government whenever possible. Kerensky did little to placate the situation in the countryside. His main concern was the war and he was wary of passing agricultural legislation which might merely cause further problems. Food supplies from the countryside were already unsatisfactory. There was also the concern that, despite the promises made to serving peasant soldiers, any beginning of land allocations during the war would result in mass desertions, as peasants would scramble back to the countryside to claim their share of the booty of the Revolution. The price of inaction was high, however: peasant risings against the estates soared throughout 1917, the only partial respite being during the harvest months of July and August:

Number of recorded peasant risings against the estates in 1917	
March	49
April	378
May	678
June	988
July	957
August	760
September	803
October	1169

(L. Volin, 'The Triumph of the Peasantry', in D. H. Pinkey (ed.), *The Russian Revolution*, 1979)

Such risings occurred throughout the empire, and took on various forms. On one estate in the Ukraine:

'The stock, equipment, furniture, etc., were divided by the peasants, each taking whatever he could. The land was divided amongst the peasants, and all the buildings burned down. In the mansion house there were many historical treasures and an enormous collection of books, which the peasants tore up to roll cigarettes.'

(L. Volin)

The Provisional Government was powerless to stop this kind of action. The revolution on the land – because that was what it amounted to – continued throughout 1917.

When Lenin and the Bolsheviks seized power, they forgot all about the land nationalisation which had formerly been so prominent a part of their revolutionary strategy. This was because they had to accept that a revolution in the land had already occurred through the individual and group actions of millions of peasants.

The national minorities

The different provinces of the empire began to collapse into chaos and anarchy as 1917 progressed: national minority activists were energetically pursuing their ambitions for independence. By September 1917 reports were flooding in of rioting, mutiny and murder, from places as far apart as Azov in the Crimea, Astrakhan on the Volga, Ekaterinburg in Siberia, and Tiflis in Georgia. The pretext for the unrest was often bread prices, occasionally nationality antagonism, and sometimes a lack of response from the Provisional Government to requests viewed by those concerned as reasonable requirements.

Lenin and the Bolsheviks realised the importance of having a coherent strategy devised which would appeal to the national minorities. At the April All-Russian Conference held by the Bolsheviks, resolution 19 declared:

'The right of all the nations forming part of Russia freely to secede and form independent states must be recognised. To deny them this right, or to fail to take measures guaranteeing its practical realisation, is equivalent to supporting a policy of seizure or annexation. Only the recognition by the proletariat of the right of nations to secede can ensure complete solidarity among the workers of the various nations and help to bring the nations closer together on truly democratic lines.'

(Lenin, *Collected Works*)

The two parts of the Tsarist empire which immediately demanded independence following the February Revolution were Poland and Finland. As Poland was under German occupation at the time, the Provisional Government was in a position to agree to

Polish demands for the simple reason that it did not have to do anything to put them into practice. Milyukov, the Foreign Secretary at the time, issued a proclamation committing the Provisional Government to bringing in an independent Poland.

The case of Finland was more complex, however, the main reason being that it lay outside the military zone of action. In addition, there were Russian troops based in Finland. A further factor for the consideration of the Provisional Government was the existence of a strong Finnish Social Democratic Party which might choose to work towards establishing a Finland loyal to revolutionary Russia, if it were given proper encouragement. The Provisional Government deliberated over what its response to Finnish nationalists should be. Lenin was convinced that, if approached properly, the Finns would agree to maintain the relationship with Russia:

> 'All the Finns want now is autonomy. We are for Finland receiving complete freedom, because then there will be greater trust in Russian democracy and the Finns will not separate . . . we say: "Any Russian socialist who denies Finland freedom is a chauvinist." '

> (Lenin, *Collected Works*)

The issue of Finland was not resolved during the short life of the Provisional Government. It was the Bolshevik government which finally took the decision in December 1917 to accept the Finnish government's demands for independence. Curiously enough, the Finnish Social Democrats subsequently attempted a coup d'état within weeks, and received assistance from the Bolsheviks in Russia in the civil war which developed as a result. Revolutionary Russia found itself in the strange position of having accepted Finnish independence, and recognising the new independent Finland – and yet, within weeks, helping revolutionaries in their attempt to overthrow it.

The Ukranian nationalists, too, expected a response to their desire for independence. The Ukranian situation was an immensely complex one, partly because of the very mixed ethnic population of the area, partly because of the economic dependence of the Ukraine on Russia – and vice versa. Ukranian nationalists were a small band of intellectuals who played upon the resentment felt by Ukranians about the excesses of Russification during the previous three decades. Their appeal had tended to be minimal because of the mixed population of the region and because of the economic inter-dependency between the Ukraine and Russia. In March 1917, a Ukranian soviet called the Rada emerged, and under the influence of nationalists it progressively adopted a more and more diverse outlook from Petrograd. By June 1917 the Rada was attempting to negotiate an independent Ukraine. The Provisional Government, desperate for the resources of the empire's richest region, was unimpressed. The Rada then issued a decree setting up a Ukranian Republic which was to operate 'without separating from Russia'. The Provisional Government could do little to stop the development. The Ukranian Republic was a fact of life by the autumn of 1917.

This pattern of the national minorities seeking to establish autonomy in the wake of the February Revolution existed throughout the empire. By May 1917 the first all-Muslim congress met in Petrograd to press, not for independence as such, but for autonomy within the new Russia. As the summer of 1917 progressed, Muslim congresses in many of the easterly parts of the empire pressed for the motion that 'Russia should become a federal democratic republic'. In Turkestan the general breakdown of authority led to demands for autonomy, and in September 1917 the Tashkent Soviet overthrew the Provisional Government representatives in the region. In Armenia the close proximity of diverse national groups saw a collapse into a situation of near civil war at times following the February Revolution.

It was to be expected that intense activity would occur following the February Revolution, bearing in mind the problems with the national minorities which had been exacerbated by insensitive Russification under the last two Tsars. No real solutions to the problems of the nationalities emerged during the time of the Provisional Government. Lenin and the Bolsheviks, during their time in opposition, had deliberated endlessly on the nationalities question and had made the kind of propositions which were most appealing to the nationalist activists. Once they were in power they were required to put their words into action – and that was to prove to be no easy task.

The overthrow of the Provisional Government

By July 1917 the Provisional Government was in grave difficulty. Lenin and the Bolsheviks were constantly seeking ways to discredit it and to bring about a situation where they could overthrow it and bring in the Bolshevik revolution. Between July and October 1917 the fortunes of Lenin and the Bolsheviks altered dramatically. They were associated with an abortive rising in July, and they appeared to be routed. Yet in October they succeeded in overthrowing the Provisional Government. The rise of the Bolsheviks can best be explained by investigating three key events: the July Days, the Kornilov Revolt, and the October Revolution.

The July Days

Between 3 July and 6 July 1917 the Provisional Government faced its gravest crisis to date. It was in danger of being overthrown by a politically motivated military rising in Petrograd. The background to this rising – referred to as the 'July Days' – is an area of some uncertainty for historians. Some historians believe that the July Days were a spontaneous protest by Petrograd-based soldiers angered about the war situation. Others believe that the Bolsheviks were behind the rising; but once it had failed, they disclaimed all responsibility for it.

Many soldiers were angry that even after the failure of the June offensive, no efforts to secure peace were being made. Soldiers in the Petrograd garrison and sailors from the Kronstadt naval base, accompanied by delegations from factory workers, marched to the Tauride Palace in Petrograd. This was where the Soviet Executive Committee was based. It had formed part of the coalition with the Provisional Government since April 1917. The protesters demanded that the soviets should take power from the Provisional Government and bring peace to Russia. 'All Power to the Soviets' became their rallying cry – a cry usually associated with Lenin and the Bolsheviks. But were Lenin and the Bolsheviks behind the July Days?

Historians sympathetic to the Bolsheviks insist that Lenin and the Bolsheviks were taken completely unawares by the developments in July 1917. Lenin, allegedly suffering from overwork, was in Finland resting at the time. News of the events in Petrograd was hurriedly delivered to him. Lenin was alarmed to hear of outbreaks of street fighting in Petrograd, and quickly made his way back to the scene of the action. He was apparently fearful of the consequences of these events: his great dread was that an unprepared attempt to establish soviet power would disintegrate, and would result in soviet collapse. The Bolshevik strategy in the summer of 1917 was to allow the full impact of the failure of the June offensive to undermine the Provisional Government, and then to strike decisively when that had happened.

But historians critical of the Bolsheviks dismiss this interpretation. Richard Pipes declares:

> 'No event in the Russian Revolution has been so wilfully lied about than the July 1917 insurrection, the reason being that it was Lenin's worst blunder, a misjudgement that nearly caused the destruction of the Bolshevik Party... To absolve themselves of responsibility, the Bolsheviks have gone to unusual lengths to misrepresent the July putsch as a spontaneous demonstration which they sought to direct into peaceful channels.'
>
> (R. Pipes, *The Russian Revolution*, 1990)

According to Pipes, the idea that Lenin would find himself in need of rest in Finland at such a time as the summer of 1917 is impossible to believe. He insists that Lenin was about to be arrested by the Provisional Government for treason – the charges related to his dealings with the Germans – and fled into hiding as a result. The July rising did not develop because soldiers and sailors were upset about the failure of the June offensive: it happened because Bolsheviks encouraged it. The soldiers who participated were involved because they were about to be shifted to the front by the government – which had realised that the Petrograd garrison was easy prey for Bolshevik propagandists.

The Bolsheviks were spurred into action because the transfer of the Petrograd garrison meant the removal of the force which they hoped to use in order to seize power at a later date. On 3 July a protest march by soldiers and sailors, supported by factory workers, was organised. In fact many regiments refused to become involved. The aim of the protesters was to overthrow the Provisional Government and to pass 'All Power to the Soviets'. The marchers headed for the Tauride Palace and the Marinsky Palace, the former being the base of the Soviet Central Committee, and the latter the home of the Provisional Government. Some rioting and looting took place, but the marchers eventually retreated to their barracks at midnight. In the early hours of 4 July Lenin crept back into Petrograd.

On 4 July a second march to the Tauride Palace took place. Lenin and the Bolsheviks were on the sidelines, not fully convinced about what they should do. Should they go all out for power now, knowing that most of the garrisoned soldiers had remained loyal to the government? What would happen if they failed?

Gradually the demonstrations got out of hand. Leon Trotsky provides one explanation of what happened:

> 'There were no few bloody encounters on that day in different parts of the town. A certain number of them were doubtless due to misunderstanding, confusion, stray shots, panic . . . But an element of bloody provocation was also indubitable in the July events . . . In attics and roofs, members of the officers' organisations were at work. They were attempting – and not without success – by firing on the demonstrators to spread panic and produce clashes between the different military units participating. The chief instigators of the bloodshed . . . were the government troops – powerless to put down the movement, but adequate for purposes of provocation.'
> (L. Trotsky, *The History of the Russian Revolution*, 1932–33)

Figure 7.7 on page 170 was taken on 4 July during this incident. When the shooting stopped, the marchers regrouped, only this time with guns at the ready. Trotsky's indignant interpretation of events could be countered by the Provisional Government pointing out that it saw itself being threatened by a Bolshevik-inspired armed mutiny. As the day progressed, the protesters seemed to be making considerable headway, seizing railway stations, attracting more regiments to their cause – and not meeting with a great deal of further opposition.

In July, according to Richard Pipes, Petrograd was there for the

Fig 7.7   Demonstrators in the Nevsky Prospect in Petrograd scattering in confusion after being fired at, on 4 July 1917.

Bolsheviks to seize. Yet Lenin hesitated. The Provisional Government was given time to launch its counter-attack. It published information which it held which clearly suggested that Lenin still had connections with Germany. Suspicions about Lenin's journey through Germany to Petrograd had never gone away, and the soldiers were readily responsive to the information.

Lenin rapidly realised that events had swung against him: the troops might have no love for the Provisional Government, but they would certainly not tolerate a German collaborator. An order for Lenin's arrest was issued on 6 July, and Lenin was not prepared to hang around and challenge it. He disappeared and eventually took refuge in the countryside. Also on 6 July order was restored in Petrograd by loyal troops from the garrison supplemented by soldiers who had returned from the front.

The charges against Lenin were never proved, and the Petrograd Soviet never accepted them. However, his flight from Petrograd did his reputation much harm.

Kerensky, now Prime Minister, was subtle in his response to the July Days. He disbanded and disarmed the regiments who had participated, reduced the size of the garrison to 100,000 men, and banned all Bolshevik publications from the trenches at the front. The offices of *Pravda* were destroyed, and prominent Bolsheviks, including Trotsky, were imprisoned.

But what alarmed Kerensky more than anything was the possibility of a right-wing reaction to the July Days. Kerensky noted the readiness with which the loyal troops of the army had emerged to crush the July riots, and he wondered what could happen if pro-Tsarist officers decided to attempt to overthrow the Provisional Government, on the pretext of saving Russia from disintegration. On 7 July he ordered the transfer of the Tsar and his family to Tobolsk in remote Siberia.

The Kornilov Revolt

Following the July Days, Kerensky appointed General Lavr Kornilov as Commander-in-Chief of the Russian Army (see Figure 7.8). Kornilov, the son of a peasant Cossack, had been a military man all his life. He was renowned for his loyalty to Russia and for his bravery in the field, but not necessarily for his intelligence: in fact one observer said of him that he had 'the heart of a lion and the brain of a sheep'.

Fig 7.8 General Kornilov speaking to Russian soldiers in the summer of 1917.

Kornilov set down certain conditions before he would take office. He insisted that full authority should be restored to Russia's military leaders; that no one would interfere with his command of the army; and that disciplinary measures, including capital punishment, should be returned to military life. He also suggested that Russia's war effort required that those aspects of the economy vital to the war – for example the ammunitions industry and the railways – should come under military control. These suggestions alarmed Kerensky, who realised that they would lessen the authority of the Provisional Government and increase the authority of Kornilov and the army. But so reliant was the Provisional Government on the army that Kerensky eventually agreed to Kornilov's terms.

Kornilov, however, immediately came up against the soviets. His proposed reforms meant a total bypass of soviet authority, but he was adamant that soviet influence had to be removed from the army if it were to have any chance of fighting a successful war. As a result of his approach to the soviets and to the Provisional Government, Kornilov rapidly became a hero in the eyes of the Liberals and Kadets, but a villain in the eyes of the left-wing groups, especially the Bolsheviks. All this made Kerensky's position very difficult. He needed the support of the political left in the Provisional Government and in the soviets to survive; but he also needed the support of the moderates; and, perhaps most pressingly of all, he needed a disciplined army.

When the soviets rejected Kornilov's proposal for the restoration of the death penalty in the army, Kerensky backed away from supporting Kornilov. Kornilov took this as further proof that Kerensky was merely a tool of the soviets. By August 1917 divisions between the two men were becoming clearly marked. Kornilov was being fêted as the potential saviour of Russia by the moderates and conservatives, and their newspapers began to deride Kerensky, noting for example his apparent unwillingness to prosecute Bolsheviks after the July Days.

Kornilov's dissatisfaction with the performance of the army reached a new low when on 20 August 1917 the Germans captured the city of Riga without any effective opposition from the Russian troops (see Figure 6.3). Coincidentally the French intelligence network began spreading information about another planned Bolshevik coup in the making. Kerensky responded by preparing to have Petrograd placed under martial law. Kornilov agreed to transfer a cavalry corps to Petrograd and to place it under the command of the Provisional Government. Both men remained suspicious of each other, but were prepared to act for what they saw as the common good. However, what they had set in motion was a situation which could clearly be pointed to as the beginnings of a counter-revolution.

In the background a group of right-wing intellectuals led by Vladimir Lvov began to become involved in the developing intrigue. Lvov and his group were insistent that some kind of order had to be restored to Russia and that an alliance between the army and a more conservative Provisional Government was a possibility. He approached both Kerensky and Kornilov. To Kerensky he said that support for the Provisional Government was so low that it needed to be upheld by the military. To Kornilov he declared that Kerensky had been receptive to his ideas, and that Kornilov and Kerensky could form a military dictatorship with the support of the nation. Kerensky later wrote that he had dismissed Lvov without promising him anything.

Whatever the truth of the case, Kornilov apparently believed that Kerensky was prepared to support a Kornilov dictatorship with a view to winning the war. Kornilov told Lvov he would be prepared to do his duty. Lvov at that stage went back to Kerensky and told him of Kornilov's stance. Kerensky was astounded. Kornilov, it seemed, was apparently attempting a military coup.

Why either Kerensky or Kornilov bothered to take Lvov seriously remains a mystery. He was a self-appointed go-between of dubious merit. However, in a desperate situation where distrust on every side was apparent, Lvov's credibility was accepted. He seemed to be conveying proof of what the respective parties believed to be the case. Kerensky called an emergency cabinet meeting and informed them that an attempt at a military coup led by Kornilov was planned. He requested full powers, that is dictatorial powers, to repel the threat. The cabinet agreed. Kerensky thus became dictator of Russia.

The next day, at the very end of August, a telegram was sent to Kornilov informing him that he had been dismissed, and ordering him to report to Petrograd. At precisely that time Kornilov, believing that he and Kerensky were working together to combat an attempted Bolshevik coup, was preparing for troops to be sent to Petrograd. When he received the Kerensky telegram, he was dumbfounded. He came to the conclusion that Kerensky could only have produced such a message under Bolshevik duress and that therefore the long-expected Bolshevik coup had begun.

He ordered the troops to hurry towards Petrograd. Then it became clear to Kornolov that Kerensky was not operating under duress, and was in fact behind a series of moves which seemed to be designed to discredit Kornilov. Kornilov was furious. His anger turned to rage when Kerensky issued a press release accusing Kornilov of treason and of an attempted military coup. Kornilov's reaction played directly into the hands of his enemies: he countered Kerensky's press release with one of his own, directed towards all military front commanders:

'. . . I, General Kornilov, declare that the Provisional Government, under pressure from the Bolshevik majority in the soviet, acts in full accord with the plans of the German General Staff . . . [it] destroys the army and convulses the country from within. I . . . declare to each and all that I personally desire nothing but to save Great Russia. I swear to lead the people through victory over the enemy to the Constituent Assembly, where it will decide its own destiny and choose its new political system.'

(Quoted in R. Pipes)

Over the next three days, Kornilov attempted to rally the nation behind him, concentrating all the while on getting army support. But although he was admired for his many qualities, the other generals were reluctant to participate in something which had got completely out of hand. The troops outside Petrograd soon realised that no Bolshevik coup was at hand. Their leader, General Krymov, saw Kerensky, and explained to him that he and his men had been responding to false information. Krymov was dismissed by Kerensky, and committed suicide rather than face court-martial.

Kornilov was arrested three days later, but subsequently escaped. So ended the Kornilov Revolt – if, indeed, there had ever been one.

The repercussions of the Kornilov Revolt were enormous. Had the Bolsheviks set out a strategy for destroying totally the credibility of moderate exponents of authority in Russia, they could not have managed better. Everyone who had been seen providing any kind of support for Kornilov was totally discredited as a result of the affair. And of course every political grouping apart from the extreme left had, at some stage, professed to see merit in Kornilov.

Kerensky's position within the Provisional Government was greatly weakened, not strengthened as he had imagined it might be, after his apparent suppression of the military coup. This was because the soviets were no longer prepared to work with him, and therefore the coalition government was finished. The Kadets were effectively isolated after the Kornilov Revolt.

Throughout Russia, Bolshevik-inspired 'Committees to Save the Revolution' sprang up. The government tried to suppress these, to no avail. The war staggered on with no end in sight. New food shortages were developing, and winter was approaching fast. It had become evident that Kerensky offered no hope of improvement in Russia's position.

The October Revolution

In his memoirs, Kerensky declared that it was the Kornilov Revolt which opened the door to Lenin and the Bolsheviks. Certainly the Bolsheviks made considerable capital out of Kornilov. However, things had been going against Kerensky and towards Lenin even before the unfortunate Kornilov episode had done so much to strip the Provisional Government of credibility.

One can gauge the shift away from Kerensky and towards the Bolsheviks during the weeks after the Kornilov Revolt in several ways. A key pointer is found in the results of the municipal elections held in Petrograd and Moscow. The Petrograd elections were held in the week before the Kornilov Revolt. The Bolsheviks increased their share of the vote from a fifth of the total to a third of the total – a significant swing, though not decisive. But the Moscow elections were held in September. Richard Pipes has produced the following table which compares the results of the elections in September with the results of similar elections held in June 1917:

Municipal elections in Moscow
(in percentage of seats)

Party	June 1917	September 1917	Change
Social Revolutionary Party	58.9	14.7	−44.2
Mensheviks	12.2	4.2	−8.0
Bolsheviks	11.7	49.6	37.9
Kadets	17.2	31.5	14.3

The result of the Moscow elections was a very important breakthrough for the Bolsheviks. It meant that they had gained municipal control of their first major city. Conversely, it was a disaster for Kerensky because it clearly pointed to the fact that popular support for the Provisional Government was waning.

How had this situation come about? Clearly the trend towards the Bolsheviks was in evidence in the Petrograd municipal elections which were held before the Kornilov Revolt, so that incident does not tell the whole story of why voters switched their allegiance to the Bolsheviks. Perhaps more telling is the fact that significantly fewer people were bothering to vote at all. For example, in the Moscow elections, the total number of votes cast in June 1917 was 640,000; but in September 1917 the number had fallen to 380,000. The Bolsheviks were gaining power partly because of increasing support, but partly because many Russians were becoming completely disillusioned by what had happened since the February Revolution, when so much had been promised and since when so little had been achieved.

Bolshevik political revitalisation was actually helped by Kerensky. On 30 August all Bolshevik prisoners, except those against whom legal charges were to be brought, were released from imprisonment. Leon Trotsky was one notable release, on 3 September, and he immediately assumed control of the Bolshevik faction in the Petrograd Soviet. Army officers, already disgusted with Kerensky over the Kornilov Revolt, looked on in dismay as he pandered to the whims of the Bolsheviks.

The army's position was especially crucial in determining the state of support for the Provisional Government. Kerensky had effectively lost the support of the officers. The support for him by the serving soldiers was, if anything, even worse. The collapse of the June offensive had destroyed much of what was left of their morale, and the prospect of another winter at the front with no sign of a peace initiative was not an attractive option for Russia's conscripts. Soldiers and sailors, as much if not more than peasants and workers, had had enough of the Provisional Government. They were also disillusioned with the continual shifts in position of the Mensheviks and the Social Revolutionaries. Lenin and the Bolsheviks continually insisted that only they could offer 'peace, bread and freedom'.

As the summer of 1917 drew to a close, and as disillusionment with the alternatives grew, the question was being asked: shouldn't the Bolsheviks be given a chance?

In the countryside, the peasants wanted official recognition that the land that they held was their own and that more land would be made available to them. In the towns, people yearned for something better, as unemployment, disintegrating industry, food shortages, and a general disenchantment with the achievements of the February Revolution to date grew.

The shift to the political left developed everywhere. The Petrograd factory committees showed clear Bolshevik majorities by July 1917. On 9 September Trotsky became President of the Petrograd Soviet, thus securing Bolshevik control of the most vital soviet in Russia. From this strong position, the Bolsheviks swept aside remaining Menshevik cadres of authority in other soviets. By late September, the Bolsheviks could fairly be said to be in control of all the soviets in Russia's major cities, especially in the centres of industrial production and in garrison cities. Remaining Menshevik areas of control tended to be second-string cities in terms of importance and of closeness to the centre of govenment. The only real challenge to Bolshevik influence was the Social Revolutionary Party, which retained the allegiance of peasant soviets and which had a considerable following among the large numbers of peasant conscripts in the army.

This apparent surge in popular support for Bolshevism lay as much in the apathy of the Bolsheviks' opponents as in support for Bolshevism itself, as has been seen in the case of the municipal elections. *Izvestiia*, the official soviet newspaper, commented often in the summer of 1917 on how fewer and fewer soviet delegates were actually bothering to turn up to meetings. But Bolshevik deputies were fastidious in attending them. Another area of concern noted by *Izvestiia* was the declining number of soviets actually operating in Russia. A new pattern of soviets was emerging: there were fewer of them, attended by fewer delegates. However, Bolshevik representation was rising and Bolshevik influence was increasing disproportionately. Little wonder that Lenin's cry of 'All Power to the Soviets' again became fashionable among Bolsheviks in September 1917.

By early October Lenin was still in exile in Finland, where he had eventually taken refuge after the July Days. But he was in constant contact with Petrograd, and was now convinced that the Bolsheviks could seize power. Other Bolsheviks, such as Kamenev and Zinoviev, disagreed, insisting that the Bolsheviks should wait to achieve the majority which they could expect in Russia's promised Constituent Assembly. Lenin proposed that if the Bolsheviks were to seize power, they could achieve immediate popular support by doing two things: by ending the war and by giving land to the peasants. Those measures alone, declared Lenin, would result in mass support for any Bolshevik coup. To await the Constituent Assembly, Lenin declared, would be fatal, because the peasants would vote for Social Revolutionaries and not for Bolsheviks. The only way that the Bolsheviks could claim to have a national mandate was through the soviets. That opportunity would be gone if elections to a Constituent Assembly were held, and the soviets were no longer viewed as organs of popular representation. Lenin proposed a Bolshevik coup under the slogan 'All Power to the Soviets'.

With the support of Trotsky, Lenin won the day. A decision was taken on 10 October 1917 that the Bolsheviks should seize power. Trotsky proposed that, in order to give the Bolshevik revolution an appearance of legitimacy, Bolsheviks should await the Congress of Soviets which had been arranged to take place in Petrograd later in October, and should organise the seizure of power so that it would appear not as a Bolshevik coup, but as a rising designed to protect the soviets. To set the scene, Bolsheviks should work relentlessly to ensure that it was Bolshevik delegates who dominated the Congress of Soviets.

A vital consideration for the Bolsheviks was the army, especially the Petrograd garrison. It had to be won over to the Bolshevik cause. Events went Lenin's way. The war situation had reached a new crisis point in mid-August when the Germans had captured Riga. As a result they were within striking distance of Petrograd. In preparation for defending the city from possible attack, the Petrograd Soviet had formed a Military Revolutionary Committee in early October. It did not take much Bolshevik manipulation to develop this Committee into one which would defend the Revolution, not only from German invaders, but also from 'counter-revolutionaries'.

Now the Military Revolutionary Committee had to win over the Petrograd garrison. An energetic propaganda campaign was launched amongst the soldiers. At the same time the Military Revolutionary Committee, acting with the permission of the Petrograd Soviet – which was, of course, led by Trotsky – declared that it exercised authority over the garrison. The Commander of the garrison, Polkovnikov, was informed that the garrison would respond to military orders only if they were countersigned by the Military Revolutionary Committee. The army officers were outraged by this turn of events, but discussions with Military

Revolutionary Committee representatives defused the situation temporarily.

By mid-October, the ingredients for the Bolshevik coup were all there. Kerensky was in no doubt about what the Bolsheviks were up to. However, he made a mistake: he underestimated the Bolsheviks. This was partly because the military commanders told him that Bolshevism had had little influence amongst the Petrograd garrison, and that if a Bolshevik rising occurred, as had happened in July, the Bolsheviks would be finished off this time. He was also in a dilemma such as he had previously experienced: if he brought in the army to crush the Bolsheviks who were so influential within the soviets, would he not be associated with counter-revolution? This dilemma meant that Kerensky delayed too long before attempting to prepare the army to defend the Provisional Government. This was fatal. The Bolsheviks had achieved some success in winning over the Petrograd garrison, but only about one man in twenty actually participated in the October coup. The rest of the soldiers did not participate in it, but they did not oppose it either.

Kerensky's minimal preparations to oppose the coup were futile. A few troops were given key strategic positions in Petrograd to defend on the morning of 24 October. Figure 7.9 shows one such group of armed sentries. A mood of tension descended on the city. Businesses closed early and people rushed home. During the night of 24–25 October 1917, government troops and their supporters relinquished their positions without any effective opposition to Military Revolutionary Committee troops.

Kerensky vainly tried to gather together the military force which he had so mistakenly assumed would protect the Provisional Government against precisely the situation it was now

Fig 7.9   Armed sentries guarding a post office against Bolsheviks in October 1917.

facing. His efforts came to nothing, and he rapidly realised that his only hope of survival lay in rapid flight. By early morning on 25 October, Kerensky had fled from the Winter Palace.

Polkovnikov reported on the morning of 25 October that his men were refusing to accept orders. Meanwhile, Bolshevik supporters were calmly assuming control of the city's vital installations – the power stations, railway stations and so forth – without a single shot being fired in anger. The men in Figure 7.9 and others like them had decided that resistance was futile.

In the afternoon of 25 October Trotsky could calmly proclaim, 'In the name of the Military Revolutionary Committee I announce that the Provisional Government no longer exists.'

Lenin now took the initiative, producing a press release:

'TO THE CITIZENS OF RUSSIA!

The Provisional Government has been deposed.
Government authority has passed into the hands of the organ of the Petrograd Soviet of Workers' and Soldiers' Deputies, the Military Revolutionary Committee, which stands at the head of the Petrograd proletariat and garrison.

The task for which the people have been struggling – the immediate offer of a democratic peace, the abolition of landlord property in land, worker control over production, the creation of a Soviet Government – this task is assured.

Long live the Revolution of Workers, Soldiers and Peasants!'
(Lenin, *Collected Works*)

At the Winter Palace, the remnants of the Provisional Government awaited the return of Kerensky with the military force which would surely put down the Bolshevik rising. By early evening, it was becoming clear that no such return was going to occur. The Military Revolutionary Committee ordered an immediate surrender of the palace, the alternative being that the battleship *Aurora*, moored within firing range, would open up on the defenders. Finally the *Aurora* was compelled to fire – a single blank shot. Artillery from the Peter and Paul Fortress, which was located on an island in the River Neva, opened up on the Winter Palace. Its ammunition was live, but wildly inaccurate. Taking the Winter Palace, the required symbol of Bolshevik success, was lapsing into farce. Finally, realising that there would be no Kerensky relief force, the defenders of the Palace decided to escape. The Palace was then virtually undefended, so the soldiers of the Military Revolutionary Committee broke into it, accepted the few arms of the remaining handful of defenders, and proceded to loot and ransack the Palace. The discovery of the wine-cellars was the high point of the occasion. Many of the revolutionary vanguard spent the rest of the night getting uproariously drunk.

The truth about this rather uninspiring sequence of events was subsequently distorted by Communist propaganda. Images such as

Fig 7.10　A soviet artist's romantic impression of the storming of the Winter Palace in October 1917.

Figure 7.10 were created to establish a myth about the taking of the Winter Palace – a myth which had no foundation whatsoever in reality.

During the night of 25–26 October, the Congress of Soviets finally assembled. The Bolsheviks declared that the Provisional Government no longer existed. Not all the delegates were prepared to accept this. The Mensheviks and some right-of-centre Social Revolutionaries declared their continued support for the Provisional Government against what was clearly in their eyes an orchestrated Bolshevik coup. Led by Martov, they expressed their disapproval by walking out of the Congress – but in so doing they handed a clear majority within the Congress to the Bolsheviks and their supporters. Of these, the supporters outnumbered actual Bolsheviks, and Lenin was required to exercise a rather delicate balancing act to retain the fragile power base which he had inherited.

Lenin was where he wanted to be: in power, in a position to manipulate events to his advantage, and able to prepare for what he saw as Russia's true revolution.

ESSAY

1. Was the Provisional Government's decision to continue Russia's involvement in the Great War a fatal mistake?

2. Did the Provisional Government have 'authority without power'?

3. Why did the Bolsheviks grow in strength throughout 1917?

4. What were the reasons for the Provisional Government's fall from power in October 1917?

A new authority

Between 1917 and 1921 Russia ended her involvement in the Great War, but suffered terribly from a widespread and damaging civil war. Because of the demands of this war, and in response to the opposition to the Bolsheviks, Lenin and his group supervised the setting up of instruments to ensure Bolshevik authority: a single party state, an army, and a state police network. In this chapter the following issues will be considered:

1. In what ways did the Bolsheviks secure their hold on power?
2. What kind of authority did they establish?

By looking at these questions, we shall be examining the methods by which Lenin and the Bolsheviks established their *authority* throughout the former Tsarist empire. To what extent were they guided by the *ideology* which they professed to adhere to? Alternatively, did they resort to terrorism and brutality to consolidate their hold on power? Were they prepared to acknowledge the distinctive *identities* of other groups, such as the national minorities?

TASK

It is 1967, the fiftieth anniversary of the Russian Revolution. The teacher of a history class of sixteen-year-old school pupils in Moscow has invited an old Bolshevik to deliver a talk about his experiences during the Revolution. His talk has reached the year 1918 and he intends to finish off his reminiscences by covering the events in which he was involved up until 1921. The old Bolshevik in question lived in Moscow in 1918, was active in promoting the aims of Bolshevism, and eventually fought for the Red Army during the Civil War.

As you are working through Issue 8, make notes which will allow you to write the speech

which the old Bolshevik would have delivered, covering such areas as:

1. how the Bolsheviks defeated their political rivals in Petrograd and Moscow.
2. how Russia's involvement in the Great War was ended.
3. what happened during the Civil War.
4. to what extent the Bolsheviks had consolidated their hold on the former Russian empire by 1921.

Then use your notes to write a speech approximately 1500 words long.

The beginnings of the one-party state

Lenin and the Bolsheviks truly believed in their ideology. So they believed that the political ideologies of all other parties were not only wrong, but were also 'counter-revolutionary'. And they insisted that those who favoured 'counter-revolutionary' policies had to be energetically opposed so that the October Revolution could be consolidated.

The All-Russian Congress of Soviets met following the collapse of the Provisional Government. This Congress set up a new 'Provisional Workers' and Peasants' Government' which was supposed to run Russia only until the Constituent Assembly, which would decide on the future political structure of Russia, could be established. Lenin himself became head of this Provisional Workers' and Peasants' Government. Government ministers were to be referred to as 'People's Commissars'. All of those appointed were prominent Bolsheviks: Leon Trotsky, for example, was given the important post of Commissar of Foreign Affairs.

For most people in the empire the October Revolution did not make much difference to how they lived their lives. In the major cities, the general assumption was that the soviets had tired of the failures of the discredited Provisional Government and had claimed power as a preliminary to setting up the long-promised Constituent Assembly. The Bolsheviks were seen as part of the soviets, and no more.

Lenin saw things differently. The Bolsheviks' task was clear to him. They had to dispense with the remnants of both Tsarism and the Provisional Government, and to construct a new Bolshevik authority over the whole empire. That would take considerable calculation, time and effort. The first task, Lenin believed, was to destroy the proposed Constituent Assembly. The second task was to ensure that the soviets came fully under Bolshevik influence and control.

The elections to the Constituent Assembly were held on 12 November 1917. The result was as bad as the Bolsheviks had feared it would be. Social Revolutionaries had an overall majority, with 410 out of the 808 seats. Bolsheviks won only 175 seats. The national minorities won 86 seats – and most of them were strongly anti-Bolshevik. Clearly the Bolsheviks were not the party favoured by the majority of voters. However, it had suited the Bolsheviks to claim support for the Constituent Assembly throughout the summer of 1917. If Lenin spoke out against it now, it would create the impression that his opposition was purely because the voters had not supported Bolshevism.

On 13 December Lenin had anonymously published an article entitled 'Theses on the Constituent Assembly' in *Pravda*. The key point made in this article was that, while a Constituent Assembly was an understandable demand by the workers at the time of the Provisional Government (which had never been elected), it was no longer necessary now that the soviets, which clearly represented the workers, had taken control of Russia. Furthermore, the era of Dual Authority between the soviets and some kind of elected government was finished; the soviets, alone, would rule. Therefore only the soviets would decide on the nature of Russia's constitution.

On 4 January 1918 an article in *Izvestiiya* continued this theme by carrying the following warning:

> 'On the basis of all the achievements of the October Revolution... all power in the Russian republic belongs to the Soviets and Soviet institutions. Therefore any attempt on the part of any person or institution whatever to usurp this or that function of state power will be regarded as a counter-revolutionary act. Any such attempt will be crushed by all means at the disposal of the Soviet power, including the use of armed force.'
>
> (E.H. Carr, *The Bolshevik Revolution, 1917–23*, 1950)

The Constituent Assembly eventually met on 5 January 1918. After a lengthy debate, the only vote on a policy issue was lost by the Bolsheviks, who then walked out of the Assembly because of the 'counter-revolutionary majority' present. The Assembly broke up, planning to meet again the next evening; but before then Lenin had declared that it was dissolved. Army Bolshevik supporters, the 'Red Guard', the forerunner of the Red Army, were placed at its meeting place, the Tauride Palace. The Constituent Assembly never met again. A few protest risings occurred, mainly in Petrograd, but Red Guards quelled these by shooting dead an unspecified number of people who were later referred to as 'armed conspirators'.

Izvestiia carried the following announcement to explain these events:

> '... The Constituent Assembly, elected according to lists which were made up before the October Revolution... gave a majority to the Party... of Kerensky... It was natural that this Party... refused to recognise the October Revolution and the Soviet régime. Thereby the Constituent Assembly broke off any connection between itself and the Soviet Republic of Russia. The withdrawal from such a Constituent Assembly of the Bolsheviks and the Left Socialist Revolutionaries, who now, as is known, make up the vast majority in the Soviets and enjoy the confidence of the workers and of the majority of the peasants, was inevitable... [Now] the parties of the majority in

the Constituent Assembly carry on an open struggle against the Soviet régime . . .

Therefore the Central Executive Committe decides:

The Consituent Assembly is dissolved.'

(Izvestiia, 28 January 1918)

In place of the disbanded Constituent Assembly, the third All-Russian Congress of Soviets met at the Tauride Palace the next day. Russia's new political structure was decreed in the opening paragraph of the resolution 'On the Federal Institutions of the Russian Republic':

'The Russian Socialist Soviet Republic is created on the basis of a voluntary union of the peoples of Russia in the form of a federation of the Soviet republics of those peoples.'

(E.H. Carr)

No longer did Lenin and the Bolsheviks feel it necessary to describe the status of their régime as 'provisional'.

Russia's constitution eventually appeared – it was the work of a Bolshevik-appointed commission – on 3 July 1918. The constitution contained most of the expected clauses – freedom of speech; no discrimination because of race or religion; and so forth – together with the duties required of the citizens, such as preparedness to give military service to protect the state. Russia was declared a republic. Supreme power was to lie with the All-Russian Congress of Soviets. The Congress would elect the All-Russian Central Executive Committee, and this Committee would appoint the Council of People's Commissars.

Local soviets could deal only with local matters. 'Questions of national importance' were to be left to the Bolshevik-controlled central authorities. And what was determined to be a 'question of national importance' was left for the central authorities to decide. In other words, local soviets only had control over what the central authority allowed them to control.

On 19 July 1918 Russia's new constitution was published in *Izvestiia*. It was entitled 'The Constitution (Fundamental Law) of the Russian Socialist Federal Soviet Republic'. The central aims of Lenin and the Bolsheviks were subtly incorporated into the wording of this 'constitution'. The Russian empire was to become a one-party state, with all real authority lying with the central Bolshevik command in Moscow. But in the summer of 1918 that remained an ambition rather than an achievement.

The Bolsheviks had won the political battles, but they still had to win control over the people of the vast former Russian empire.

The Treaty of Brest-Litovsk

Lenin was adamant that the most pressing task for the Bolsheviks was to end the war. He had promised peace to the Russian people. He was determined to keep his promise – a major reason being that the Bolsheviks required peace to consolidate their authority over Russia.

Lenin believed that Russia had absolutely nothing to gain from continuing the war. The Russian army was patently unable to win back the territory lost to the Central Powers (Germany and Austria-Hungary). According to Lenin, the Bolshevik priority was to accept peace on any terms, so that the Bolsheviks could use all their energy for securing their hold on Russia and for building up their defences. The need to build up defences was emphasised by Lenin, who suggested that, irrespective of who won the Great War, all the other European powers might well unite in opposition to Bolshevism. The Bolsheviks needed a breathing space to prepare for this.

Another consideration which Lenin had to bear in mind was that the Germans had financed the Bolsheviks throughout the war, had allowed Lenin to return to Petrograd to participate in the overthrow of the Provisional Government, and had continued to divert money to them after the October Revolution. The Germans, understandably, required a return on their investment. The Bolsheviks were being financed by Germany as part of a strategy which would allow the Central Powers to close down the main theatres of war on the Eastern Front and divert all their attention westwards. Ludendorff and Hindenburg, the German generals who had masterminded German successes on the Eastern Front, were already preparing a major offensive on the Western Front for the spring of 1918 – the assumption being that the Eastern Front would be calm by then.

But Lenin had a major problem. Most of the Bolsheviks, as well as members of the other political groupings, disagreed with his idea of peace on any terms. The idea of giving up huge tracts of Russian territory to the Germans was absolutely repugnant to them. Not only that, most Bolsheviks believed that their revolution would gradually spread to other European nations and that this process would be helped by continuing the war. They argued that Germany and Austria-Hungary were as much on the point of collapse as Russia, that the Socialist parties in these countries were very developed and were within sight of having revolutions, and that Socialist revolution within the Central Powers would consolidate the hold of Socialists in Russia. Trotsky was a very outspoken exponent of this idea.

On 20 November 1917 talks with the Germans and Austrians opened at Brest-Litovsk in Poland. Three days later a ceasefire was agreed, and the Germans fully expected to have the deal that they wanted by Christmas. They expected that the Bolshevik delegates, inexperienced in international diplomacy and desperate to get out of the war, would create no problems. They were mistaken. The Bolshevik delegates immediately demanded as a prerequisite for peace that Germany should withdraw from occupied territory won since 1914. The Germans had been expecting that the

Russian delegation would offer an unconditional peace. They were astonished. Hindenburg expressed the view that the Bolsheviks were deliberately frustrating the talks with a view to stirring up unrest in Germany and Austria, where expectations of peace on the Eastern Front were intense. He also pointed out, angrily, that the Bolsheviks were promoting fraternisation between Russian and German troops on the front as part of a deliberate ploy aimed at destroying army morale. He insisted that Germany must adopt a much stronger line with Russia.

Talks resumed on 27 December, this time with Trotsky at the head of the Russian delegation. Trotsky had been shocked to learn that on 19 December the Germans had opened up separate peace talks with the Ukranians. The Ukraine, producer of a third of Russia's grain and of almost three-quarters of its coal and iron, was vital to Russia. On 30 December the Central Powers declared their recognition of the Ukraine, with the Rada as its official government. (On 9 February 1918 a separate peace was duly arranged, under which the Ukraine became a German protectorate.) Trotsky was presented with a further shock: the Germans told him that they intended to hold on to the territories which they currently occupied. Trotsky called for a twelve-day adjournment and returned to Petrograd.

The split within the Bolsheviks now hardened. Lenin continued to advocate acceptance of Germany's terms; other Bolsheviks refused to agree. Lenin suggested a new possibility: that the Central Powers would come back with even worse terms if what was presently on offer were not accepted.

Further talks with Trotsky at the head of the Bolshevik delegation proved fruitless, and the German generals decided that they had had enough. The Russians were told that hostilities would begin again on 17 February. On that day, they began their advance, taking Dvinsk without meeting any opposition from the Russians. It now became perfectly clear to Lenin that the Germans could easily advance to Petrograd, overthrow the Bolsheviks, and install a puppet régime. The whole revolution had come under dire threat. Still the majority decision about peace terms went against him. Trotsky finally gave in and allowed the Central Committee a majority of one vote on the Lenin programme. The information was relayed to the Germans – who carried on with their advance. By 21 February the Bolsheviks were in such a panic that they tried to re-establish relationships with France and Britain. On that day, the Germans contacted them and informed them that peace talks could reopen on a new basis: Russia should concede the loss of the territories taken by Germany and Austria-Hungary since the breakdown of the last talks; in addition, she would have to evacuate the Ukraine and Finland, to demobilise, and to make financial concessions to Germany.

Lenin's warning had thus been proved correct. He convened the Central Committee and insisted that the German terms must be accepted before something even worse was placed on the table. After all, he declared, Germany's conditions did allow the Bolsheviks to remain in power; the next German surge into Russia might see Bolshevism itself overthrown. Finally, when he was still facing opposition, Lenin threatened to resign unless his wishes were agreed to. At last he got his way. Opponents to the German terms either abstained from the vote or walked out of the meeting.

The decision was relayed to the Germans – who still had a point to make. Despite the fact that the old Bolshevik, Sokolnikov, was despatched to Brest-Litovsk to sign the humiliating peace treaty, the Germans continued their advance. Bombs were actually dropped on Petrograd. The city was in a state of panic by early March, and Lenin ordered the government to be evacuated to Moscow. On 10 March Lenin himself fled to Moscow and set up his base in the Kremlin, which thereafter became the seat of Bolshevik power.

The Treaty of Brest-Litovsk was signed on 1 March 1918. The enormous tracts of territory lost are shown in Figure 8.1. Poland, Finland, Latvia, Lithuania, Estonia and Transcaucasia all became part of the German protectorate. The Ukraine was

Fig 8.1 Map showing territories ceded to the Germans by the Treaty of Brest-Litovsk in 1918.

recognised as an independent republic. These terms meant that the former Russian empire had lost over a quarter of its population, a similar amount of its factories, and a third of her agricultural land. Furthermore, punitive financial clauses were applied by the Germans, who also demanded the demobilisation of Russia's army and navy. Russia was pushed back from the Black Sea and the Baltic Sea. As one historian said of the cumulative impact of the treaty, 'It swept away at one stroke the fruits of two centuries of expansion towards the West and South' (W.H. Chamberlain, *The Russian Revolution 1917–1921*).

Russia was outraged by the terms accepted by Lenin and the Bolsheviks. However, Lenin addressed the Central Committee and, eventually, the All-Russian Congress. His message was clear. Brest-Litovsk should be regarded only as a temporary measure which would allow the consolidation of the revolution. It would allow Russia time to organise proper defences. Both the Central Committee and the Congress had to accept what had in reality already happened. With bad grace they did so.

Within months, Lenin's prediction had been proved correct. The Germans had launched their western offensive, but they were stopped short of Paris. The entry of America into the Great War proved to be decisive against Germany and Austria-Hungary. Germany surrendered on 11 November 1918. Two days later, the Communists renounced the terms of the Treaty of Brest-Litovsk. Lenin was able to review his approach to the question of peace terms from the very beginning and to point out that he had been right all along and that everyone else had been wrong. His reputation soared. Never again did he feel compelled to offer his resignation over any issue.

The Bolsheviks become Communists

During the seventh All-Russian Congress of Soviets held in March 1918, the Bolsheviks named themselves the 'Russian Communist Party'. They wanted to break any remaining connections with Social Democrats, both in Russia and in other parts of Europe. The word 'Communist' will replace 'Bolshevik' for the remainder of this text, except when reference is made to an event prior to the seventh All-Russian Congress.

The formation of the Red Army

Lenin was always acutely aware of the importance of the Russian army for his plans. Once the October Revolution had occurred, he watched the Russian army warily, as he did not trust the officers. The Russian army was in disarray, but Lenin wanted Communist Russia to have its own reliable force. He believed that in the foreseeable future Russia would be called upon by workers everywhere to help to establish Communism in their countries, as the socialist revolution became widespread throughout the world. More pressingly, however, the Communists in Russia required a reliable army to protect the revolution and to consolidate it throughout the former Tsarist empire. As *Izvestiia* declared:

'The complete and final triumph of the proletariat is unthinkable without the triumphant conclusion of a series of wars on the external as well as domestic fronts. For this reason, the Revolution cannot manage without its own, socialist army.'
(*Izvestiia*, 28 January 1918)

In March 1918, Trotsky was given the job of creating a professional army. His task was enormous. He had the nucleus of an army in the form of the Red Guards who had provided military support for the Bolsheviks during and after the October Revolution. However, this was not the large, disciplined army which Russia clearly needed. Trotsky set to work to build up such an army.

One irony was that, in order to establish a working army with an effective command structure, Trotsky had to reverse most of the concessions won by Russian soldiers since the February Revolution. He expressed the view that soldiers' committees could not lead regiments in time of war; he insisted that a return to military discipline was required; and he demanded that the Red Army should have proper, central control. The suggestion which always accompanied these demands was that a properly run army under the Communists did not need things such as soldiers' committees because Russia itself was being run by the soviets which had the soldiers' interests at heart in any case.

Administration of the Red Army required Trotsky's energetic attention too: recruiting centres, barracks, and supplies were needed. Under the slogan, 'Work, Discipline and Order will save the Soviet Republic', Trotsky sought full soviet support for the construction of a Red Army. Recruitment began. There was no consistency in the quality of the early Red Army units: some were very well disciplined and effective, while others were little better than a rabble. Figure 8.2 on page 190 shows one of the first Red Army detachments marching through Red Square in Moscow soon after the launch of Trotsky's recruiting campaign in April 1918. Notice the haphazard marching and the careless way in which hats are worn. This was very much a makeshift army.

Quality officers were at a particular premium, and Trotsky had to accept former Tsarist officers who were prepared to serve in the Red Army. Precautions were subsequently used during the Civil War to ensure that these officers would think twice about switching allegiance. For example, a register of their families was kept and Trotsky made it known that their families would be used as hostages if they deserted from the Red Army. In addition, a Communist commissar was placed at each officer's side to ensure the politically correct nature of judgements made.

Fig 8.2   One of the first Red Army detachments marching through Red Square in Moscow in 1918.

There were immense problems involved in all this, and it is to Trotsky's credit that an effective fighting force did emerge during the years of the Civil War. At the end of the Civil War, the Communists could claim victory – and could point to an army of five million men.

The background to the Civil War

The most pressing reason why the Red Army was needed was that a state of civil war existed in Russia. The starting point of this Civil War is difficult to determine: because it was a civil war, no actual declaration of war was ever made. However, certain points of departure can be identified, such as the situation in the Ukraine and in Finland.

Both the Ukraine and Finland were designated as German protectorates by the terms of the Treaty of Brest-Litovsk. Russian troops were compelled to withdraw from the Ukraine and from Finland. Both areas had been controlled by their own national soviet régimes. In the Ukraine, German and Austrian troops helped to remove these soviets from positions of influence. Government of the Ukraine was placed in the hands of a congress made up of big landowners who had been picked by the Germans. The leader, Skoropadsky, energetically set about ensuring the complete separation of the Ukraine from Russia.

But Ukranian peasants were infuriated when Skoropadsky began to restore confiscated land to big landowners. They were angered further when the Germans began expropriating massive amounts of grain and other foodstuffs from the region. As a result, peasant guerrilla bands began to appear, attacking the landed estates and small bands of enemy soldiers. Ukranian Communists who had fled to Russia established and maintained contact with the rebels, and gradually a sustained guerrilla war built up in the region. The commander of the German forces in the Ukraine, General Eichorn, was eventually assassinated. The German response was brutal. Figure 8.3 shows one of the many public hangings of captured insurgents in the Ukraine. Actions such as these infuriated the Ukranians. By the late summer of 1918 the whole region was seething with discord.

Fig 8.3   The public hanging of captured insurgents in the Ukraine by the Germans in 1918.

The terms of the Treaty of Brest-Litovsk also required Russian troops and warships to be withdrawn from Finland. German troops were sent in to oppose Finnish soviet supporters, who were eventually forced to flee to Russia. Finland continued to have many supporters of the soviets, and the enemies of these soviet sympathisers carried out a campaign of terror and intimidation against them. Finland became an angry and divided nation which could be held in check only for as long as German troops remained there to keep order.

Other aspects of the developing Civil War were already under way in the immediate aftermath of the October Revolution. For example, General Kornilov managed to arrange to escape after his alleged attempted rising, and he joined up with a 'Volunteer Army' of anti-Bolsheviks in Cossack country on the River Don.

Kornilov was killed in an early skirmish, and eventually General Denikin became the leader of the Volunteer Army. This army was just one of many groups in opposition to the Bolsheviks which were already in existence before any Civil War was acknowledged to have begun.

As well as the fact that there are difficulties in defining when the Civil War began, there are problems in defining the nature of the opposition to the Communists. All the opposition groups tend to be referred to as the 'Whites', because they were opposing the 'Reds'. The general tendency is to assume that these 'Whites' were supporters of the Tsar, white being the royal colour, and that therefore the Civil War was about Tsarist supporters wanting to overthrow Communism and bring back the Tsar. Undoubtedly there were royalist supporters engaged in the war against the Communists; equally there were many anti-Communists who sought different things. For example, some 'Whites' were national minority groups which wanted to achieve independence from Moscow; others were Social Revolutionaries or Kadets who wanted to restore the Constituent Assembly.

A further complexity was foreign involvement in the Civil War. Initially this was because the First World War was still on the go, and the warring nations had a vested interest in what was going on in Russia. After November 1918, when the armistice was signed to signify the end of the Great War, the nature of foreign intervention changed. As a measure of the sheer variety and complexity of 'White' resistance to Lenin and the Bolsheviks, it can be noted that by August 1918 there were some twenty different governments of one type or another operating within the former Tsarist empire.

In looking for a point of departure for the beginning of the Civil War, many historians emphasise an episode involving a group of Czech and Slovak soldiers. In 1914, during a successful campaign against Austria-Hungary, the Russians captured hundreds of thousands of prisoners, including over 50,000 Czechs and Slovaks. (Czechoslovakia did not exist as a country until it was set up under the Treaty of Versailles in 1919. The captured Czechoslovaks were reluctant subjects of the Austro-Hungarian empire.) The Russians offered them the chance of fighting alongside Russian soldiers on the Eastern Front, and over 30,000 of them did so, distinguishing themselves in the spring offensive of 1917. In December 1917, the Czechoslovaks were recognised by France and Britain as a separate army operating in Russia. Once the Treaty of Brest-Litovsk had been signed, arrangements were made to evacuate them to the west. The task took on some urgency because at that time the Czechoslovaks were based in the Ukraine, which had become a German protectorate.

As it had become impossible to evacuate the Czechoslovaks from the western side of the empire, arrangements were made for them to use the trans-Siberian railway to get to Vladivostok in the east and to be evacuated from there. The Czechs set off, in armed trains for their own protection, as the Communists had agreed. Such units, crossing terrain which was already rife with unrest, were always likely to become embroiled in local troubles. In the Siberian town of Cheliabinsk fighting broke out between the Czechs and some Hungarian prisoners-of-war. When the local soviet arrested some Czechs, their compatriots took up arms to release them. Trotsky, meanwhile, as Commissar of War, saw the potential of the Czechs as an experienced fighting unit for his Red Army. On the pretext of the Cheliabinsk disturbance, he ordered the disarmament of the Czechs, the cessation of their move eastwards, and their compulsory enlistment in the Red Army.

The Czechs were infuriated. They were militarily the strongest unit in the region and Trotsky had no immediate way to make his order work. Some 14,000 Czechs had already reached Vladivostok, but another 20,000 were still spread along the length of the trans-Siberian railway. Figure 8.4 shows one of the trains carrying Czechs on the trans-Siberian railway in May 1918. The Czechs showed their strength by seizing control of the railway, and by overthrowing Communist authority in the key cities through which it passed. Their actions allowed the enemies of Lenin and the Communists to set up new governments. By early June 1918 the length of the trans-Siberian railway was not in Communist control. The Red Army was in its infancy, and the Communists had no ready means of winning back the railway. But already Trotsky was enlisting forces massively in response to the challenge. On 29 July compulsory military service for all males between the ages of eighteen and forty was declared, and all officers of the old army were ordered back into service. Discipline was unceremoniously returned in full, although the Red Army soldiers were rewarded with higher pay and rations than the industrial workers. Trotsky energetically pursued an army of the old type, introducing for the first time a massive military display in Red Square in Moscow in 1919.

Fig 8.4   Czechs on the trans-Siberian railway in May 1918.

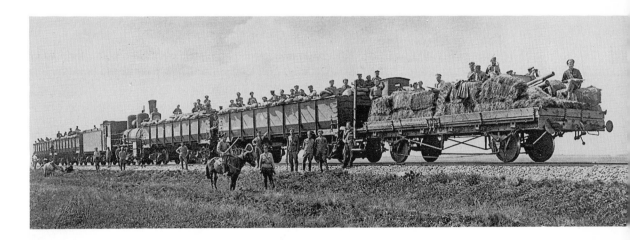

The Czech advance continued unabated. By the end of June 1918 they had taken control of Vladivostok itself. Meanwhile, other opponents of the Communists were adding to the Communists' problems. A 'Committee of the Constituent Assembly' was developed by disillusioned Social Revolutionaries in Samara in Siberia. Their proclaimed purpose was to break away from Moscow.

Yet a further complication to all this was the attitude of the warring powers. For example, the Germans were debating whether or not their best interests would lie in removing the Communists from control in Russia. While this situation existed, Trotsky found it impossible to transfer the few effective troops that he had to where they were needed because he had to prepare for a possible German invasion. Eventually the Germans assured the Communists that they had no intention of interfering in Russia, and Trotsky could shift his men to the key trouble spots.

By this time the situation was beginning to get out of hand. Encouraged by the actions of Social Revolutionary rebels in Siberia, the many enemies of the Communists were progressively coming out into the open. The Volunteer Army under General Denikin was fighting in the Caucasus region in the South. Admiral Kolchak, the former head of the Black Sea Fleet, became active in Siberia. In November 1918 Kolchak declared himself the 'Supreme Ruler of Russia' in opposition to Communist claims. Meantime Skoropadsky was in control of the Ukraine. Other White units rapidly sprang up, emphasising how fragile was the Communist control over the former empire. However, the very disparate nature of all of these White units was to be their undoing. As the Civil War developed, the Red Army grew in strength and organisation under the energetic leadership of Trotsky. The Whites had no overall plan or structure of campaign.

One source of White support was foreign assistance. British troops and subsequently French and Americans as well landed at the northern port of Murmansk. Their express purpose was to prevent the Germans getting hold of the military supplies there. In April 1918, on the other side of the former Tsarist empire, Japanese troops landed at Vladivostok. By July 1918 British and American detachments had joined them. Again, there was a specific reason provided for the invasion: to allow the Czechs to make their escape and get to the war on the Western Front. In July 1918, British, French and American troops occupied Archangel, apparently of the opinion that they could get the Czechs out from the north. In Archangel they oversaw the setting-up of an anti-Communist government, mainly of Social Revolutionaries, led by Chaikovsky. Another White government was set up with British assistance at Ashkabad in Turkestan.

At first the foreign powers, especially Britain and France, became involved in Russia because of anxiety that the Bolsheviks would make a separate peace with Germany. After November

1918 that was clearly not a reason for their continued assistance to the Whites. They were there to fight Communism and to stop it spreading. Another reason was the Communist decision to cancel all repayments of foreign loans and to nationalise all foreign companies in Russia: the foreign powers were reacting to this.

The progress of the Civil War

Figure 8.5 shows areas of action in the Civil War.

Until the armistice with Germany was signed in November 1918, the involvement of other nations in the Civil War could be explained in the context of the Great War as a whole. After November 1918 the actions of the foreign invaders were quite clearly to oppose Communism by assisting the Whites. Britain and France sent arms to General Denikin. Other White generals were given assistance with their supplies. A French naval division landed

Fig 8.5   Map showing Russia during the Civil War, 1918-20.

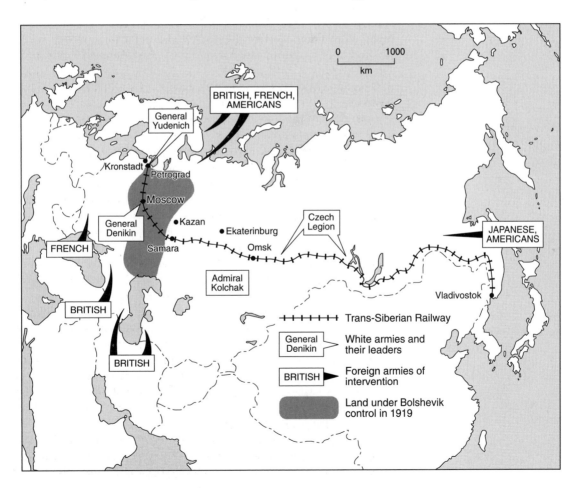

Fig 8.6   Czech, American, Japanese and British troops in Vladivostok.

at the Black Sea port of Odessa, and Britain moved troops into Batum and Baku. Figure 8.6 shows Czech, American, Japanese and British troops in Vladivostok. Troops such as theses were soon involved in fierce warfare. Figure 8.7 shows Japanese troops with the bodies of Communists. Actions like these infuriated Lenin and the Communists and reinforced what they knew already: the developed world was vehemently against them and all that they stood for.

Both sides in the Civil War engaged in extensive propaganda to vilify their opponents. Figure 8.8 is a White poster showing Trotsky at the Kremlin. Trotsky is presented not just as an ogre, but as a Jewish ogre. Notice further racist imagery: the Communists at the bottom of the poster are all presented with Asiatic features. A Communist poster of Trotsky (see Figure 8.9) uses Christian symbolism: Trotsky is St George, slaying the capitalist counter-revolutionary dragon.

Fig 8.7   Japanese troops with the bodies of Communists.

Fig 8.8   *A White poster showing Trotsky at the Kremlin.*

Fig 8.9   *A Communist poster showing Trotsky as St George, slaying the capitalist counter-revolutionary dragon.*

Propaganda posters such as these were designed to persuade people that good was fighting evil during the Civil War. In reality, atrocities abounded on both sides. For example, Figure 8.10 shows White officers under the command of Kolchak posing beside the heads of decapitated Communists. This horrific image can be set alongside an extract from a decree passed by the Cheka, the Communist secret police (see page 205), in September 1918:

'A considerable number of hostages must be taken from among the bourgeoisie and the officers. Mass shooting must be applied upon the least attempt at resistance . . . Administrative departments through the militia . . . must take all measures to detect and arrest all who hide under foreign names and surnames, with unconditional shooting of all who are involved in White Guard activity.'

(Quoted in R. Pipes, *The Russian Revolution*, 1990)

Historians are divided in their opinions about how Whites and Reds behaved during the Civil War. Some historians detect bias in the coverage of the Civil War written by others. Richard Pipes states in the same book:

'The White armies did, indeed, execute many Bolsheviks and Bolshevik sympathisers . . . sometimes in a barbarous manner.

Fig 8.10   Officers under the command of the White General Kolchak posing beside the heads of Communists.

But they never elevated terror to the status of a policy and never created a formal institution like the Cheka to carry it out. Their executions were as a rule ordered by field officers, acting on their own initiative, often in an emotional reaction to the sights which greeted their eyes when they entered areas evacuated by the Red Army.'

However, Peter Kenez takes issue with Pipes:

'Richard Pipes' . . . hatred of the revolutionaries is so great that he ceases to be a historian and becomes instead a prosecutor of revolutionaries . . . Apparently . . . in his mind the Bolsheviks were uniquely evil . . . It is, however, far from clear that the number of innocent victims of one side was lower than that of the other . . . We know that in a single year (1919) in the Ukraine alone one hundred thousand Jews were killed, largely, though not exclusively, by soldiers of the White army. It was Denikin's Cossacks who buried Jews up to their necks and rode horseback over their protruding heads . . .'
(Peter Kenez, in '*The Russian Review*', July 1991)

Incidents such as those just referred to occurred extensively during the Civil War. While it may be controversial to apportion degrees of blame to one side or another, the evidence would seem to suggest that neither side could derive much credit from their behaviour.

In early 1919 General Kolchak, who was probably the Allies' greatest hope for forming an alternative government to the Communists, began an advance in earnest. He crossed the Ural Mountains, and headed for Moscow. The bulk of Trotsky's Red Army was in the south, holding back Denikin. Kolchak's progress was steady until the end of 1918, but then he suffered a reverse. By the end of 1919 his army had disintegrated. Kolchak himself was captured, and he was executed in 1920. Meanwhile Denikin was making spectacular gains in the south. By June 1919 his advance had allowed him to take Kharkov and Tsaritsyn. By August he had captured the major Ukranian city of Kiev. By October he was in Oriel, only 450 kilometres south of Moscow. The Communists' troubles increased when Yudenich launched an attack on Petrograd from Estonia. Trotsky rallied the Red Army in time and managed to stave off the advances of both Denikin and Yudenich. He was assisted because Denikin was losing popular support because of the behaviour of his soldiers and because of the obvious corruption of his administration. By the end of 1919 Denikin and Yudenich were finished as active forces. Meanwhile the British and the French had had enough of the war and had evacuated their troops.

As foreign support ebbed away, it was only a matter of time before the Red Army would win. The Reds never lost control of the vital centre of the former Tsarist empire. Figure 8.11 shows

Fig 8.11   Red Army soldiers on one of their armoured trains.

Red Army soldiers on one of their armoured trains. Notice the coffin on the gun turret – and how the turret has been shelled. In all probability, a Red Army soldier had recently been killed in action, and a burial was about to take place. Red Army soldiers such as these won the Civil War for the Communists. The one real success for the Whites and their foreign allies was in the Baltic provinces. Estonia, Latvia and Lithuania succeeded in their long-held ambition of achieving independence from Russia.

The final offensive of substance against the Communists came from Pilsudski and the Poles. He advanced into the Ukraine, expecting the Ukranians to rise with him. The rising failed to materialise, and the Red Army rapidly pushed back the Poles. By this stage the Red Army was so much in the ascendency that Lenin believed that he could push further westwards and bring on the revolution which he hoped was likely to occur in Germany. The Polish capital Warsaw was never taken, however, and the Treaty of Riga in 1921 ended the war between Russia and Poland.

All that remained for the Communists to do was to tidy up the remnants of the Civil War, safe in the knowledge that the capitalist West had failed in its bid to overthrow Communism. A succession of White governments fell in 1921: in Georgia, Armenia, Azerbaijan, Khiva, Bokhara, and Turkestan. In 1922 Red Army troops finally entered Vladivostok, the last White stronghold.

The Civil War, following Russia's involvement in the Great War and the Revolutions of 1917, had totally exhausted the former Tsarist empire. What was left of the economy in 1917 was destroyed by 1921. The devastation of the countryside had resulted in widespread starvation. However, Lenin and the Communists had held on to power. Not only that, they had built up the essential instrument for maintaining their authority: a strong army. They had also added to their methods of controlling the internal situation in Russia using the war to isolate and vilify their enemies.

In order to explain how the Communists had added to their authority in Russia by 1921, it is necessary to go back over the years of the Civil War and to examine how the Party's economic policies were adapted to take account of the emergency situation, and how the Party's machinery for maintaining order was improved.

Grain (harvest in million tonnes)

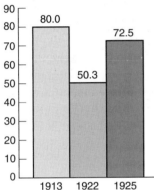

Coal (in million tonnes)

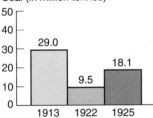

Steel (in million tonnes)

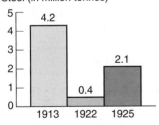

Fig 8.12   Bar graphs showing the production of key commodities - grain, coal, steel - from 1913 to 1925.

Economic policy: from War Communism to NEP

When the Bolsheviks seized power in October 1917, the Russian economy was in an appalling situation:

'The cultivated area had been reduced by the war by a sixth, the number of horses available for agriculture by nearly a third, the cereal harvest was down by fourteen per cent . . . The product of industry was a little more than three fourths of what it had been in 1913. The railway system had suffered severely from the strain of war, and from the lack of replacements and repairs . . . The money in circulation was twelve times as much as in July 1914. In the country, the paper rouble was worth from a tenth to an eighth of the pre-war rouble . . . A fall in real wages, calculated at twelve to fifteen per cent, had occurred: and the cost of living in October 1917 was five times that of a year earlier.'

(Sir John Maynard, *The Russian Revolution and Other Studies*, 1942)

The years up until 1921 – years of political uncertainty and civil war – saw this situation greatly deteriorate. By 1921 agricultural land under crop production was less than half what it had been in 1913, and numbers of livestock had dramatically fallen away. In industry the picture was even worse. Key industrial indicators such as coal and steel output, textile production, and the manufacture of consumer goods, showed huge declines in comparison with the 1913 data (see Figure 8.12). In addition the transport and communications systems was in a state of collapse.

Industrial cities such as Moscow and Petrograd lost hundreds of thousands of inhabitants as former industrial workers headed back to the villages from where they had come. The period of greatest disaster was between 1920 and 1921 when, on top of all the other problems, drought and famine struck the Volga region again. Figure 8.13 shows some of the victims of this famine. Five million people died at this time. Indeed, it is estimated that the population of the former Tsarist empire fell by 28 million people between 1913 and 1921. This was the base from which Lenin and the Communists had to build the new Russia.

The Communists required an economic plan which would tackle these enormous problems. They favoured state control of the economy. As Russia's wartime economy was in large part under government control when they staged their coup, they inherited a situation where banks, the war industries, and the grain trade, were all centrally supervised. They decided to build upon this base. In May 1918 the Communists began putting their policy of nationalisation into action.

The first industries to be nationalised were those of sugar and oil. In late June 1918 a decree of General Nationalisation was passed, affecting all large-scale enterprises. This decree is usually regarded as the measure which set in motion the policy generally referred to as 'War Communism'. By War Communism, the Communists took it upon themselves to control the entire resources of the state in order to defend their revolution. This allowed them, for example, to appropriate the personal wealth of individuals, to direct manpower to where it was needed, and to pass measures allowing the compulsary purchase of essential commodities, notably grain. These measures clearly increased the extent of Communist authority over people's lives.

Fig 8.13   Famine victims in devastated southern Russia in 1921.

A pressing problem for the Communists was the agricultural situation. Small peasant farmers had seized land from the big landowners, but their primitive farms were not producing enough to feed either the industrial population or the army. To tackle this problem, the Communists issued a decree bringing the peasant allotments under state control. The idea was that the Communists would thereafter be empowered to seize surplus grain from the countryside – but the peasants responded by growing only enough to feed themselves. As if that was not bad enough, peasant revolts against Communist actions were rife by the autumn of 1920.

War Communism did not improve Russia's economic position, and it was finally dropped following a revolt near Petrograd in March 1921. The Kronstadt Revolt, as it was called, was sparked off by the peasant recruits in the Kronstadt military and naval bases. It was a clear rebellion against what were seen as the excesses of Communist authority. The demands of the rebels reflected this, especially the cry for 'Soviets without Communists'. The Communists had been experiencing considerable criticism of their policies for some time, and even from within their own ranks there were protests that they were losing contact with the people. Strikes developed in Petrograd.

On 27 February 1921 a poster which emphasised workers' disillusionment with the Communists appeared on walls:

'A complete change is necessary in the policies of the Government. First of all, the workers and peasants need freedom. They don't want to live by the decrees of the Bolsheviki: they want to control their own destinies. Comrades, preserve revolutionary order! Determinedly and in an organised manner demand:

Liberation of all arrested socialists and non-partisan working men.

Abolition of martial law; freedom of speech, press and assembly for all who labour . . .

Call meetings, pass resolutions, send your delegates to the authorities and work for the realisation of your demands.'

(A. Berkman, *The Russian Tragedy*, 1942)

This was a very worrying development for the Communists. After all, the Kronstadt base had provided much support for them in 1917. Now Kronstadt rebels were seeking a 'Third Revolution' which would give a voice to trade unions, peasant organisations and other political parties, such as the Social Revolutionaries and the Mensheviks.

An open letter sent to *Izvestiia* elaborated on disillusionment with the Communists:

'With the October Revolution the working class had hoped to achieve its emancipation. But there resulted an even greater enslavement of human personality. The power of the police and gendarme monarchy fell into the hands of usurpers – the Communists – who, instead of giving the people liberty, have instilled in them only the constant fear of the Cheka [see page 205], which by its horrors surpasses even the gendarme régime of Tsarism . . . It is now become clear that the Russian Communist Party is not the defender of the labouring masses, as it pretends to be. The interests of the working people are foreign to it. Having gained power it is now fearful only of losing it, and therefore it considers all means permissible: defamation, deceit, violence, murder . . .'

(Quoted in A. Berkman)

The Kronstadt Revolt was very much the acid test for Communist authority. Trotsky proposed no compromise with the rebels and demanded unconditional surrender from them. Ten days of bitter fighting occurred before the rising was eventually put down. Communist propaganda tried to suggest that the Kronstadt rebellion was the work of White counter-revolutionaries. The Communists themselves knew otherwise: the people whom they had forcibly put down and whose leaders they had had executed were Socialists who had become disillusioned with Communist government. The lesson was clear: unless the Communists could find some way of appeasing restless workers, peasants, soldiers, and sailors, more unrest would come. First and foremost, the economy would have to be improved so that people could be fed, clothed, and housed.

Lenin had already been dwelling on a new approach to provide short-term relief for the beleagured Russian economy. Within a week of the Kronstadt Revolt being crushed, the New Economic Policy – the NEP – was being implemented. The chief aim of the NEP was to restore to the peasants the kind of incentives which would encourage them to grow more food for sale in Russia's cities. Industrial productivity also needed to be improved. Furthermore, some more effective means of commodity exchange between town and country were necessary.

The NEP was supposed to work in this way. The state took a fixed proportion of the peasants' surplus production, that is the amount grown over and above the needs of the peasant and his family, and the peasant could sell the rest for his own profit. The incentive for the peasant was that he could grow a surplus and make a profit – and the bigger the surplus he grew, the bigger the profit would be. Surplus grain would go for sale, handled by commercial businessmen who were referred to as Nepmen. By 1923 these Nepmen controlled 75 per cent of the retail trade in grain in Russia.

On the industrial side of the economy, large-scale energy industries such as coal, oil and electricity, were to remain under state control, as were iron and steel production, and the railway network. However, private enterprise was allowed in smaller industries. Labour incentives were to apply, in order to encourage workers, just as the prospects of making profits were designed to stimulate investment and enterprise. Systems of bonuses were introduced to encourage hard work, and the compulsory direction of labour by the government was abandoned.

Study Figure 8.12 again to see the extent of Russia's economic collapse after 1913 and the way that improvements were slowly made after the introduction of the NEP. By restoring aspects of capitalism to the Russian economy, the Communists began to make progress. However, they had to compromise with their own ideology to allow this to happen. Lenin was quite content to adapt his ideology to accommodate this apparent shift in direction. He declared that there was no possibility of Russia moving directly to Communism while it was still primarily a peasant economy. This being the case, a short-term solution to Russia's problems caused by the years of war and destruction was perfectly acceptable, as long as it did the vital thing: maintain intact the achievements of the revolution.

The Communist police state

Economic distress alone was not the reason behind the Kronstadt Revolt, of course. Any analysis of the complaints made by the rebels – and the poster and letter on page 203 are clear pointers to these – indicates a colossal antagonism towards some of the things that the Communists were doing to ensure that they retained power.

One of the most feared and hated institutions, already briefly referred to, was the Cheka, the secret police, which was formed in December 1917. The Cheka brought a new enthusiasm and urgency to policing activities within the former Tsarist empire. They inaugurated what has become known as the period of 'Red Terror'.

The term 'Cheka' was a shortened form of the name of an organisation: its full name serves admirably to describe its purpose: 'The All-Russian Extraordinary Commission for Fighting Counter-Revolution, Sabotage and Speculation'. The Cheka had 'extraordinary' powers, which meant that it did what it liked, as long as its activities fitted in with broad Communist aims. Those aims required the Cheka to engage in 'fighting counter-revolution', which meant that it actively opposed all non-Communists, because Lenin and the Communists were absolutely convinced that their ideology was utterly, absolutely and incontestably correct. The Cheka was also required to fight 'sabotage', which meant actively opposing any person or group who attempted in any way to inflict damage on the Communist state.

Finally, the Cheka was entrusted with combating 'speculation', by which was meant the activities of individuals engaging in any economic activity, the benefits of which were not transferred directly to the Communist state. This attack on speculation was specifically designed to ensure that peasants would deliver their surplus grain to where it was needed at a price determined by the Communists; it also allowed Communist supervision of all industry and enterprise in order to ensure that manufacture fitted in with the overall Communist strategy for Russia.

The head of the Cheka was Felix Dzershinsky, a ruthless and committed Communist of Polish aristocratic origin. Dzershinsky accepted without question the Communist call for active repression of anyone or anything deemed by Lenin to be a threat to the revolution. Lenin, in turn, was quite open and adamant about the necessity for ruthless treatment of anyone designated as a 'class enemy', and if the Cheka made a few mistakes in ensuring that 'class enemies' were rooted out and dealt with, then that was regrettable but unavoidable. In 1919 during the Civil War and when Cheka activities were at their height, he observed to a Menshevik critic:

> 'I judge soberly and categorically what is better – to put in prison a few dozen or a few hundred incitors, guilty or not, conscious or not, or to lose thousands of Red Army soldiers and workers? The former is better.'

> (Quoted in R. Pipes)

During the Civil War atrocities were commonplace on both sides, and the Cheka's activities should be examined in this light. But the Cheka was responsible for much more than the actual physical exterminations it engaged in. It created a mood of fear and repression throughout Russia. Anyone classified as fitting into a category regarded as being against the revolution – for example, either those who owned property or those who had even once owned property – was a likely target. The biggest threat of all was to the Tsar and his family.

The Romanovs had been sent to Tobolsk in Siberia by Kerensky. There they lived in modest comfort until April 1918. By then the Treaty of Brest-Litovsk had been signed, but there remained considerable doubt in Communist minds about future German actions. One possibility which the Communists feared was that the Germans might see some benefit in overthrowing Communism and restoring Tsarism in Russia. Another developing problem was the Civil War. The Communists feared that White forces might see the Tsar as a rallying point in their campaign against them. From the point of view of the Communists, the Romanovs remained a threat as long as they remained alive.

The Tsar and his family were transferred to Ekaterinburg in the Urals, and they arrived there by rail on 30 April. During the next few weeks, the Communists debated what to do with the Tsar and his family. Trotsky favoured a trial which would make public the 'crimes' committed by the Tsar. But this was regarded by Lenin as a risky tactic. Instead, the Cheka was given the task of dispensing with the Romanovs.

The precise sequence of events which occurred on the night of 16 July 1918 is the subject of intense historical debate. Recently, a grave allegedly containing the bodies of the Romanovs was discovered near Ekaterinburg. DNA tests carried out in 1993 confirmed beyond reasonable doubt that the remains were those of the Tsar and most of his family. The remains of Alexis and of one daughter were missing. This discovery has led to new interest in what happened at Ekaterinburg. The most widely accepted interpretation is as follows.

The Tsar and his family went to bed before 11 p.m. At 1.30 a.m. they were awakened: they were told that shots had been heard in the vicinity, and that they should take refuge in the cellar of the house in which they were living. Nicholas, Alexandra, their children and their servants, all descended to a cellar room from which all the furniture had been removed. Twelve armed men entered the room. An astonished and alarmed Nicholas was told that, as he and his family had continued to oppose the revolution, the executive committee of the Urals Soviet had ordered their execution. The slaughter took place immediately, with the armed guards turning their guns on to the Tsar, his family and the servants. The confined space ensured that the task was not carried out easily. Handguns and bayonets had to be used to finish off six of the victims, including three of the Tsar's daughters. The bodies were then burned and destroyed with acid and the remains buried several kilometres outside Ekaterinburg.

An official announcement published in *Izvestiia* on 19 July 1918 declared that, as Ekaterinburg was under threat, and as a plot had been discovered to overturn the revolution, the Urals Soviet had decided to execute the Tsar. The article also stated that the Tsar's family had been transferred to a more secure location.

The execution of the Romanovs was the most noted excess carried out by the Cheka, but there were many, many more. By the summer of 1918 its policy of political extermination was well under way. In July over 1000 Cheka executions occurred: typical targets were former army officers – military conspiracy was always a great Bolshevik fear – and outspoken political opponents. The terror then spread to the countryside to ensure that supplies of grain were sent to the towns. A particular target for the Bolsheviks were the Kulaks, the better-off peasants who owned tracts of land. Probably thousands of unnamed peasants were disposed of between 1918 and 1921: the true figures are never likely to be known.

Following an assassination attempt on Lenin on 30 August 1918, the Red Terror intensified. Victims seemed to be chosen at random, designated as 'class enemies' because of their wealth. In September a decree was issued which allowed the taking of 'hostages' – relatives of known White sympathisers and the like – who could be executed at will. Many subsequently were, often on the whim of local soviet deputies.

By 1920 the Cheka had become the established enforcement agency of what was in reality a Communist police state. It actually extended its range of activities. For example, to ensure that 'speculation' did not occur in key economic sectors, it took over control of the transport and communications sector, including the railways. In April 1921, Dzershinsky was appointed Commissar of Communications. Forced labour became part of the Cheka remit too – and those not prepared to work properly could be summarily shot. A Cheka security army appeared, in order to patrol the 'home front' and to supplement the activities of the Red Army.

The Cheka was probably the most powerful institution in Russia.

Dzerzhinsky later expressed the view that the activities of the Cheka had saved the revolution. Certainly it could be said that the Cheka established rigid Communist authority in Russia. Lenin continued to justify and praise the Cheka, because he believed that any price was worth paying to ensure the survival of the achievements of the Communist revolution. In reality Communist ideology had become a secondary consideration. A ruthless police state had come into being in Russia.

The Communists and the national minorities

Lenin and the Bolsheviks had been vociferous in their support for the national minorities when they were in opposition both to Tsarism and to the Provisional Government. This was understandable. When Bolshevism was in its infancy, representatives of national minority groups had been amongst the most active revolutionaries against Tsarism, and Lenin did not want to detach himself from such a strong pro-revolutionary element. However, a fundamental problem existed in the minds of Lenin and the Bolsheviks. They believed that world revolution was inevitable, and that eventually national differences would amount to very little once Communism existed everywhere. Marx had ended the Communist Manifesto with the rallying call: 'Workers of the World – Unite'. When the Bolsheviks seized control of Russia in 1917, they took over the former Tsarist empire of some two hundred different nationalities located in a sixth of the land mass of the world. Lenin was not prepared to relinquish Communist control of such a significant part of the world because of nationalist demands for independence.

When he returned to Russia in April 1917, Lenin wrote

extensively explaining his position with regard to the national minorities. His writings on the nationalities question overlapped his criticisms of the Provisional Government's war policy. He demanded 'Peace without annexations or indemnities on the basis of self-determination of the peoples'. The implication of this was that he was opposed to the occupation of the territory of any national group by another, and that the peace between Russia and her enemies should be drawn up by all parties concerned on the basis of this principle. The logical follow-through from this was that any national minority group who wanted to break away from the control of an occupying power, including those in the former Russian empire, were free to do so. Subsequently, however, Lenin amended his approach. He declared that what he was opposing was the enforced hold of one nation over another. He now stated that, once people were free, they could readily join with other national groups in voluntary bonds of comradeship:

> '... the proletarian party strives to create as large a state as possible, for this is in the interests of the workers; it strives to bring the nations closely together, to fuse them ... by a free brotherly union of ... the toiling masses of all nations.'
>
> (Lenin, *Collected Works*)

According to Lenin's view of the world, 'nation' could mean several things, but the only real 'nation' was the workers. Certainly, different nationalities had different cultures, languages and so forth – but the workers of the world had more in common than they had differences. Once this was realised, national minorities of the former Russian empire would appreciate that, under Communism, they were not oppressed peoples ruled over by an alien state: they were workers, like all other workers. After October 1917 Lenin regarded calls for independence in the former Russian empire as the intrigues of 'counter-revolutionaries'. He suggested that these 'counter-revolutionaries' wanted to re-establish 'bourgeois' control of territories which, now that the revolution had happened, were in sight of becoming truly liberated. It was the duty of the Communists to fight such attempts at re-establishing 'bourgeois' control of the former subject nationalities of the Tsarist empire. This fight was necessary, in order to consolidate as much Communist control of the world as possible, because, with a strong base from which to operate, it was only a matter of time before Communism could be exported to the rest of the world.

On the day that the Winter Palace fell and Lenin's Provisional Workers' and Peasants' Government came into being, a new government post was created: Chairman of the National Minorities. The chairmanship went to Joseph Dzhugasvili, better known as Stalin. As the one-party state came into being, and as Communists moved towards central control of government in

Russia, the official attitude towards the national minorities began to take shape.

National minority representatives had expressed their desire that Russia should become a federation, as this would allow each nationality to have considerable control over its own affairs while the substance of a united Russia would be retained. The Communists' hold on the empire was fragile at the time, so the position of the national minorities in the constitution had to be expressed sensitively.

On 3 April 1918, Stalin set out his definition of the nature of the Russian federation in *Pravda*. He described Russia as 'a union of historically distinct territories differentiated by a special way of life, as well as by their national composition'. The Soviet Federation would oversee a transition from 'forced unification' under the Tsars to 'the voluntary and fraternal union of the working masses of all nations and peoples of Russia'. The implication was that the Federation was a temporary, transitional stage which would eventually disappear once a more acceptable form of unity than that which had operated under Tsarism had come into being.

In the years 1917–21 the situation of many of the national minorities of the former Tsarist empire changed. Estonia, Latvia and Lithuania became independent of Russia: their independence was established by the terms of the 1919 Treaty of Versailles. Poland, too, was recognised as an independent nation in 1919, although it was not until 1921 that a border between Russia and Poland was established by the Treaty of Riga. Finland's independence was accepted by the Communists by the terms of the Treaty of Tartu, signed in October 1920.

But the ambitions of the other national minority activists were not realised under Lenin's rule. The western European powers had failed to achieve anything of note from their involvement in the Civil War, and were content to establish a line of 'buffer states' separating the Communist sphere of influence from themselves. After 1921 Lenin and the Communists were free to work towards incorporating all the remaining national groups of the former Tsarist empire into a Union of Soviet and Socialist Republics. Propaganda images such as that shown in Figure 8.14 promoted Lenin as the wise and compassionate leader of all the proletariat of the former Russian empire, irrespective of nationality. Notice how the men are clearly identified as being of different origins by the clothing they are wearing – and how all of them are looking to Lenin as their leader and guide.

The reality of Communist control over the former Tsarist empire was rather different from the cosy image promoted in pictures such as Figure 8.14. Central direction from Moscow ensured that any challenge to Communist supremacy in the Soviet Union was rapidly suppressed. Lenin and the Communists had fought long and hard to get themselves to the point where they were in 1921. They genuinely believed that the future would lie with them and their ideology, not just in Russia, but all over the world. They were in control of a sixth of the land mass of the world. They were surrounded by enemies, but by 1921 they had won a reprieve from active opposition. They could now plan and move forward.

Fig 8.14   A cosy image of Lenin.

ESSAY

1. Did Lenin establish a 'dictatorship *over* the proletariat' (see page 74)?

2. How accurate would it be to suggest that Russia gained more than she lost by the terms of the Treaty of Brest-Litovsk?

3. Why was the Red Army able to defeat the Whites during the Civil War of 1918–21?

4. How was Communist authority established throughout the former Russian empire by 1921?

Conclusion

The transformation from Tsarism to Communism had largely been completed by 1921. However, it is the similarities in the régimes which stand out rather than the differences between them. The centrally-controlled Tsarist state, unwilling to accept any kind of challenge to Tsarist ideology or authority, had been replaced by a centrally-controlled Communist state, unwilling to accept any kind of challenge to Marxist-Leninist ideology or authority. Through policies such as Russification, the Tsarist régime had attempted to force the many different nationalities to alter their identities so as to make them more controllable as subjects of the Tsar. Through policies such as the Red Terror, Lenin and the Communists forced the subject peoples of the former Tsarist empire to abandon any perception of themselves outside the Marxist view of class differentiation.

The instruments of Tsarist control – loyal ministers, a secret police force, and an army capable of uncompromising brutality – became the instruments of Communist control. Lenin and the Communists believed themselves to be the vanguard of world revolution. They saw themselves as overthrowers of an unjust régime which deprived the mass of ordinary people of any kind of life worth living. They wanted to develop a better Russia, a better world. They were convinced that the logic of history, as

Fig C.1   The head of a giant statue of Tsar Alexander III lying smashed on the ground.

defined by Karl Marx, ensured that the future which they envisaged would inevitably come about. In the short term, they had to protect the revolution in any way possible, therefore they could justify the excesses to which the Kronstadt sailors had taken such exception in 1921. They could justify the military-style police state which they had brought into being, in which all opposition, political or otherwise, could be brutally suppressed. One day, they believed, the world which they envisaged would come into being.

That world never did materialise. Instead, the police state which had been developed by 1921 became the reality of Communist Russia thereafter. So rigid was Communist control of the Soviet Union that few observers in the West imagined that it would ever collapse. In recent years that assumption has been proved dramatically wrong, and now the problems of the former Soviet Union are depressingly similar to what they were under both Tsarism and Communism: economic backwardness and inefficiency; an inability to provide adequate food; national antagonism and intolerance.

Fig C.2   Two Romanian citizens shaking their fists at the head of a giant statue of Lenin after it had been removed from its base in Bucharest in March 1990.

Figure C.1 has often been used to signify the collapse of Tsarism in Russia. The photo was taken in Moscow in 1917, and it shows the head of a giant statue of Tsar Alexander III, broken off and smashed on the ground. Amongst the most lasting images of the late 1980s and early 1990s were similar pictures – only the smashed statues were of Lenin and other Communists (see Figure C.2).

We have traced the path from Tsarism to Communism in Russia and the empire. In recent years that path has changed direction. No one is entirely sure where it will now lead to.

General essays

The essays at the end of each Issue in this book are related specifically to the content of that Issue. The essay titles provided here are more general, and require you to draw upon your knowledge and understanding of larger areas of the book. Essays such as these may well appear in your Paper 1 examination.

As part of your revision, examine each of these essays. Draw up plans of how you would tackle each essay. Do as many of the essays as you can. Each essay should be approximately 1200 words long.

1. Did the policies of Alexander III help or hinder the development of the Russian empire?

2. In what ways did industrial developments in Russia between 1881 and 1904 create new challenges to the authority of the Tsarist state?

3. How effectively did Russia's last two Tsars deal with the problem of the national minorities?

4. Did the Tsarist state deal effectively with opposition to its authority in the years before 1905?

5. Why was the Tsarist autocracy able to survive the 1905 Revolution?

6. Did the Tsarist state change significantly after the 1905 Revolution?

7. How accurate was Stolypin in identifying the sources of the problems of the Russian empire, and how successful was he in providing solutions to those problems?

8. Were the Bolsheviks a significant threat to Tsarist authority before 1917?

9. How important a factor in the downfall of the Tsarist state was Russia's involvement in the First World War?

10. Did the position of the national minorities in the Russian empire improve between 1917 and 1921?

11. Explain how the Bolsheviks were able to exert their authority throughout the former Russian empire between 1917 and 1921.

12. To what extent was Lenin successful in achieving his ambitions for Russia by 1921?

Extended essays

The transformation of Russia from Tsarism to Communism is an area of study which offers considerable scope for preparing an extended essay. The extended essay is intended to provide evidence of investigatory skills such as:

- the ability to identify an issue and place it in context;
- the ability to select and organise information from a variety of sources;
- and the ability to present the findings in a form that shows some attempt at analysis.

There are over forty essay titles in this book. These titles reflect the areas of this period of Russian history which are most commonly discussed by historians. As a result, there are many books available which will allow a similar or related topic to be tackled as an extended essay. It may well be useful to go over the essay titles provided in this book: perhaps an area of investigation related to one of these essay titles will appeal as an extended essay topic. Some areas which could be considered are:

1. A consideration of the importance of an *individual* in the period of study. Two people about whom a great deal has been written are Tsar Nicholas II and Lenin. Essay titles could be:

> a) To what extent was Tsar Nicholas II responsible for his own fall from power?
> b) Assess the role of Lenin as a revolutionary leader.

2. An evaluation of the reasons for particular *events*, for example:

> What caused 'Bloody Sunday' in 1905?

3. A discussion of the *relationships* between political events and the context provided by social, political, economic, military, or other world affairs, for example:

> What were the political implications of the rapid industrialisation of Russia in the 1890s?

4. A comparison between ideology and events, for example:

> Was the October Revolution of 1917 a Marxist Revolution?

5. An evaluation of the reasons for the nature and effectiveness of *particular policies*, for example:

> a) Did Tsar Alexander III's policy of Russification bring stability and prosperity to the Russian empire during his reign?
> b) Why did Kerensky's leadership of the Provisional Government end in failure?

Bibliography

The following titles may help you to do the research for an extended essay. They are just a few of the many books available about Russia between 1881 and 1921.

Shorter texts covering all or part of the period

Kochan L and Abraham R 1962 *The Making of Modern Russia* Penguin.

McKean R B 1977 *The Russian Constitutional Monarchy, 1900–1917* The Historical Association.

Service R 1986 *The Russian Revolution, 1900–1927* Macmillan Education.

Williams B 1987 *The Russian Revolution* Basil Blackwell Historical Association Studies.

Wood A 1987 *The Origins of the Russian Revolution* Methuen.

More lengthy texts

Carr E H 1950 *The Bolshevik Revolution, 1917–1923* Macmillan.

Pipes R 1987 *Russia Under the Old Régime* Penguin.

Pipes R 1990 *The Russian Revolution, 1899–1919* Collins Harvill Press.

Seton-Watson H 1967 *The Russian Empire, 1801–1917* Oxford University Press.

Biographies

Deutscher I 1948 *Stalin* Oxford University Press.

Deutscher I 1970 *Trotsky* Oxford University Press.

Ferro M 1991 *Nicholas II: the Last of the Tsars* Penguin.

Radzinsky E 1992 *The Last Tsar: the Life and Death of Nicholas II* Doubleday.

Shub D 1948 *Lenin* Doubleday.

Eye-witness accounts

Denikin General AI *The White Army* Ian Faulkner Publishing Limited.

Reed J 1966 *Ten Days That Shook The World* Penguin Modern Classics.

Trotsky L 1932–33 *The History of the Russian Revolution* Victor Gollancz.

Revolutionary ideology – brief introductory texts

Conquest R 1972 *Lenin* Fontana Modern Masters.

Lenin VI *What Is To Be Done?* Penguin Twentieth Century Classics.

Marx and Engels *The Communist Manifesto* Introduced by A J P Taylor Penguin Classics.

McClellan D 1975 *Marx* Fontana Modern Masters.

Singer P 1980 *Marx* Oxford University Press Past Masters.

Economic history

von Laue TH 1963 *Sergei Witte and the Industrialisation of Russia* Columbia University Press.

Nove A 1976 *An Economic History of the USSR* Penguin.

The First World War

Stone N 1975 *The Eastern Front* Hodder and Stoughton.

The Civil War

Mawdsley E 1987 *The Russian Civil War* Allen and Unwin.

Documents

Golder A F 1927 *Documents of Russian History, 1914–1917* The Century Company.

Laver J 1991 *Russia 1914–1941* Hodder and Stoughton History at Source Series.

Robottom J 1984 *Russia in Change, 1870–1945* Longman Modern Times Sourcebooks.

Rothnie N 1991 *The Russian Revolution* Macmillan Education Documents and Debates.

Photographs

Fitzlyon K and Browning T 1992 *Before the Revolution* Penguin.

Index

Alexander I, 15, 17, 52
Alexander II, 26–33, 36, 39, 45, 46, 47, 49, 56, 64,
    76, 77
Alexander III, 6, 21, 28, 33, 34–58, 64, 76, 77, 83,
    84, 86, 93, 96, 212, 213
Alexandra, Tsarina, 87, 88, 136–137, 206–207
Alexis, Tsarevich, 136–137, 206–207
All-Russian Central Executive Committee, 184, 188
All-Russian Congress of Soviets, 152, 165, 177, 180,
    182, 184, 188
All-Russian Social Democratic Party, see under
    Social Democrats
All Russian Unions, 135
America, 188, 194, 196
April Theses, 155–157, 158
Archangel, 130, 194
Armenia, 13, 53–54, 167, 200
Assembly of Russian Factory Workers of
    St Petersburg, 100
Aurora, 179
Austria-Hungary, 44, 46, 48, 50, 129, 130, 136, 140,
    141, 158, 160, 185, 186, 190, 192

Baku, 90, 196
Baltic provinces, see under Estonia, Latvia,
    Lithuania
Belorussia, 13, 29, 50
'Bloody Sunday' (1905), 91, 99–103
Bobrikov, N.I., 52, 53, 98
Bogolepov, N.P., 96
Bolsheviks, 60, 74–76, 80, 111, 123, 147–148, 149,
    151, 152, 154–157, 165, 166, 167, 172, 173,
    174–180, 181, 182–188, 198, 199, 201, 208 (see
    also under Communists)
Boxer Rebellion (China), 98
Britain, 68, 70, 134, 186, 192, 194, 195, 196
Brusilov, General A.A., 141, 142, 159
Brusilov Offensive (1916), 141, 142
Bund, 58, 81

Capital, 66, 68–70
Catherine the Great, 10, 16, 20, 48
Chaikovsky, N.V., 194
Cheka, 198, 199, 204, 205–208
Cheliabinsk, 193
Chernov, V.M., 65, 163–164
China, 96–99, 141
Civil War, 189–201
Coalition Government, see under Dual Authority
Committees to Save the Revolution, 174
Communist Manifesto, 66–71, 80, 208
Communist Party, 157, 188
Communists, 188, 201, 202, 203, 204, 205, 209, 210

Constituent Assembly, 150, 177, 182, 183–184,
    192
Cossacks 30, 48, 49, 102, 113
Crimean War (1854–56), 26, 84
Criminal Code (1845), 32
Curie, Marie, 47
Czechoslovak Legion, 192–194, 196

Decembrist Rising (1825), 24, 31, 42, 61
Denikin, General A.I., 192, 194, 195, 199
Dual Authority, 150, 153–154, 157, 183
Duma (first, 1906), 79, 82, 104, 106–115, 116,
    119
Duma (second, 1907), 117
Duma (thrid, 1907–12), 117–127
Duma (fourth, 1912–17), 127, 134–136, 137, 138,
    141, 145–146, 147, 148
Dzershinsky, F.E., 206–208
Dzhugasvili, J.V., see under Stalin

Eichorn, General H von, 191
Ekaterinburg, 165, 206–207
Emancipation of the serfs (1861), 27–28, 31, 32,
    41, 83, 116, 119
Engels, F., 66, 67, 71
Estonia, 13, 30, 50–51, 187, 199, 200, 210

Feudalism, 15, 26, 27, 67–69
Finland, 13, 30, 51–53, 111, 124, 155, 165–166,
    168, 176, 186, 190–191, 210
Finland Station, 155
France, 44, 66, 90, 134, 186, 192, 194, 195
Franco-Russian Convention (1892), 44
French Revolution (1789), 24
Fundamental Laws, 14, 21, 108, 109

Galicia, 136
Gapon, Father G., 91–92, 100–101
Georgia, 13, 84, 165, 200
Germany, 13, 44, 46, 48, 72, 90, 130, 132, 136, 140,
    155, 158, 170, 185–188, 190, 191, 194, 206
'Going to the People', 63, 64
Golitsyn, B.A., 54
Goremykin, I.L., 138
Gorlice, 136
Guchkov, A.I., 110, 119, 125, 126, 127, 145, 146,
    152, 154, 155, 158, 159
Gurko, V.I., 47, 113

Hegel, G.W.F., 66, 69
Herzen, A., 62
Hetman (Ukraine), 48
Hindenburg, General P. von, 132, 134, 185, 186

Ignateyev, Count, 40, 41
Iskra, 72
Ivan the Great, 9, 10, 20, 22, 24
Ivan the Terrible, 9, 10, 14, 15, 16
Izvestiia 145, 148, 151, 176, 183, 184, 189, 203, 207

Japan, 57, 82, 96–99, 103, 104, 122, 125, 194, 196
Jews, 13, 21, 30, 48, 56–58, 79, 80–81, 124, 199
Judiciary Law (1864), 33
July Days (1917), 167–171, 172, 177
June offensive (1917), 159–163, 168, 176

Kadets, 110–111, 113, 118, 119, 145, 150, 172, 174, 175, 192
Kamenev, L.B., 154, 177
Kerensky, A., 111, 145, 146, 151, 158, 159–163, 164, 170–171, 172–174, 175, 178, 179, 183
Khabalov, General S., 144
Kiev, 8, 9, 29, 48, 57, 99, 199
Kokovtsov, Count, 112, 127
Kolchak, Admiral A.V., 194, 198, 199
Korea, 97
Kornilov, General L.G., 160, 162, 163, 171–174, 175
Kornilov Revolt, 167, 171–174, 175
Kremlin, 187, 196, 197
Kronstadt naval base 168, 203–204, 213
Kronstadt Revolt, 203–204, 205, 213
Krymov, General A.M., 141, 174
Kulaks, 207
Kuropatkin, Governor-General, Turkestan, 56
Kurds, 54

Land and Freedom, 63, 64
Land commandants, 41
Latvia, 13, 30, 50, 51, 187, 200, 210
League of the Three Emperors, 44
Legal Marxists, 78
Lena goldfields 122–123, 143, 147
Lenin, 71–76, 80, 94, 123, 147–148, 151, 154–157, 165–170, 174–180, 181, 184–188, 193, 201, 202, 204, 205, 206, 207, 208–211
Leninism, 71–76, 209, 212–213
Letters From Afar 154–155, 157
Liberals, 39, 59, 60, 61, 76–79, 99, 110–111, 172
Lithuania, 13, 30, 50, 51, 135, 187, 200, 210
Loris-Melikov, 40
Ludendorff, General E., 132, 185
Lvov, Prince G.E., 138, 145, 147, 150, 152, 153, 155, 157, 163
Lvov, V., 172–173

Makarov, S.O., 122
Manchuria, 97, 98
Marinsky Palace, 169
Martov, L., 80–81, 180
Marx, K., 63, 66–76, 80, 153, 208, 213
Marxism, 59, 61, 66–76, 80, 93, 153, 212, 213
Masurian Lakes, Battle of (1914), 132–133

Mensheviks, 60, 74–76, 111, 113, 147, 152, 153, 154, 175, 176, 180, 203
Michael, Tsar, 10–11
Military Revolutionary Committee, 177, 178, 179
Milyukov, P.N., 78, 99, 111, 125, 145, 146, 150, 151, 154, 157, 158, 166
Mir, see under Obshchina
Mirsky, D.S., 98–99
Mongol invasion, 9
Moscow, 9, 12, 16, 18, 19, 38, 65, 76, 85, 88, 93, 96, 99, 139, 146, 147, 175, 184, 187, 189, 193, 199, 202, 210, 213
Muscovy, 9, 48
Muslims, 13, 21, 53, 54, 55, 79, 124, 140–141, 167

Napoleonic Wars, 15, 51
National League (Poland), 48
New Economic Policy (NEP), 204–205
Nepmen, 204
Nicholas I, Tsar, 24–26, 31, 42, 45
Nicholas II, Tsar, 21, 35, 36, 48, 52, 53, 54, 56, 57, 58, 77, 82, 87–89, 96, 98, 99, 101, 103–105, 108–110, 112, 115, 126–127, 136–137, 142, 145, 146, 171, 206–207
Nikolay Nikolayevich, Grand Duke, 136, 140

Obshchina, 28, 29, 62–64, 70
October Manifesto, 104, 106, 107, 108, 115, 117
Octobrists, 110, 113, 116, 118, 125, 126, 145, 150
Okhrana, 42
Order Number One, 150–152, 160
Orthodoxy, 8, 21–26, 29, 36, 38, 45, 46, 50, 51, 53, 54, 56, 100
Osvobozhdenie, 78–79

Pale of Settlement, 56
'Paris Bloc', 99
Peasant Land Bank, 120–121
'People's Will', 33, 64, 65
Peter and Paul Fortress, 179
Peter the Great, Tsar, 11–12, 14, 18, 21, 22, 36, 48, 84, 88
Peter III, Tsar, 20
Petrograd, 129–130, 139, 143–144, 146, 147, 151, 154, 157, 163, 166, 167–170, 172–180, 183, 185, 186, 187, 199, 202, 203
Petrograd Soviet, 147, 150–153, 155, 158–159, 168, 170, 175, 176, 177, 179
Pilsudski, J., 140, 200
Plehve, V.K., 78, 98
Plekhanov, G., 71
Pobedonostsev, K., 26, 36, 38–41, 45, 51
Pogroms (Jews), 56–58
Poland, 13, 14, 29–30, 46–48, 51, 79, 80, 118, 124, 134–135, 139, 140, 165–166, 187, 200, 210
Police (Tsarist), 31, 42, 94
Polkovnikov, G.P., 177, 179
Populists, 59, 61–65, 84

Port Arthur, 97, 98, 99, 100
Pravda 123, 170, 183, 210
'Progressive Bloc', 137
'Proletariat', 48
Provisional Government, 145, 147, 149–180, 183, 185, 208
Provisional Workers' and Peasants' Government, 182, 209
Putilov steelworks, 100, 123

Rada, 166, 186
Rasputin, 136–137, 142
Red Army, 183, 188–190, 193, 194, 199, 200, 206, 208
Red Guards, 183, 189
Red Terror, 205–208, 212
Redemptiom payments, 28, 89, 119
Rodichev, F.I., 78, 79
Rodzianko, M.V., 134–135, 145, 147
Russification, 29–30, 45–58, 78, 111, 124, 167, 212
Russo-Japanese War (1904–05), 96–99, 103

St Petersburg, 11, 18, 19, 33, 38, 50, 63, 65, 71, 72, 76, 79, 80, 82, 83, 84, 88, 90, 92, 93, 94, 96, 99–103, 107, 112, 122–123, 129 (now see under Petrograd)
Sarajevo assassination, 129
Schlieffen Plan, 132
'Sealed train', 155
Senate of Nobles, 15
Serfdom, 16–18, 27–28, 31
Siberia, 6, 42, 43, 71–72, 85–86, 97, 104, 109, 121, 122, 165, 171, 193, 194, 206
Sipyagin, D.S., 96
Skoropadsky, H.P., 191, 194
Social Democrats, 72–76, 78, 79, 80–81, 93, 99, 111, 113, 118, 157
Social Revolutionaries, 60, 65, 79, 93, 98, 99, 111, 116, 153, 163, 164, 175, 176, 177, 180, 182, 183, 192, 194, 203
Sokolnikov, G., 187
Somme, Battle of the, 141
Soviets, 94, 147, 150–154, 155, 157, 158, 159, 160, 167–169, 172, 176, 177, 183, 184, 203
Stalin, J.V., 154, 209, 210
'Stariki', 71
Steppe region, see under Turkestan
Stolypin, P.A., 89, 106, 115–127
Straits Convention (1841), 98

Struve, P.B., 77–79, 111, 117
Sturmer, B.V., 138

Tannenberg, Battle of (1914), 132–134
Tatars or Tartars, 6, 14, 54
Tauride Palace, 110, 115, 168, 169, 183, 184
Tolstoy, D., 40–42, 56
Tolstoy, L., 62, 63, 84
Trans-Siberian Railway, 85–86, 96–97, 192–193
Treaty of Brest-Litovsk (1918), 184–188, 191, 192, 206
Treaty of Portsmouth (1905), 103
Treaty of Riga (1921), 200, 210
Treaty of Tartu (1920), 210
Treaty of Versailles (1919), 210
Trotsky, L., 151, 169, 170, 175, 176, 177, 182, 185, 189–190, 193, 194, 196, 197, 199, 204, 207
Trudoviks, 111, 113
Tsushima Straits, 97, 103
Turkestan, 6, 54–56, 139, 140–141, 167, 194, 200
Turkish empire, 53–54

Ukraine, 13, 30, 48–50, 56, 118, 124, 165, 166–167, 186, 187–188, 190–191, 192, 194, 199, 200
Ulyanov, A., 64, 71
Ulyanov, V.I., see under Lenin
Union of Liberation, 79
Union of Soviet and Socialist Republics (USSR), 210
Union of the Russian People, 57, 58, 111, 113, 118
Urals Soviet, 207
Uvarov, S., 25, 26, 29, 45

Varangians, 8
Vladivostok, 85, 97, 131, 192, 193, 194, 196, 200
Volonsky regiment, 144

War Communism, 201–203
What Is To Be Done?, 73
White armies, 192, 194, 195, 198–200, 206
Wilhelm II, Kaiser, 44, 90, 130
Witte, S., 37, 84–86, 89–91, 94, 96

Yudenich, General N.N., 195, 199
Yusupov, Prince F., 142

Zasulich, V., 33
Zemstva, 32, 41, 57, 76–78, 99, 104, 119, 126, 134, 135, 136, 137, 138
Zinoviev, G.E., 177
Zubatov, S., 94–96, 100, 122